PROBLEMATIC COMMUNICATION

PROBLEMATIC COMMUNICATION

The Construction of Invisible Walls

C. David Mortensen

Westport, Connecticut
London

Library of Congress Cataloging-in-Publication Data

Mortensen, C. David.
    Problematic communication : the construction of invisible walls /
C. David Mortensen.
       p. cm.
    Part of the text is based on a series of working papers,
conference papers, and informal talks presented at several
universities.
    Includes bibliographical references and index.
    ISBN 0–275–94632–0
    1. Interpersonal communication. I. Title.
P94.7.M67 1994
302.2—dc20   93–23671

British Library Cataloguing in Publication Data is available.

Library of Congress Catalog Card Number: 93–23671
ISBN: 0–275–94632–0

First published in 1994

Praeger Publishers, 88 Post Road West, Westport, CT 06881
An imprint of Greenwood Publishing Group, Inc.

Printed in the United States of America

The paper used in this book complies with the
Permanent Paper Standard issued by the National
Information Standards Organization (Z39.48–1984).

10 9 8 7 6 5 4 3 2 1

Contents

Preface

Communication theorists claim it is just as legitimate to study everything from one point of view as to study one thing from all possible points of view. The study of face-to-face interaction is a case in point. At issue is whatever can be sustained by one source among many in a mutually accessible environment. The critical task of each entity is to take into account just noticeable changes in complex and elaborated relations with other entities in the system. For every expressed act, there is some margin of opportunity for multiple modes of interpretive response. As a corollary, each source constructs a frame of reference from a unique position and place within the larger system. What is open to question, in each instance, is a distinct style of personal presentation that cannot be duplicated or replicated by any other source. In effect, separate yet related entities construct unique versions of what transpires between them. As a consequence, the personal conduct of each source is constrained by the expressive freedom and interpretive slant of every other source. At issue is the goodness of fit between the respective versions of multiple frames of action. In dynamic fields of shared action, any notion or presumption of "complete" or "total" communication is strictly ruled out as a matter of principle.

The purpose of this book is to examine the one-source-among-many problem from a standpoint of elaborated modes of complication and complexity. When a great deal of activity takes place in a very short period of time, the potential for face-to-face interaction to become problematic is great. Much depends on (1) the compatibility of the lived circumstances of the respective parties, (2) the clarity of relational development, and (3) the possibility for sustaining a climate of agreement and understanding.

At issue is how various sets of interactants deal with unspoken implication, uncertainty, risk, disruption, confusion, ambiguity, and archriding personal concerns that operate beyond the immediate locus of personal control. Eight chapters are arranged in a typography of communicative possibilities. The first two chapters provide a theoretical framework for inquiry. The next six chapters examine a typology of prototypic instances of mutual exploration, struggle, and concern. Central themes in Chapter 1 are based on a series of working papers (Asilomar Conference in Honor of Gregory Bateson, Pacific Grove, California; Seminar on Communication Theory from Eastern and Western Perspectives, The East-West Center, Honolulu; and Eighth Conference on Communication and Culture, Temple University, Philadelphia) and informal talks presented at the University of Illinois, Urbana, the University of Iowa, Northwestern University, Ohio State University, Purdue University, Temple University, and the University of Wisconsin, Madison. The central construct in Chapter 7 is based on several conference papers (International Conference on Semiotics, Indiana University, Bloomington; International Society for the Study of Aggression, Turku, Finland, and Evanston; International Communication Association, New Orleans; International Humor Conference, Arizona State University, Phoenix; National Cultural Association, San Antonio; and the Speech Communication Association, Chicago, New York, New Orleans, and Houston).

Acknowledgments to the following kindred spirits for engaging in probing conversations scattered over two decades to help light my path: Paul Arnston, Carter M. Ayres, Arthur P. Bochner, Don Cegala, Robert T. Craig, Paul P. Cushman, Jesse G. Delia, James P. Dillard, Mary Anne Fitzpatrick, Dean Hewes, John O. Greene, Lawrence Grossberg, Allen S. Gurman, Doug Maynard, Peter Monge, Barnet Pearce, Morton S. Perlmutter, L. David Ritchie, Robert E. Sanders, Kenneth K. Sereno, Herbert Simons, and 20,000 students (Bethel College, University of Minnesota, University of Washington, Temple University, and University of Wisconsin) who became my teachers. Catherine A. Lyons, Production Editor, James Dunton, Editor, and the fine staff at Praeger Publishers deserve all the credit in the world for acting in good faith, and treating the manuscript so well, from start to finish. Finally, to my wife, Morgan, for inspiration without measure.

Problematic Aspects of Face-to-Face Interaction

A *problematic* proposition asserts that something may be the case. (Brody, 1967, p. 69)

When individuals come into the immediate presence of one another, what transpires may or may not be construed as 'problematic' in Brody's sense of the term. Individuals who engage in face-to-face interaction need not encounter linguistically mediated difficulties or complications when they do so. Nonetheless, one fascinating aspect of direct human encounters is the ways in which they can be so disarmingly simple, automatic, and even mindless in one situation and still become so complicated, intricate, difficult, or vexing the next. This recognition leads to paradox because the very process that enables human beings to speak "thousands of different, mutually incomprehensible tongues" (Steiner, 1975, p. 49) is one we declare with Scheff (1990) to be "awesomely complex" but nonetheless worthy of being taken for granted because we are all so adept at it (p. 27).

At issue is the central question of *why* face-to-face interaction has such great potential to become problematic across a diverse spectrum of shared activities, projects, and routines. The approach taken here appeals to conditions presumed to be intrinsic to language use in public settings. The logic of the essay presupposes just as the language to be taken most seriously is instantiated as language-in-use, perhaps conversation that is real (as opposed to abstract notions) should also be privileged as the paradigm case of human communication. If so, each instance is a model that (potentially) sheds light on the larger significance of how problematic issues emerge in concrete form.

There is growing recognition that "language use and communication are in fact pervasively and even intrinsically flawed, partial, and problematic" (Coupland, Giles & Wiemann, 1991, p. 3). Such an important principle may be (re)interpreted to show how brief or seemingly uncomplicated segments of face-to-face interaction give rise to much more complicated, intricate, inexplicable, or intractable episodes of miscommunication. One exemplar is a lover's quarrel sparked by something trivial before shifting into a spiral of harsh criticism and recrimination in which the lovers suddenly find themselves suspended in a web of irreconcilable linguistic differences.

It probably is not an exaggeration to suppose a great deal of face-to-face interaction is potentially *problematic* whether it in fact turns out that way or not. (This is a softer version of claims that "all communication is problematic" [Kellerman, 1992, p. 292] or that "many problematics are universal" [Babrow, 1992, p. 107]). One of Alfred Schutz's (1967) great insights is that our interactions with others are "constituted in an immensely complicated network of dimensions, relations, and modes of knowledge" (xxvii). We should, therefore, expect nothing less when examining the interface of events, processes, and activities produced at varying levels of clarity and explicitness. The goal is to take advantage of such complexity-in-practice as a way of being better prepared to recognize and integrate fuzzy, messy, or untidy considerations into the fabric of our theoretical schemes.

Only complex living creatures are qualified to produce discourse, engage in dialogue, and endow the world with meaning. As a consequence, the realities of language and communication are far too complicated to be examined in any one neat and tidy theoretical framework (Chomsky, 1957, p. 17). Stated bluntly, "the more complex the system, the more uncertain of its state an observer necessarily must be" (Platt, 1989, p. 655). This progressive differentiation of complexity is what makes sustained coordination difficult and the efficacy and effectiveness of the system so potentially problematic (Hamilton & Biggard, 1985; Hudson, 1984). This is particularly the case for an array of face-to-face encounters extended widely in time and space (Babrow, 1992; Giddens, 1984, 1989, 1991; Mouzelis, 1989).

It follows that face-to-face interaction may produce translational or interpretive achievements of considerable magnitude but never to a point of being immutable or infallible. Making sense of interaction either occurs or it doesn't but the difference between success and failure is ordinarily a matter of more or less rather than all or nothing (Taylor, 1992). Ordinary conversation can be expected to revolve around a multiplex of initial impressions, generalized notions, abstract characterizations, analogues, metaphors, exemplars, protocols, and appeals to global or universal considerations (Bradioc, Bowers & Courtright, 1980, p. 196; Bunge, 1973, p. 92; Ericsson & Simon, 1984). After all, human events *are* infinitely describable and what an evolving set of individuals presumes to be "reality" is simply a model of some designated or conceptualized sense of shared stance in the wider scheme of things (Arndt & Janney, 1987; White & Carlston, 1983; Wierzbicka, 1992). Hence, there need be no simple (isomorphic) relationship between our conceptions (of what to call things) and the object of our appeals (to the way things are). The central task is to measure what transpires on a human scale in accessible terms.

Since all accounts produce a gloss (degrees of abstraction), the ultimate quest of social scientific and humanistic inquiry is to establish a maximum goodness of fit (translatability) between what we study as problematic and various constructions or accounts of others (Tudor, 1976, p. 491). What counts as data, as Geertz (1973) claims, "are really our constructions of other people's constructions of what they and their compatriots are up to" (p. 9). One is led, therefore, to a basic recognition. Any theoretical conception of what makes human communication problematic runs the risk of being as troublesome as the complicated phenomena it seeks to explain or understand because whatever places limits, constraints, limitations, and boundaries on our personal participation in such an inexhaustible subject matter is fashioned out of the same indeterminate stuff that constrains the communicative value of our precious theories (Jacobson, 1991; Kellerman, 1992; Pearce, 1991; Tehranian, 1991).

THE CENTRAL CONSTRUCT

In an effort to sort out what may *become* problematic from what may not, Callon (1980) invokes a view of individuals who engage in a never-ending struggle "to impose their own definitions and to make sure that their view of how reality should be divided up prevails" (p. 198). Relevant activities operate in systematic fashion. First an initial frontier is traced to separate what is to be analyzed from what is not, what is considered relevant from what is to be suppressed and taken as tangible or given from what is problematized as uncertain, unproven, or unknown. Thereafter, amidst concerted effort to formulate problems and mark off sequestered "zones of ignorance," the "protagonists necessarily take as their basic concepts, systems of interpretation and reasoning which are then given the force of certainties and thus totally escape suspicion" (p. 206). In effect, to formulate a problematic is, among other things, "to produce social context for oneself and for others" (p. 216).

Such notions lead to a tentative and provisional conception of the central construct. A problematic centers around any complicated or unsettled question over the definition and direction of expressed relations between separate entities. The central dynamic emerges as a definitional, conceptual, or explanatory inquiry into the elaborated significance of particular states-of-relations sustained by those who address one another in a conventional idiom or code.

Critical themes are instantiated in terms of (1) whether sense-making practice has occurred in any form, or (2) whether something in particular (an X factor) has any communicative value when framed from multiple viewpoints and alternative vantage points. An "expressed" problematic registers as an archriding concern that does not lend itself to any self-evident means of articulation, course of action, or mode of resolution. Hence, such matters surface in explicit relations between interactants and/or in their own implicit involvements with unspoken aspects of manifest subject matter. In effect, face-to-face interaction gives rise to the opportunity for mutual engagement in shared practices that remain somehow in question as unsettled, unfinished, or incomplete.

Stated differently, problematic interchange may be construed in terms of the degree to which the *process* can itself be called into question. After all, just because people interact with one another does not necessarily assure they will remain in a position to make clear and coherent sense out of whatever transpires between them. It has been almost three decades since Watzlawick, Beavin, and Jackson (1967) reminded us that individuals may presume to be engaged in a constant state of communication without any one participant being able to say exactly what *is* conveyed (collectively) and that such conditions constitute a major problem in society. Similarly, Wilden (1980) acknowledges that "no communication can be properly defined or examined at the level at which it occurs" (p. 113). Hence, there is "no assurance that communication will be certain or even relatively trouble free (Fish, 1989, p. 42).

What has been stated so far is advanced in an inquisitive and explorative spirit. The central theme can be subject to 'thick description' across a wide range of possibilities. At issue is who, what, why, where, or when anything in particular has any expressive or communicative value within the expansive parameters of a relatively open-ended system. Specifically, the movement from nonproblematic to problematic forms of interchange may be construed as a shift in the focus of direct or mediated episodes of interaction from (1) what is simple (effortless) to what is difficult (strenuous) to achieve or sustain; (2) what is obvious and self-evident to (a) what *may* be the case or (b) what cannot be presumed or taken for granted; (3) what is expedient or expendable (optional) to what is insistent, demanding, necessary, critical, or urgent; (4) what is inconsequential and fully manageable to what is risky and highly consequential; and (5) what is abundant and easily affordable to what is valued but in scarce supply. All manner of tentative and provisional considerations invite protracted struggle to "put things into words" and "figure out what transpires." The value of the problematic can be expected to correspond roughly with the total magnitude of what is still at issue, outstanding, or what still stands before us as yet unresolved, unsettled, or unknown. It is, in other words, a matter of the capacity and willingness to attend to the accumulation of unfinished discursive business.

Human problematics are construed here to operate at three embedded levels of behavioral complexity—ontological, relational, and discursive. Ontological (first-order) concerns revolve around conditions in which the lived circumstances of one individual remain inaccessible or incommensurate with those of any other. Prior to the point of initial contact, insofar as participants have spoken separate vocabularies and lived in different worlds, what matters most is precisely what is lacking at the very outset, namely a tacit sense of common ground. This presumably makes it much more difficult for clear and coherent sense-making practices to occur. Such conditions tend to foster or reproduce (second-order) relational confusion in the unfolding definition and direction of the interpersonal activities or encounters in question. Moreover, relational confusion interferes with shared effort to define what transpires (immediately) and to chart or direct the possible course of future interaction in light of whatever has already taken place. Finally, (third-order) sources of linguistic ambiguity undermine mutual effort to promote or foster a climate of agreement and understanding. In effect, problematic interchange may be expected to produce a higher level of disruptive circumstance, relational confusion, and linguistic ambiguity than what characterizes nonproblematic modes of exchange. Such extraordinary points of disruption in the perpetuation of tradition, habit, and routine coincide with an inability or unwillingness to maintain what Giddens (1991) describes as a clear sense of continuity of personal identity through "interchanges with persons or objects on the level of daily practice" (pp. 42–43).

INCOMMENSURATE CIRCUMSTANCE

An incommensurate circumstance may be construed in operational terms. At issue are a wide spectrum of interruptions or disruptions in the performance of an *existing* habit, project, ritual, or routine. This standard applies equally for individuals and *collectivities*. The baseline—the degree of continuity in the fulfillment of intentional, strategic, and goal-directed tasks. By such a standard, one might describe any given segment of one's entire existence as relatively in or out of sync or alignment with any other. The same principle applies in the course of everyday interactions in which given modes of conduct of any one source depart from a state of alignment or synchrony with accompanying sequences of actions of any other. Presumably, disruptive and discontinuous circumstances undermine or subvert shared effort to foster or maintain a clear and transparent climate of mutual influence.

The most inclusive question is the manner in which the lived circumstances of any one source are discovered to be compatible, accessible, tolerable, or commensurate with those of any other. The urge to make connections implicates risk and change as well as the subsequent possibility of disintegration and disconnection. So perhaps one's lived circumstances are at issue in direct proportion to the magnitude of unresolved complications brought to light in any public situation. Such conditions presumably complicate issues of relational definition and direction and thereby tend to diminish the efficacy, transparency, and clarity of what transpires.

In successful problematic confrontations, unfinished business and unresolved issues are worked through in a sequence of communal exchanges designed to overcome individual sources of resistance and restraint. It is a matter involving the capacity and willingness to fulfill the potentialities of shared moments despite all that would hold back the respective participants or stand in their way. By this standard, successful means of handling problematic concerns enable us to overcome together, while unsuccessful methods encourage us to give in or let go alone. Perhaps this shifting alignment of what is individually *constituted* within a collaboratively *constructed* framework helps explain the enormous potential for symbolized interaction to be construed in equivocal terms.

The lived circumstances of given individuals become potentially problematic in direct proportion to the full magnitude of unsettled or unresolved questions and issues that emerge as focal points of symbolized interaction. In this most inclusive sense, direct human encounters have the potential to become problematic in direct measure to the total weight of involvements and concerns left unresolved before any given sequence of direct encounters unfold. Here an important ecological principle applies. The sheer magnitude of what is possible gathers individual and collective momentum. In any developmental or evolutionary process both the conditions of potentiality and possibility are important in establishing the conditions for future elaboration. Each new capacity unfolds step by step, thereby allowing for more insightful forecasting and a more accurate fit between knowledge about human reality and real-world circumstances.

Ordinary face-to-face interaction is extraordinary in one primordial sense. Every expressive act with any distinct communicative value is instantiated from at least two or more distinct points of view: the producer of the expressive act and the interpretive observer of that same act (reframed from an equally distinct angle). It follows that each source of reference must connect with multiple points of view to make any real connection at all. By these standards, concrete acts of collaborative action are produced in situated activities sustained by multiple source of orientation who *can* be expected to produce incrementally or radically shifting points of view and altered trajectories of personal conduct. A changing mix of personal alignments and misalignments define the threshold of mutual tolerance for movement toward consensus or divergence. Presumably, then, the interplay of competence and performance factors is observed for effects produced on self and others and repeated (in the manner of trial and error) for the sake of those effects (Mortensen, 1991).

By these premises, a human being, for communicative purposes, may be conceived as an entity capable of calling its shared existence with others into question. Communication between one source and another is problematic insofar as (1) the lived circumstances of one or the other are at issue or otherwise called into question in a disruptive manner; (2) what each one expresses (or interprets) is at issue (to be analyzed); or (3) the interactants are "free" to be one way or another. What remains open to question is the aspiration of the self in relation to the demands and commitments to others (Peters, 1989, p. 387).

In this regard the question of who defines what for whom is potentially burdensome because human beings speak to one another in pragmatic and strategic vocabularies slanted, skewed, and weighted by the imprint of vested interests sustained within the surrounding community at large. At issue are all manner of serious and casual conversations that require a considerable investment of time, space, and energy in the pursuit of matters affecting the definition of personal presentation (by one) and alterative representation (by every other one).

The power to signify is not a neutral force in society but is rather, as Hall (1982, 1989) claims, the result of a struggle for mastery in discourse over what accents will prevail and gain credibility across diverse practices where meaning is intrinsically polysemic and remains therefore inextricably context bound. Public life, as Powell (1988) suggests, "consists essentially of constantly negotiating our understandings with other people, establishing and maintaining by social controls and resistances our own virtue and those of our kind . . . and the immorality and irrationality of others" (p. 99). Hence, effort to give expression to one's lived circumstances is not conceived here as merely an episodic or provisional test of fluent articulation or appropriate decorum under favorable or adverse conditions. It is envisioned rather as an all-inclusive reality test of one's capacity and resolve to make maximum level of discriminate sense out of the experience of interacting with others who may, at any time, express varying gradations of interpretive resistance, directly or indirectly, to what one seeks to reveal before them.

RELATIONAL CONFUSION

Within the inclusive parameters of one's lived circumstances as an issue that may be open to question, there is also a second domain, what might be construed as "relational problematics." What is in question here is the degree of clarity/confusion in the goodness of fit between source and subject matter. In this regard interpersonal relations may be viewed as systems that occur both *between* and *within* interactants (Branham & Pearce, 1985; Polanyi, 1962; Sillars, 1989). Relational problematics involve struggle and strain over the definition and direction of the subsequent course of human events. The potential for mutual influence diminishes as the respective parties endeavor to engage in relational activity in light of each member's own stockpile of first-level difficulties and unresolved complications acquired from prior interactions. Such disruptive circumstance lead to confusion at the level of (1) tacit implicature, (2) constraints on alternatives, and (3) matters of indeterminacy.

Implicature: Here there is definitional and conceptual tension between what is expressed overtly and tacit implications that register from within. Such a conception presupposes (1) intentional acts have unintended consequences (Chaffee & Berger, 1987; Giddens, 1984, 1989, 1991; Held & Thompson, 1989) and (2) observable (accessible) conditions are linked to underlying, nonobservable (inaccessible) implications. In a review of constructivist positions in cognitive psychology, Mandler and Nakamura (1987) make four major claims: (1) the capacity of consciousness is limited in such a way that any description or report displaces or changes salient aspects of its contents (p. 300). (2) Consciousness is *constructed* out of activated unconscious structures (p. 301). (3) "We are customarily conscious of the important aspects of all the evidence that enters the sensory gateways or of all our potential knowledge of the event" (p. 301). (4) Choices are based on selective and strategic activation of complex unconscious mechanisms (p. 302).

Constructivist claims hold at two levels, observation and participation. Arndt and Janney (1987) outline several relevant considerations. The number of interpretable audible and visible activities conveyable at any given point of interaction is "virtually uncountable" (p. 13). Certain neurological screening mechanisms filter and channel our attention and preconceptions in such a bewilderingly complex way that "it ultimately becomes impossible to distinguish internally-generated perceptions from externally-generated ones" (p. 15). Moreover, what we take to be our *conceptualized reality* is infiltrated with introspection—inferences, intuition, imagination, hunch, and educated guesswork (pp. 16–19). "Language and communication may be modeled in virtually any number of ways" (p. 19). Finally, "assumptions about language tacitly involve assumptions about man" (p. 28). The point, therefore, is not to reject whatever is "messy" about face-to-face interaction but rather to take advantage and integrate complex insights into our conceptual frameworks (Arndt & Janney, 1987, p. 38; Grace, 1987, pp. 55–72; Halliday, 1978, p. 38; Pike, 1982, pp. 135–136; Schrag, 1986, pp. 38–39; Sperber & Wilson, 1986, pp. 15–21).

Of immediate relevance is how diverse sets of interactants make sense and endow the personal conduct of one another with meaning. Here the position of Scheff (1990) is particularly instructive. The capacity and willingness of interactants to make sense together depends upon implicature because (1) what individuals articulate to one another ordinarily leaves some aspects (of content and form) unarticulated; (2) for this reason it is "almost impossible for the interactants to understand fully *what* they are talking about, at its various levels, or to understand the implications of the *form* their talk takes" (p. 27); and (3) what gets worked out in interpretation is a highly imaginary effort to link explicit affordances with their accompanying implicit inferences and implications. Here Scheff appeals to Peirce's (1955, pp. 151–156) concept of abduction (rapid and expansive cycling between observation and imagination) as active effort to locate relevant patterns (reference) upon which many cognitive search operations are predicated.

A similar principle is echoed in Grice's (1989, pp. 138–143) notion that cognitive schemes incorporate elements of implicature insofar as they contain explicit reference to words and gestures that are not explicitly expressed in any form. Also relevant are studies of the indexical and reflexive (conscious self-referencing) aspects of expression underscoring the contextual, provisional, and tentative fit between overt acts and their expansive tacit contexts (Atkinson & Heritage, 1984; Mills & Kleinman, 1988; Platt, 1989). Participants in communicative systems do not express everything that matters explicitly. Some things are implied. Having the ability to understand articulations and their intended meanings is difficult enough. Very often the intended meaning of a speech act does not register in the interpreted meaning. Members of close relationships, for example, may be under relatively greater pressure to be sensitive to words and gestures and their underlying implications. In a fast-paced society, human beings are limited in their ability to pick out other people's implications.

The notion that behavior acquires definition through implication is consistent with Schutz's (1967) insistence that the meanings produced by interaction are polymorphic, complex, and multilayered. From such a vantage point, the study of face-to-face interaction is suspect insofar as it presupposes that a constant or optimum level of convergence or attunement is being sustained between interactants over extended time frames. Although such a condition may appear to be the case at the surface, Scheff (1990) concludes "it seems untrue and misleading when applied to the many layers of meaning and implication below the surface of discourse: feelings, motives, and long-range intentions. Attunement at these deeper levels is difficult enough at the personal level; at the group level it may be precarious indeed" (p. 35).

Magnitude of Constraint: The mix of discourse and dialogue facilitates and enables but also inhibits and constrains. No case is friction free. Microanalysis of just noticeable differences in the stream of ordinary conversation are shown to be slanted, skewed, by underlying urges, tensions, intentions, strategies, and unspoken goals. Ethnographers and discourse analysts marshal impressive evidence for the notion that even mundane talk is subject to a bewildering array of implicit constraints and explicit sanctions on the process, form, and content of interaction (Grimshaw, 1990; van Dijk, 1987; Maynard, 1991; Philipsen, 1989). Here situated activities give rise to varied conditions of contextual embeddedness where matters of comprehension depend upon immediate circumstances and where "our best laid descriptions, categories, and explanations always leave something out, need fudging, or are replete with inconsistencies" (Maynard & Clayman, 1991, p. 397). Participant enactment of turn taking provides shifting latitudes of restrictive or expansive opportunity to "compete for the right to be able to talk, and respond to the moment-by-moment emergence of enormously consequential and diverse exigencies, including gaps, overlaps, hesitations, false-starts, errors, topical trajectories, and so on" (p. 400).

Indeterminacy: Conversation generates interpersonal logic that can be sustained or undermined in relation to partially unknown, indeterminate, or unpredictable demand characteristics that cannot be fully anticipated in advance nor deciphered fully within the boundaries of the absolute present tense. Since there is no fixed point in the social system but rather a series of actions relative to one another, and since the state of those relations are changing in magnitude, scope, and salience among the respective parts (Porpora, 1989), what transpires cannot, in the words of Dudley and Brown (1981) "be estimated as an object of fixed determination" (p. 321). Hence, from any given individual viewpoint, what transpires collectively is not an "ultimately knowable object" (p. 321).

One crude measure of relational problematics is simply the proportion of total interaction time where some highly salient aspect of interpretation or understanding is called into question by one or more of the respective parties. After all, exchange relations involve a succession of conjoint activities on behalf of someone or something that matters to someone else. By this standard, three main types of possibilities may be envisioned: relational centered interaction that is (1) nonproblematic, (2) problem- solution- centered, and (3) problematic in definition and direction. Here the central lines of demarcation must be construed as fluid and provisional rather than static or constant over space and time.

Nonproblematic, relational-centered interaction emerges as tacit ground rules, implicit assumptions, reflections, expectations, and inferences are taken for granted (as given) by one or more sources of expressed activity. When things go smoothly and everything seems to fit, interactants maintain a natural attitude toward what each one expresses or interprets in response to the personal conduct of the others. Therefore, interactants may or may not be completely aware of what is being taken for granted on the part of any other. Under such conditions, preconstituted assumptions remain nonproblematic insofar as interactants maintain a state of coordination or synchrony with one another that sustains the basis for common ground. In nonproblematic interchange, the assumptive ground is not at issue. Instead it provides implicit support for interaction that is (in a provisional sense) settled, sedimented, and deeply grounded. In effect, when face-to-face interaction serves to facilitate, legitimate, and sustain what is presumed or taken for granted about relations between (or among) the respective parties, it is, for all intents and purposes, nonproblematic.

When difficulties arise in what one source expresses or another interprets, the respective parties are placed in a position where tacit assumptions (implicature) become an object of explicit, overt focus. Hence, it is a mistake to insist that interaction occurs exclusively at overt or manifest levels of interpersonal behavior because a wide array of implicit and tacit elements may themselves become the focus of explicit involvement and concern. When this happens, the very process of interaction is susceptible to remedial effort at definitional and interpretive negotiation or reform.

When there is a problem in the conduct of individuals who are in the immediate presence of one another, the respective parties may search for alternatives in the manner of a goal-oriented, problem-solving exercise, ritual, or routine. Whenever there is tension, stress, or strain amidst conjoint effort to resolve some felt difficulty, either the difficulty is resolved or it is left unresolved. Insofar as felt difficulties are resolved at the time and under the initial circumstances in which they arise, it is appropriate to characterize the process as a problem-solving exercise executed in the manner of a negotiated settlement. In an important study of the subject, Aldous and Ganey (1989) examine research on the factors that influence families' definition of behavior in problematic situations. Often there is only a vague sense that something is wrong before family members retrospectively define it as a problem (Aldous & Ganey, 1989; Weick, 1971). Sometimes problems do not lend themselves to a technical solution but must simply be lived through (Hewitt & Hall, 1973). Moreover, problems are often deeply "embedded" in the context of other concerns (Weick, 1971). Negative affect is common. So are denial, avoidance, preoccupation with individual concerns, sketchy situational definitions, and discussion cover-ups, particularly when there is an uneven distribution of power. Finally, families, like other groups, continuously face extraordinary events with potentially significant negative consequences (Aldous & Ganey, 1989, p. 858; also, Olson & McCubbin, 1983; Reid, 1985; Reiss, 1981).

In problematic relationships, felt difficulties are not resolved at each step along the way or in the spirit of once-and-for-all. At the level of conversation, individuals make choices in light of the total magnitude of complexities in a situation in which multiple goals and strategies come into play (Tracy, 1989). In the collective search for a "solution" or "cure," individuals are prone to rely on quasi-theories, ritualized causal explanations, and well-known interpretations as a means of addressing unconventional issues (Aldous & Ganey, 1989; Hewitt & Hall, 1973). Hence, problems become problematic insofar as they must be confronted repeatedly in the context of some institutionalized habit, ritual, or routine.

It is appropriate to think of relational problematics as struggle and strain that are manufactured at each step along the way. As soon as one relational difficulty disappears (in the manner of problem-solving exercise, truce, or negotiated settlement of some unfinished business), another soon arises to take its place. The question of whether one should be open and trusting at this particular time and place may be a problem, but it becomes problematic only if the question becomes salient during widely extended sequences of interaction construed by the participants to be never or rarely amenable to resolution or solution. If one source is in a position of having to confront over and over the basic question of whether to trust someone else, then the issue of trust is not a problem but a problematic. From this angle some central object of involvement and concern is at issue in the manner of a hidden agenda that does not go away or as unfinished business to be confronted over and over again but without much prospect of ever being amenable to a mutually satisfying method of resolution. Initial difficulties may well multiply in the manner of a conflict without a technical solution.

LINGUISTIC AMBIGUITY

The third subdomain of problematic communication unfolds at the level of symbol, discourse, or symbolization. Where the lived circumstances of various interactants are not in question, and where the definitions and directions of a given relationship are also taken for granted, what each source expresses to others may still be at issue. Here is where unfinished business and hidden agenda involve ambiguous or distorted subject matter that transcends the immediate relationship between the respective parties. Since communication is fundamentally a sense-making, meaning-endowing activity, it is inherently risky and subject to gradations of noncomprehension, moments of incoherence, and lapses into somewhat inexplicable domains of misinterpretation and misunderstanding (Branham & Pearce, 1985; Branham, 1989).

Here the ideal is purely hypothetical, the vision of a universal translator of all the individual translations in question—one who is presumed to be in a sovereign or privileged position to know. Such an ideal type may be construed as one who is able and willing to take the expressed activity of every other one consistently and predictably into full and unconditional account. This implies the capacity to make no translational or interpretive mistakes (miscommunication) while moving back and forth from one language to another and from one source of language use to another. Here competence (in ideal form) presumes the use of principles and mechanisms assuring for all intents and purposes that anything stated in one language can be restated in any other, both under familiar and foreign circumstances. Grace (1987) calls this the postulate of "intertranslatability," an idea that makes it particularly difficult to recognize the incommensurate, uncertain, and undecidable features of all human translation (Brown, 1984).

The concept of "universal" translation presumes that whatever individuals can experience in their own language they can and will translate interchangeably into the language of one another. Unfortunately, such an idea does not allow for elements of the indeterminate, the ineffable, the diffuse, and the things of which we cannot speak. Moreover, it allows no provision for an individualized sense of wonder and awe that things are what they are. At all times it is supposed that the encoded interpretive schemes of one interactant match the decoded interpretive schemes of any other and, hence, nothing is left undecided when conceptual terms are placed in opposition to one another (Platt, 1989). In point of fact, human discourse is as fuzzy as thinking in general because everyday words are, as Lyons (1981) claims, somewhat polysemic, indeterminate in meaning, and therefore undefinable (pp. 73–74). The basic insight is that lexical variation reflects cultural differences across diverse speech communities. The form of talk follows the flow of thought and different conceptual universes so that, as Wierzbicka (1992) states, "not everything that can be said in one language can be said (without additions and subtractions) in another, and it is not just a matter of certain things being *easier* to say in one language than in another" (p. 20). The same principle applies, perhaps in a weaker sense, to interchange between any two or more interactants within the *same* speech community.

Real life complexities assure "not everything two persons signal to one another in a given situation is perceived, and not everything that is perceived is shared intersubjectively" (Arndt & Janney, 1987, p. 63). Because human actions integrate manifest conditions together with what Schrag (1986) calls "meanings hidden and submerged, scarred by self-deceptions, and infected with ideology" (p. 38) and forces that surpass the intentions of the participants, thereby "announcing patterns of ideation and valuations that remain opaquely entrenched within the habitual behavior of everyday life and delivered processes of social formation" (pp. 38–39), a science of human behavior must indeed do a "double duty," namely to attend to "conscious motivation and calculated actions . . . but also . . . the resources of . . . tacit and repressed meanings" (pp. 38–39).

To examine problematic aspects of face-to-face interaction, it seems sensible to abandon the overly idealized and mythical presumption that the lived circumstance of any one individual can ever be fully shared with the lived circumstances of any other. What is required is a movement away from the optimistic myth that pure communication is even possible. In the study of face-to-face interaction, it is important to recognize that the (phenomenological) status of any given participant or observer is not completely afforded by any other one. Moreover, what constitutes exchange for one source need not constitute the basis for exchange for any other (Graumann, 1988). This does not mean simply that everyone sees things in their own unique way. It leads rather to something far more important. The presence of each and every single observer alters the cumulative definitions of the shared situation as a whole. This suggests we are all suspended in webs of significance that *we* and *others* have spun.

In the final analysis, everyone sees things in their own way because of invariant and structural conditions in the immediate environment that affect each one who is coimplicated (within observable limits) in charting the respective definitions and directions of what collectively transpires. First, there is the minimal presumption that each individual in question is located in a position to be a source of what is manifest to others. Second, in any shared circumstance the respective parties are able to construe things, to take the larger stream of events into account, from a unique vantage point. This, in turn, implies that one's point of view molds and shapes whatever viewpoint there is to be acquired. Third, everyone is presumed to have some margin of freedom, a range of vantage points from which to construe things. Fourth, there is a universal consideration that every inter-actant has *no* choice but to see things in relation to the various positions and places in which they and no one else is situated.

Stated another way, discourse becomes problematic because each inter-actant is equipped with a single set of interpretive parameters, an archrid-ing frame of reference that sets the limits of all context-bound frameworks of activity. In this connection Rommetveit (1980, 1988) points out that interactants do not merely assume or adapt to a given stance or position but rather actively inhabit the perspective from which events are framed, an insight that echoes the insightfulness of Schutz's (1967) claim "I live in my acts." So, of course, does everyone else. This is the one context from which we cannot even remotely conceive of escape. Each one of us has, as Moore (1987) puts it, "a perspectival conception of the world which we cannot rise above—but without which we cannot otherwise depict ourselves from having" (p. 20). Since "the possibility of description itself implies a point of view . . . this implies, in turn, niche oriented, imperfection, and partial representation" (Clark, 1984, p. 486). In this regard Levenson (1972) refers to what we perceive of the real world as a "creation" with boundaries and limits that make it an epistemological fallacy "to think that we can stand outside of what we observe, or observe, without distortion, what is alien to our experience" (p. 8). Levenson underscores the fact that "we inhabit a world of synaptical connections, obscure, interrelated and tampered with at great risk" (p. 26).

This basic principle of "perspectivity" serves to underscore the localized and positional dependence of linguistic construction as constrained by (1) the immediate location of the source, (2) the larger biographical stance from which all concrete events are construed, and (3) the tacitly accepted, taken-for-granted array of background conditions, situatedness, em-beddedness, and total immersion in interest-relative and goal-oriented projects and routines (Barwise & Perry, 1983; Graumann, 1988; Hanney,

1987; Putnam, 1978; and Rommetveit, 1980, 1988). By these standards, no one source or version of any one source constitutes the ultimate standard by which to judge all the respective versions because the very question of what transpires is always somewhat beyond each one's interpretive grasp. In other words, "communication is seldom what it seems," as Reilly and DiAngelo (1990, p. 129) claim, because of the dynamic interface between what is visible and what is invisible or hidden in unevenly permeated degrees and textures of sedimented symbolic form.

To assert that individuals see things in their own unique way is a tacit admission that individuals do not see exactly the same arrangement of things at all. At the level of symbolization, Grace (1987) points out that it is virtually impossible to discuss subject matter with anyone who "has not previously been aware of the existence of that subject (*qua* subject)" (p. 17). Moreover, since the rules of language use are not identical from one speaker to another, "each language has a unique potential for reality construction—each subtends a different set of potential realities" (p. 70). In short, language is not only used but is also put to use in two fundamental ways: to construct a world and to operate with others within it (Bruner, 1984; Deely, 1978). We are left with a universal set of possibilities to be filled in by each and every one.

The distinction between "participant" and "observer" is critical here. The crucial recognition is that "the observer cannot make an observation without an intrusion on the observed" (Dudley & Brown, 1981, p. 320). In matters affecting both the mix of explicit vantage points and deeply embedded viewpoints, the interpretive frame of any given observer is not presumed to coincide or duplicate the interpretive frame of any other. In other words, there is always slippage—some fragmented, lost, misplaced, or missing elements—implicit in the shift from one interactant's frame of reference to the interpretive frame of any other. In matters affecting the interplay between expressivity and responsivity, there can be no such thing as infallibility. All translations, all interpretations, are subject to alteration, reinterpretation, and revision by one member or another. Hence, the most competent forms of human interchange *must* fall short of the mythical ideal of complete fidelity in the transformation of who-expresses-what-to-whom in shared circumstances. What matters most here is fidelity to the unfolding expression of human possibilities.

While a given physical setting may be fully shared, it is nonetheless subject to a principle of differential sensitivity. Lines of action, their accompanying intentions, goals, and effects, arise within prior environmental structures and constraints. As Knowles and Smith (1984) note, the process for each participant is rich, complex, and differentially sensitive. Moreover, there is what Fischer (1988) terms "an overwhelming amount of evidence" that communication between individuals, even under ideal circumstances (identical levels of information and interpretive-processing capacity, identical goals, unlimited time) will "almost unavoidably, within some reasonable time span, eventuate in misunderstandings, misinterpretations, different conclusions, different cognitive adaptations and variations, and disparity of perception in certain domains" (p. 194).

As a rule, if two individuals have different internal standards, if they occupy distinct positions, places, and lines of orientation and engage in the mutual production of fused and unfused spheres of activity in a shared situation, it cannot be expected they will grasp, comprehend, or react in the same way to any given mode of expressed intent or have equal effects on other things (Bhaskar, 1978; Brown, 1984; Dascal & Berenstein, 1987; Knowles & Smith, 1984; Mandler & Nakamura, 1987; Senchuk, 1986; Smith & Ginsborg, 1989; Vollmer, 1986). Total communication does not exist in this sense. As Prodi (1988) recognizes, there will never be total interaction because the possibility of meaning and attribution of meaning presuppose "both a world to be explored and a structure capable of exploring, and, in all cases, the limited and specialized possibilities of this experience" (p. 195).

In matters involving the management of meaning, Coupland, Giles, and Wiemann (1991) take the position that semantic "slippage" is common because conversation occurs under real-time processing constraints and within the use of ordinary linguistic codes "we must doubt that there are such entities as pure, unsullied, and perfect semantic representations" (p. 5). While the measure of meaning may *potentially* vary on a continuum of possibilities ranging from the transparent to the opaque, practical considerations assure that even where there is considerable conjoint effort to be as clear, direct, and explicit as possible, interactants are bound to be affected by subtle pressures associated with the intrusion of tacit, inexplicit, and indirect features of ordinary language use.

The urge to make perfect sense notwithstanding, there is considerable potential for misdirection, indirection, and equivocation because symbolic processes, as Foster (1980) states, are "largely covert and extremely complex" (p. 395). As a case in point, humor is prototypic of discourse that exploits ambiguity instead of minimizing it. Hence, it is very responsive to incongruity, ambivalence, and subtrafuge when the respective parties give themselves (temporary) permission to escape from task-oriented literal-mindedness into the domain of verbal play to explore implicit meanings, exchange subtle, semisecret feelings that trace hidden analogies, condense and compress the strange, uncertain, irregular, or unfamiliar deviations from straightforward and conventional modes of address. Humor is enigmatic by definition. It is full of surprises because it thrives on deflection, sleight-of-hand, magic, tricks, and misdirection—whatever is irregular, nonlinear, open-ended, maniform, paradoxical, or self-contradictory about what registers at the outer fringes of the prevailing social order (Apte, 1985; Mulkay, 1988; Raskin, 1985).

In an innovative study of equivocal matters on the literal-minded, serious side of conversation, Bavelas, Black, Chovil, and Mullett (1990) describe equivocal messages that change before our eyes. "We can see it one way, then another. It makes sense, then it doesn't. It doesn't make sense, then it does" (p. 13). Like reversible figures with opposite yet reconcilable properties, equivocal messages can "say something without really saying something" or "say nothing while saying something" (p. 21). They do this by means of denial and avoidance of direct communication in situations where alternative choices would lead to negative consequences. Hence, it is a good solution to a bad situation.

In effect, the critical matter of who-and-what-matters-to-whom is subject to all manner of ambiguation and discontinuity in complex situations that vary from literal sense to ludicrous nonsense. At all times A and B may assume, ascribe, or deny (continuously or discontinuously) the various positions and places that are assumed toward or away from one another, but none of the positions are to be construed as exhaustive, privileged, or sovereign. Said another way, there is always something about the visible effects of direct human encounter that cannot be subsequently conveyed or reproduced in terms of the initial conditions that produced them. Communication is problematic for all of the reasons that make it difficult to express what is communicated on its own terms. These contingencies render the question of establishing what Gergen (1982, p. 64) calls the "supremacy of interpretation" entirely problematic and is therefore consistent with Mannheim's (1952) view of human existence as radically problematic. Here one's room to move is as inclusive as one's worldview. On this issue Petrilli (1986, pp. 225–226) describes meaning as the product of a dynamic interpretation and a potentially infinite process of semiosis that is never fully encapsulated by a single interactant.

What is affordable to any one source may or may not be aligned with the focus of any other. Source A cannot and does not escape what surrounds A, and source B cannot and does not escape what surrounds B. Moreover, since A and B remain *uniquely* situated in *commonly* inhabited communities of time and space, so also must their respective definitions of what takes place remain uniquely situated, spontaneous, fresh, and autonomous. From this perspective fascination with the interplay of discourse and dialogue is reserved not so much for those who take the mechanisms of conversational life for granted as for those as yet still capable of feeling a sense of wonder and awe that communication (between one source and another) should happen in any sense at all.

In the domain of personal conduct perhaps it is possible to become more "mindful" of what other human beings construe as having or not having any distinct communicative value. In the domain of inquiry it is important to be in a position to formulate or construct a humanistic logic for communication theory that strives to remain sensitive to matters of individual competence and realization of ideal levels of performance but also to practices that reveal real-time pressure, constraint, limitation, lack of enablements, or the neglect or abuse of precious linguistic resources.

The model of problematic communication envisioned here has a central focus—the movement in and out of disruptive circumstance, relational confusion, and linguistic ambiguity. It is as important to know how individuals-as-interactants explore what remains elusive, uncertain, or unknown as it is to examine conventional routines. Careful study of the transition from the ordinary into the extraordinary (and back again) sheds light on what transpires along a wider portion of the spectrum.

REFERENCES

Aldous, J., & Ganey, R. (1989). Families' definition behavior of problematic situations. *Social Forces, 67*, 870–896.

Apte, M. L. (1985). *Humor and laughter: An anthropological approach*. Ithaca, NY: Cornell University Press.

Arndt, H., & Janney, R. W. (1987). *InterGrammer: Towards an integrative model of verbal, prosodic, and kinesic choices in speech*. Berlin: Mouton de Gruyter.

Atkinson, J. M., & Heritage, (Eds.). (1984). *Structures of social action: Studies in conversational analysis*. Cambridge: Cambridge University Press.

Babrow, J. (1992). Communication and problematic integration: Understanding diverging probability and value, ambiguity, ambivalence, and impossibility. *Communication Theory, 2*, 95–130.

Barwise, J., & Perry, J. (1983). *Situations and attitudes*. Cambridge, MA: MIT Press.

Bavelas, J. B., Black, A., Chovil, N., & Mullett, J. (1990). *Equivocal communication*. Newbury Park: Sage Publications.

Bhaskar, R. (1978). *A realist theory of science*. Sussex: Harvester Press.

Bradioc, J. J., Bowers, J. W. & Courtright, J. A. (1980). Lexical variations in intensity, immediacy, and diversity: An axiomatic theory and causal model. In St. R. H. St. Clair & H. Giles (Eds.), *The social and psychological context of language* (pp. 193–223). Hillsdale, NJ: Erlbaum.

Branham, R. J. (1989). Speaking itself: Susan Sontag's town hall address. *The Quarterly Journal of Speech, 75*, 259–276.

Branham, R. J., & Pearce, W. B. (1985). Between text and context: Toward a rhetoric of contextual reconstruction. *The Quarterly Journal of Speech, 71*, 19–36.

Brody, B. A. (1967). Logical terms, glossary of. In P. Edwards, (Ed.), *The encyclopedia of philosophy*, Vol. 5 (pp. 57–77). New York: Collier Macmillan.

Brown, H. L. (1984). Incommensurability. *Inquiry, 26*, 3–29.

Bruner, J. (1984). Pragmatics of language and language of pragmatics. *Social Research, 51*, 969–984.

Bunge, M. A. (1973). *Method, model, and matter*. Dordrecht, Holland: D. Reidel Publishing.

Callon, M. (1980). Struggles and negotiations to define what is problematic and what is not. In K. D. Knorr, R. Knohn, & R. Whitley (Eds.), *The social process of scientific investigation. Sociology of the sciences*, Vol. 5 (pp. 197–219). Dordrecht, Holland: D. Reidel Publishing.

Chaffee, S. H. & Berger, C. R. (1987). What communication scientists do. In C. R. Berger & S. H. Chaffee (Eds.), *Handbook of communication science*. (pp. 99–122). Newbury Park: Sage Publications.

Chomsky, N. (1957). *Syntactic Structures*. The Hague: Mouton.

Clark, A. J. (1984). Evolutionary epistemology and ontological realism. *The Philosophical Quarterly, 34*, 482–490.

Coupland, N., Giles, H., & Wiemann, J. M. (1991). *"Miscommunication" and problematic talk*. Newbury Park: Sage Publications.

Dascal, M., & Berenstein, I. (1987). Two modes of understanding: Comprehending and grasping. *Language & Communication, 7*, 139–151.

Deely, J. N. (1978). Toward the origin of semiotic. In T. A. Sebeok (Ed.), *Sight, sound, and sense* (pp. 1–30). Bloomington: Indiana University Press.

Dudley, C. J., & Brown, E. (1981). Social relativity: The motion of groups and actors. *The Sociological Quarterly, 22*, 313–326.

Ericsson, K. A., & Simon, H. A. (1984). *Protocol analysis*. Cambridge, MA: MIT Press.

Fischer, K. (1988). The functional architecture of adaptive cognitive systems—With limited capacity. *Semiotica, 68–3/4*, 191–248.

Fish, S. (1989). *Doing what comes naturally*. Durham, NC: Duke University Press.

Foster, M. L. (1980). The growth of symbolism in culture. In M. L. Foster & S. H. Brandes (Eds.), *Symbol as sense: New approaches to the analysis of meaning* (pp. 371–397). New York: Academic Press.

Geertz, C. (1973). *The interpretation of cultures*. New York: Basic Books.

Gergen, K. J. (1982). *Toward transformation in social knowledge*. New York: Springer-Verlag.

Giddens, A. (1984). *The constitution of society: Outline of the theory of structuration*. Berkeley: University of California Press.

Giddens, A. (1989). The orthodox consensus and the emerging synthesis. In B. Dervin, L. Grossberg, B. J. O' Keefe, & E. Wartella (Eds.), *Rethinking communication: Vol. 1. Paradigm issues* (pp. 53–65). Newbury Park: Sage Publications.

Giddens, A. (1991). *Modernity and self-identity*. Stanford, California: Stanford University Press.

Grace, G. W. (1987). *The linguistic construction of reality*. London: Croom Helm.

Graumann, C. F. (1988). Phenomenological analysis and experimental method in psychology—The problem of their compatibility. *Journal for the Theory of Social Behaviour, 18*, 33–50.

Grice, H. P. (1989). *Studies in the way of words*. Cambridge, MA: Harvard University Press.

Grimshaw, A. A. (Ed.). (1990). *Conflict talk: Sociolinguistic investigations of arguments in conversations*. Cambridge: Cambridge University Press.

Hall, S. (1982). The rediscovery of 'ideology': Return of the repressed in media studies. In M. Gurevitch, T. Bennett, J. Curran, & J. Woodacott (Eds.), *Culture, society and the media* (pp. 56–90). New York: Methuen.

Hall, S. (1989). Ideology and communication theory. In B. Dervin, L. Grossberg, B. J. O' Keefe, & E. Wartella (Eds.), *Rethinking communication: Vol. 1. Paradigm issues* (pp. 40–52). Newbury Park: Sage Publications.

Halliday, M.A.K. (1978). *Language as social semiotic*. London: Arnold.

Hamilton, G. G., & Biggart, N. W. (1985). Why people obey: Theoretical observations on power and obedience in complex organizations. *Sociological Perspectives, 28*, 3–78.

Hanney, A. (1987). The claims of consciousness: A critical survey. *Inquiry, 30*, 395–434.

Held, D., & Thompson, J. B. (Eds.). (1989). *Social theory of modern societies: Anthony Giddens and his critics.* Cambridge: Cambridge University Press.

Hewitt, J. P., & Hall, P. M. (1973). Social problems, problematic situations, and quasi-theories. *American Sociological Review, 38*, 367–374.

Hudson, J. R. (1984). Mills & Hawley on power. *Sociological Perspectives, 27*, 371–393.

Jacobson, T. L. (1991). Theories as communications. *Communication Theory, 1*, 145–150.

Kellerman, K. (1992). Communication: Inherently strategic and primarily automatic. *Communication Monographs, 59*, 288–300.

Knowles, P. L., & Smith, D. L. (1984). The ecological perspective applied to social perception: Revision of a working paper. *Journal of the Theory of Social Behavior, 12*, 53–78.

Levenson, E. (1972). *The fallacy of understanding: An inquiry into the changing structure of psychoanalysis.* New York: Basic Books.

Lyons, J. (1981). *Language, meaning, and context.* Bungay, Suffolk: Fontana.

Mandler, G., & Nakamura, Y. (1987). Aspects of consciousness. *Personality and Social Psychology Bulletin, 13*, 299–313.

Mannheim, K. (1952). On the nature of economic ambition and its significance for the social education of man. In P. Kecskemeti (Ed.), *Essays on the sociology of knowledge* (pp. 230–275). London: Routledge and Kegan Paul.

Maynard, D. W. (1991). Interaction and asymmetry in clinical discourse. *American Journal of Sociology, 97*, 448–495.

Maynard, D. W., & Clayman, S. E. (1991). The diversity of ethnomethodology. *Annual Review of Sociology, 17*, 385–418.

Mills, T., & Kleinman, S. (1988). Emotions, reflexivity, and action: An interactionist analysis. *Social Forces, 66*, 1009–1027.

Moore, A. W. (1987). Points of view. *The Philosophical Quarterly, 37*, 1–20.

Mortensen, C. D. (1991). Communication, conflict, and culture. *Communication Theory, 1*, 273–293.

Mouzelis, N. (1989). Restructuring structuration theory. *The Sociological Review, 37*, 613–635.

Mulkay, M. (1988). *On humor: Its nature and place in modern society.* New York: Basil Blackwell.

Olson, D. H., & McCubbin, H. I. (1983). *Families: What makes them work.* Beverly Hills: Sage Publications.

Pearce, W. B. (1991). On comparing theories: Treating theories as commensurate or incommensurate, *Communication Theory, 1*, 159–164.

Peirce, C. S. (1958). *Philosophical writings of Peirce.* New York: Dover Publications.

Peters, J. D. (1989). John Locke, the individual, and the origin of communication. *The Quarterly Journal of Speech, 75*, 387–399.

Petrilli, S. (1986). On the materiality of signs. *Semiotica, 62* (3/4), 223–245.

Philipsen, G. (1989). An ethnographic approach to communication studies. In B. Dervin, L. Grossberg, B. J. O' Keefe, & E. Wartella (Eds.), *Rethinking communication: Vol 2. Paradigm Exemplars* (pp. 258–268). Newbury Park: Sage Publications.

Pike, K. L. (1982). *Linguistic Concepts.* Lincoln, NE: University of Nebraska Press.

Platt, R. (1989). Reflexivity, recursion, and social life: Elements for a postmodern sociology. *The Sociological Review, 37*, 636–667.

Polanyi, M. (1962). *Personal knowledge: Towards a post critical philosophy.* New York: Harper and Row.

Porpora, D. V. (1989). Four concepts of social structure. *Journal for the Theory of Social Behaviour, 19*, 195–210.

Powell, C. (1988). A phenomenological analysis of humour in society. In C. Powell, & G. Paton, (Eds.), *Humour in society* (pp. 86–105). London: Macmillan Press.

Prodi, G. (1988). Material biases of signification. *Semiotica, 69* (3/4), 191–241.

Putnam, H. (1978). *Meaning and the moral sciences.* London: Routledge & Kegan Paul.

Raskin, V. (1985). *Semantic mechanisms of humor.* New York: D. Reidel Publishing.

Reid, W. J. (1985). *Family problem solving.* New York: Columbia University Press.

Reilly, B. J., & Di Angelo, J. A. (1990). Communication: A cultural system of meaning and value. *Human Relations, 43*, 199–210.

Reiss, D. (1981). *The family's construction of reality.* Boston, MA: Harvard University Press.

Rommetveit, R. (1980). On 'meanings' of acts and what is meant and made known by what is said in a pluralist social world. In M. Brenner (Ed.), *The Structure of Action* (pp. 108–149). Oxford: Basil Blackwell.

Rommetveit, R. (1988). Meaning, context, and control: Convergent trends and controversial issues in social-scientific research on human cognition and communication. *Inquiry, 30*, 77–99.

Scheff, T. J. (1990). *Microsociology: Discourse, emotion, and social structure.* Chicago: University of Chicago Press.

Schrag, C. O. (1986). *Communicative praxis and the space of subjectivity.* Bloomington: Indiana University Press.

Schutz, A. (1967). *The phenomenology of the social world.* (G. Walsh & F. Lehnert, trans.). Evanston, IL: Northwestern University Press.

Schutz, A. (1970). *On phenomenology and social relations.* Chicago: University of Chicago Press.

Senchuk, D. M. (1986). Privacy regained. *Philosophical Investigations, 9*, 18–35.

Sillars, A. L. (1989). Communication, uncertainty, and understanding in marriage. In B. Dervin, L. Grossberg, B. J. O' Keefe, & E. Wartella (Eds.), *Rethinking communication: Vol. 2. Paradigm exemplars* (pp. 258–268). Newbury Park: Sage Publications.

Smith, D. L., & Ginsburg, G. P. (1989). The social perception process: Reconsidering the role of social stimulation. *Journal for the Theory of Social Behaviour, 19*, 31–45.

Sperber, D., & Wilson, D. (1986). *Relevance: Communication and cognition.* Cambridge, MA: Harvard University Press.

Steiner, G. (1975). *After Babel: Aspects of language and translation.* London: Oxford University Press.

Taylor, T. J. (1992). *Mutual misunderstanding: Scepticism and the theorizing of language and interpretation.* Durham, NC: Duke University Press.

Tehranian, M. (1991). Is comparative communication theory possible/desirable? *Communication Theory, 1,* 44–59.

Tracy, K. (1989). Conversational dilemmas and the naturalistic experiment. In B. Dervin, L. Grossberg, B. J. O' Keefe, & E. Wartella (Eds.), *Rethinking communication Vol. 2. Paradigm exemplars* (pp. 411–423). Newbury Park: Sage Publications.

Tudor, A. (1976). Misunderstanding everyday life. *Sociological Review, 24,* 479–503.

Van Dijk, T. A. (Ed.). (1987). *Handbook of discourse analysis* (Vols. 1–4). London: Academic Press.

Vollmer, F. (1986). Intentional explanation and its place in psychology. *Journal for the Theory of Social Behaviour, 21,* 285–298.

Watzlawick, P., Beavin, J. H., & Jackson, D. (1967). *Pragmatics of Human Communication.* New York: W. W. Norton.

Weick, K. C. (1971). Group processes, family processes & problem solving. In J. Aldous, R. Hill, M. Straus, & I. Tallman, (Eds.), *Family problem solving: A symposium on theoretical, methodological, and substantive concerns.* Holland: Dryden.

White, D. J., & Carlston, D. E. (1983). Consequences of schemata for attention, impressions, and recall in complex social interactions. *Journal of Personality and Social Psychology, 45,* 538–550.

Wierzbicka, A. (1992). Semantics, culture, and cognition: Universal human concepts in culture-specific configurations. New York: Oxford University Press.

Wilden, A. (1980). *System and structure: Essays in communication and exchange* (2nd ed.). New York: Tavistock Publications.

2

The Risk of Noncommunication

One way to study face-to-face interaction is to locate a given set of instances on a continuum ranging anywhere from "simple" (effortless) to "difficult" (strenuous) to sustain as a sense-making practice. It is possible with this strategy to trace movement from what is simple, obvious, optional, inconsequential, and easily affordable to what is difficult, uncertain, demanding, risky, and highly valued but in short supply. Such a shift greatly complicates the skills required for interactants to make goal-directed sense out of the personal conduct of one another.

It is possible, after all, to engage in a great deal of interaction and still produce little or no sense of significance, import, or meaning, as in the case of a fuss or commotion. The relevant distinction is between the sheer magnitude of shared activity (what transpires) and what is brought to light as a consequence (when looking back upon it). Stated another way, what has communicative impact is contingent on (1) how much, (2) in what way, (3) by what means, and (4) with what unforeseen consequences various sequences of interaction are grasped, comprehended, and understood. The ideal model is a situation in which what we do clearly reveals who and what we are to ourselves and others. At the opposite end of the spectrum is where we reveal an inability or unwillingness to make clear sense of who and what we are to one another.

The central issue can be phrased in this way: Have you ever been in a public setting where you suddenly found yourself (momentarily) incapable or unwilling to express what you were experiencing with others who were present at the time? In many ways and in different forms over a fifteen-year period, this sort of issue has been posed by the author to several thousand individuals enrolled in a wide variety of educational institutions ranging all the way from junior and senior high school to several undergraduate and graduate (social science) courses in large, urban, Midwestern and East Coast universities. Within this larger collaborative effort, over the course of a decade, under conditions of strict anonymity, several hundred respondents completed an open-ended questionnaire containing single-spaced lines traced on both sides of a sheet of paper. The question reads: "Have there been times/circumstances in your life where you felt that what you were experiencing at the time was not something that you could express to anyone else? Yes ____ No ____ Explain."

The central question is subject to a diverse range of open-ended interpretations. In a preliminary study, fifty individuals enrolled in a course in communication theory were asked to interpret specifically what the question meant to them. Responses tend to cluster around four basic modes of interpretation: (1) forces and factors that constrain the clarity and transparency of observed behavior; (2) inferences about implicature—what does not take place explicitly, overtly (and why); (3) misuse of personal resources; and (4) what is presumed to be lacking or missing from the interchange between the respective parties.

Salient issues are defined so that a presumption of noncommunication can enter into the calculation of the larger communicative equation. For just as the vital matter of what happens is relative to what does not happen within a larger array of possibilities, so basic considerations of what can, should, or ought to take place between separate but interdependent entities are strictly relative to what cannot or will not (as a matter of principle) take place. At issue is the overall goodness of fit between a state of "being" (the condition one is in) and a process of "doing" (what one does). Such vital matters acquire definitional force in relation to what other individuals are in or out of a position to *be* or *do* for the sake of one another.

Specifically, by examining a wide spectrum of interpretive frames, it is possible to address a critical but mostly ignored issue in social science (but not humanistic) literature. Of interest is what makes it possible for human beings to come into the immediate presence of one another, then intermittently or continuously alter or redefine the personal conduct of one another, and eventually leave the boundaries of the immediate situation with an incomplete, unresolved, or faulty sense of what transpired from multiple vantage points.

If the opportunity to engage in face-to-face interaction gives rise to the very possibility of achieving a state or condition of communication between separate entities, then surely the question or definition of what qualifies as the communicative significance of any given aspect of the system can itself become an issue. There is much to be gained from multiple levels of inquiry into the dynamics of elaborative systems. Such a stance makes it possible, for example, for the question of the risk of noncommunication to be addressed *within* the parameters of the framework of inquiry. Presumptions of human connection do not, after all, preclude the possibility for discovery of points of disconnection along the way.

ASSUMPTIVE GROUND

Personal assumptions are crucial as implications. Specifically, personal assumptions may not be observable, accessible, or applicable to anyone other than the one who produces them. The first generalized interpretive stance is optimistic, unconditional, and unqualified. As an approximation, the following formula could be proposed:

Source A presumes:

(a) my direct contact with source B: $(A\rightarrow(A\leftrightarrow B) + (A\leftrightarrow B)\leftarrow B)$

(b) creates a mutual connection $(A\leftrightarrow B)$

(c) constant or consistent over time

(d) as a source of common ground.

This presumptive stance is all-inclusive. The position smacks of secular pantheism—the locus of communication is inside, outside, between, all around, and the circle is never broken. Interpersonal boundaries are construed in elastic and permeable terms. Hence, there is no presumption of any communicative breakdown, lapse, blank spot, or empty space in the emergent structure of human relations. In other words, there is no provision or possibility for a sense of loss. Nothing is construed to be irreversible. When operating in such an idealized speech community, each member is presumed to be able to say something about anything that matters to virtually anyone else. As a matter of faith it is presumed that whatever is subject to human experience can and will be articulated in one form or another. Nothing falls through the cracks. Such a position, in effect, rules out consideration of communicative failure or, for that matter, any serious form of miscommunication between two or more sensate beings.

The second interpretive stance involves tension between two oppositional types of working assumptions. The first presupposes that a point of noncommunication emerges within the framework of the immediate situation (insiders) while the second presumes that an alternative set of individuals (outsiders—who were not present at the time) could make sense of what is taking place—if only they were located with the province of the here and now. Somehow one gets caught up in the mixed movement, going back and forth, in and out of a state of connection with direct or mediated sources of expressed reference. As an approximation, the following formula could be proposed:

Source A presumes:

(a) my direct contacts with others (source B, C, D, & E)

(b) create a disruption in the continuity of mutual influence

(c) that changes over time

(d) for at least one of the respective parties (A)

(e) as a source of uncommon ground.

Such a stance, in effect, appeals to any number/circumstance in which one is presumed to be unable to express, by way of words and gestures, what is being experienced to the *particular* individuals who are involved. This does not mean, however, that one could not have expressed certain things to other individuals who were not present at the time. Moreover, the legitimacy of this position presupposes (1) a heavily reactive position where (2) the conduct of others—what they do or do not do—is framed as the all-powerful source of causation in the total dynamic of human relations. It is as if one's own expressive capacities and communicative activities are driven from the outside, as it were, by other autonomous sources. Others are viewed as obstacles to the fulfillment of one's own expressive urges. Where the demand characteristics of the immediate situation are presumed to rule the mutual exploration of individual possibilities, options, and alternatives, one may be tempted to take psychological refuge in a litany of imaginary conversations where those who are absent from the scene are construed as the only individuals who would be capable and willing to help one make sense out of existing circumstance.

The third interpretive stance invites one to attempt to (re)define what was once presumed to be undefinable or inexplicable. As issue is the capacity and willingness to reconstruct, through reflection, memories of previous direct encounters with unintended, unsettling, or unforeseen consequences. In response to puzzling features of public dialogue, there is considerable effort to produce an integrated and synthetic grasp of some unresolved domain or issue. As an approximation, the following formula could be proposed:

Source A presumes:

(a) direct contacts with other individuals

(b) create an undefinable or inexplicable lapse in the continuity of connection—an X factor

(c) that is a source of concern, paradox, contradication,

(d) and uncommon ground.

Such a stance suggests a double-sided set of possibilities: (1) just because one could not or did not express "X" back then does not mean one could not express it now or (2) one may ask that "if I couldn't express X at the time, what makes you think I can express it now?" In other words, if the X factor was ruled out then, surely it must be ruled out now. I may be able to relate the approximate circumstances that accompany the X factor, but not the precise definition of the X factor itself. Both types of options rest on alternative assumptions about the degree to which the past can be reclaimed within the confines of subsequent or distant circumstance. While the former privileges the original event as unreclaimed now and forever, the latter rests on implicit faith in one's capacity to come to terms with what was once apprehended, but only in vague and nonspecific terms.

The fourth interpretive stance appeals to presumed discrepancies between individual abilities and actual levels of performance. Any one course may not measure up to the expectations of self and/or others. Sooner or later the magnitude of unfulfilled moments begin to add up. In effect, there are circumstances where one is capable (in principle) of doing X, but not under the particular conditions and demand characteristics that prevail at the time. As an approximation, the following formula could be proposed:

Source A presumes:

(a) my communicative capacities was/is/will not be fully manifest

(b) in the actual level of my performance,

(c) and the magnitude of discrepancy

(d) remains somewhat inexplicable

(e) as a source of unfulfilled ground.

Here the focus shifts to what could occur but does not because of whatever is still unknown, uncertain, vague, or otherwise in doubt. Such conditions involve heightened sensitivity to the possibility that one's powers to define, classify, explain, predict, and control are severely circumscribed by the sheer magnitude of what is unknown. Irony: complicated efforts at uncertainty reduction may actually increase awareness of even more vexing types of uncertainty that still remain. Uncertain, unproven, or unprovable possibilities register at the fringes of consciousness as a presumption of not knowing what to feel, think, say, or do in relation to the complex interplay of behavior and environment.

In effect, one is subject to a wide range of intervening (cognitive) conditions—confusion, ambiguity, or uncertainty—that serve only to distort further the communicative significance of what transpires. Appeals to mitigating circumstance are mainly exercises in self-justification for failure to live up to one's own or someone else's standard of personal conduct. One imagines what one would have felt, thought, said, or done if only things had been different at the time. One searches through personal reconstructions and signs of unresolved complication and complexity for a necessary and sufficient account or explanation, but such efforts are largely in vain. What matters most is the vague sense of all that did not happen but might have happened if only the respective parties had found a way to work through the compelling or pressing issues at work at the time. One remains aware, through retrospective glances, of the full measure of what will never be reclaimed.

The fifth interpretive stance applies where there is some form of *discontinuity* in the relation of feeling, thinking, saying, acting, or doing X while in the immediate presence of someone else. As an approximation, the following formula could be proposed:

Source A presumes:

(a) a lack of alignment

(b) in what I feel, think, say, and do

(c) while in the presence of others

(d) as a source of disrupted or disputed ground.

For whatever cause or reason, there is a sudden disruption in the back-and-forth movement from (the proactivity of) self toward other or (the reactivity of) the other as turned toward self. Over time some participants may get out of sync with the expressive styles of one another. So instead of mutual engagement over the integration and synthesis of various basic modes of interpersonal conduct, there is merely a periodic sense of distraction and divergence from conventional alignments and rhythms of conversation and dialogue. Such a principle holds at transitional modes of sensory activation when: (1) feelings do not align with thoughts; (2) thoughts do not align with talk; or (3) what one says does not match what one does. It is this acute sense of fragmentation in one's experience of being in the presence of others that turns out to be so unexpected, bracing, or jarring. Psychological dislocations come out of nowhere and disappear the same way. A repeated theme involves the sense of discontinuity from being in a position in which something you want to express very much is precisely what cannot be put into the right words and gestures at the time. Likewise, one may monitor the flow of interaction and still not be able to make distinct sense out of what happens to oneself, much less to anyone else. The key exemplar is a case of speechlessness, in which someone is at a loss for words.

The sixth interpretive stance is heavily evaluative. It implicates severe forms of self-censorship—what one ought or should not feel, think, say, or do in relation to the expressed activities of others. There is a tentative or provisional sense that some matters of discourse and dialogue are missing, lost, left out, or discarded along the way. Primitive presumptions coalesce around tacit, covert, and implicit urges to rediscover and reclaim a way out of the maze of largely self-imposed inhibitions, restrictions, constraints, rules, requirements, multiple valuations, and unspoken criticisms that hold one back from expressing more explicitly and directly (than before) the particular means, strategies, or goals associated with the attainment of some personal end before others. As an approximation, the following formula could be proposed:

Source A presumes:

(a) my personal conduct does not measure up
(b) to some private standard or source of evaluation
(c) found to be wanting or lacking in some way
(d) as a source of discredited or disqualified ground.

Somehow the respective parties fail to live up to some self-imposed criterion, valuation, or stipulation: the assumption, for example, of a lack of comprehension, mutual reference points, or common ground between interactants. What enters the picture are mostly chronic episodes of misinterpretation, disagreement, misunderstanding, verbal conflict, or other unwelcome forms of personal confrontation. When evaluative urges overflow the experiential field, various notions of the real and ideal clash as discordant spheres in the ambiguous rule of give-and-take.

The seventh interpretive stance is based on an implicit presumption: no one else sees things just the way I do. Moreover, no other observer is in a position to interpret my course of action in a way that corresponds to my own framework of interpretation. There is severe dislocation in the interplay of various frames of action. What appears to be the universal, similar, different, or unique features of mutual exchange matter not in the slightest because all that really counts is "my own" definition of shared reality. As an approximation, the following formula could be proposed:

Source A presupposes:

(a) my position and place is utterly unique
(b) and no one else is in the position
(c) to be able to take into account
(d) my own stance or conduct
(e) as a source of distinctive ground.

Here the unique, similar, different, or constant factors governing the flow of interaction are subject to considerable reinterpretation within a forcefield of hierarchical rearrangements that underscore the primacy of the presumed uniqueness of one's own position and place within the parameters of the larger communicative system. The key presumption privileges the first person perspective of the source in question above all else. Others are objectified as objects so one member can remain in the center of the action. Initially the aspirations of 'I' prevail over commitments to the claims of 'We' and 'Us.'

The eighth interpretive stance invokes heavily monitored forms of (re)interpretation. In this type of instance, however, tacit assumptions, implications, and attributions multiply in a disproportionate and highly fabricated manner. In effect, implicature floods the perceptual field. The tendency is to become overtly interpretive, read much into little, and supply other people's desire, motives, wants, intentions, and hidden agendas for them. The sheer multiplicity of meanings is overly determined, for example, where everyone talks around the subject in the manner of an all-inclusive metaphor. Members adapt expressive styles designed to (1) conceal more than they reveal and (2) permit wide latitude of tolerance for divergent moves of equivocation, misdirection, deliberate confusion and ambiguity when it comes to matters of meaning what I say and saying what I mean. Individuals may be tempted to fill the air with words, create heavy symbolic cover, or play fast and loose with syntaxic, semantic, and pragmatic principles. The main point is to feel, think, say, or do whatever it takes to fill the time when little of what transpires can be taken at face value. Implication: the literal-minded are sure to suffer at the discordant play of nonsense, noise, and chatter. As an approximation, the following formula could be proposed:

Source A presumes:

(a) my expressive/interpretive stance

(b) is subjected to excessively complicated

(d) conceptual weight and symbolic loadings

(e) that interfere with effort to be as explicit and articulate as possible

(f) as a source of inarticulate ground.

Here events are infused with far more symbolic loadings or surplus conceptual weight than what anyone can possibly expect to express or convey to anyone else within a short period of time. Here one gives expression to far more than what any other one can grasp or comprehend within a short amount of time. One is left with a profound sense of the sheer weight of information overload in relation to what is left unsaid. More goes on than meets the eye. Appearances can be deceiving insofar as they simplify and categorize in crude and primitive frames that miss the explicit mark but fill an implicit void.

The ninth interpretive stance involves diverse states of psychological fatalism: no matter what one says or does, it surely will not affect the final outcome and therefore make no difference, no real impact in the end. Beneath the surface of public appearance are generated all sorts of implicit urges, undifferentiated, free-floating and aimless, a tacit means of undermining, subverting, or neutralizing any explicit intention, strategy, or goal. One no longer presumes to be a full participant, only a spectator who likes to watch the public marketplace from the sidelines of the street or the far corner of the room. As an approximation, the following formula could be proposed:

Source A presumes:

(a) my personal conduct
(b) has no influence
(c) on what others feel, think, say, or do;
(d) in effect, it makes no difference in the end
(e) tacit implication: give up/don't bother
(f) as a source of unclaimed or abandoned ground.

One becomes immobilized, transfixed, by the sheer magnitude of what transpires in a very short time. The hectic or frantic pace can take your breath away. It would not matter what you do or how you decide to do it because the final verdict would be the same in any case. The participants, after all, are going to do whatever they can do. So maybe it is just better to be still and keep quiet and let the world go by. Whatever will be will be. Nothing that one feels, thinks, says, or does will do a thing to change matters in the end. Better to seek solace in a mute stance of passivity toward the accelerated pace of activity that unfolds on all sides.

The tenth interpretive stance invokes the transcendent image of an individual in a state of wonder and awe. Here the mystery of what we formulate together is cause for celebration despite (or because of) the inexplicable or ineffable qualities and textures. As an approximation, the following formula could be proposed:

Source A presumes:

(a) I am in the midst
(b) of a world of wonder and awe
(c) shared with other living creatures
(d) as a source of integrated or unified ground.

In this sense human problematics are not really a problem but rather a living testament to the miracle of life as sustained on planet earth. Themes of the miraculous: while it is true that no system is friction free, a life-affirming temperament is important so that eventually the "courage to be" will enable one to confront the worse problems that may arise. The pleasure of the human text envelops each one who has shared in the composite formulation. This is the best of all possible worlds, after all, because it is our world, the only world, the one true world in which human subjects survive and flourish.

The eleventh interpretive stance celebrates diverse and divergent movement into uncertain, uncharted, and unknown aspects of the future characterized as a lifetime quest or unfinished journey. The universal movement is fourfold: birth, living, dying, and death in a distinctive developmental pathway. Individuals acquire definition and direction in relation to the sort of world each one has pursued along the way. As an approximation, the following formula could be proposed:

Source A presumes:

(a) my face-to-face interactions

(b) produce mutual movement

(c) into an uncertain future

(d) that is still outstanding

(e) as a source of unexplored ground.

Here is the possibility of conceiving of one's lived circumstances as an ongoing, demanding, and insistent struggle to articulate (make explicit) a complex array of intuitions, sensations, feelings, thoughts, reflections, and expectations toward whoever one happens to encounter. Here the communicative urge emerges in the urgent desire to transform tacit elements into explicit distinctions. It is, in effect, the desire for significance. One strains to express oneself despite all that would hold one back.

The twelfth interpretive stance invokes the primacy of magic, mystery, and mythos in the fabric of social life. The literal use of words and gestures slowly gives way to the transliteral, the ordinary transformed into the extraordinary. Here it is necessary to speak of startling revelations that help one break free of the constraining presumptions and implicature that once held one back in the past. We free ourselves and one another of hidden, private unspoken burdens that slow us down and hinder our pace. Expressive freedom is rare and precious as a prerequisite for healing and renewal. A spirit of spontaneity neutralizes deeply ingrained habits, mechanical routines, and a stance of mindlessness associated with living an unfulfilled life or just being content to go through the motions. As an approximation, the following formula could be proposed:

Source A presumes:

(a) interaction moves

(b) from the ordinary to the extraordinary

(c) in the manner

(d) of an intervention or transformation

(e) as a source of liberated, transcendent, and heroic ground.

Life becomes an expansive allegory in which the urge to overcome the possibility of noncommunication and disconnection and the waste of precious human resources is subject to idealized resolution through a litany of transcendent symbolic forms that appeal to the outer reaches of imagination.

The point is to show the relevance of twelve different types of "assumptive ground" to the complex matter of how firmly connected or unsettled various sets of interactants become in their direct dealings with one another. The presumption of shared or common ground coincides with (1) an expectation of mutual connections sustained over changing circumstance and extended time frames; (2) faith in one's capacity to be explicit, clear, articulate, and transparent; (3) the effacious use of communicative resources in modes of personal conduct that measure up to the expectations of self and other; (4) mutual exploration of unknown or uncertain matters in multiple trajectories of performance and interpretation; and (5) opportunity for personal engagement in the constructive interplay of discourse and dialogue with the potential to transform or liberate in the manner of a collective movement to higher (more humane) ground. Where each interactant acts out of a presumption of common ground, the risk of disconnection is minimized or neutralized to the point where it need not hold one back nor be allowed to stand in one's own way. Conversely, the risks of noncommunication multiply where the assumptive ground is taken as uncommon, inexplicable, discontinuous, disrupted, disqualified, inaccessible, inarticulate, unfulfilled, or unclaimed.

The twelve interpretive slants are introduced as mechanisms for further exploration. Each one describes the achievement of a state or condition of communication between separate entities in relation to uncertain or unknown risks of noncommunication or miscommunication—as in the case of missing out or falling short of the mark. Hence, the risk of personal exposure to the sort of diffuse sense of disconnectedness envisioned here includes (1) a primordial urge, longing, desire, or intent to be explicit, articulate, and discriminating, a source of significance in shared situations, together with (2) the possibility the desire or urge will remain unfulfilled because of interference from incompatible circumstances, relational strains, or unresolved linguistic issues. At various levels of presumption, intuition, implication, and attribution, the possibility arises that the very urge for solid and substantial connection and connectedness with other beings will only lead to further episodes of disconnection and disconnectedness. Hence, there may be any number of breaks, gaps, blank spots, empty spaces, bad luck, or poor timing in the future definition and direction of the various lines of coordinated action.

To establish strong ties with others, it is necessary to be able to tolerate some measure of failure, misalignment, and discontinuity in the organization of human events. The risk of not being able to make singular sense together is, therefore, a source of protection and security against the remote odds of overcoming the possibility of the risk by personal engagement in activities that would transform us into being virtual robots, cyborgs, or clones of one another. The point is to show why the image of perfect communication is merely a mythical embodiment of a pervasive fantasy of total or permanent connection in human relations.

WHY THERE ARE NO CLONES

Try to imagine the conditions to be satisfied for perfect or total communication to occur between two or more sources of language use. Whatever qualifies as an individual in this context is an entity with a distinctive set of definitional features and criteria attributes. By this primitive standard, an individual is an entity capable of being a source of origin (of expressed activity) for any other source of origin. A rock can become a source of origin for a rock thrower without the rock thrower becoming a source of origin for a rock. For any degree of communication to be achieved, some potential must exist for mutual definition or recognition to occur between any set of individuals who serve as agents (models) for one another.

Hypothetically, two or more sources of origin would be able to communicate perfectly if only they could become both fully interdependent and thereby interchangeable with one another. This presumption could be fulfilled only if the lived circumstances afforded to each one could be afforded completely by the other one. If what A takes to be the case about A's lived circumstance could become a precise replica of what B assumes to be the case about A's lived circumstance (or the other way around), then both A and B, as a matter of definition, would be in an equally favored position quite literally to take the experiential place of one another. Moreover, if A's lived circumstance should ever coincide precisely with B's lived circumstance, then A and B would be in the unique position of being able to experience the lived circumstances of one another as a matter of course. Said another way, each source would have complete and unconditional access to whatever is given by way of definition to the other one. In effect, A and B would be capable and willing to reproduce whatever the other source makes manifest. Hypothetically, this would create the precise conditions for total interaction to unfold in the fullest sense of the term. This, of course, is the one possibility in human relations strictly ruled out as a matter of definitional principle. So the illusion of total communication does not square with empirically demonstrable fact.

A domain of perfect communication would eliminate the very possibility of creating a lie. The world would no longer suffer the presence of fools because no one would be capable of becoming someone else's fool. To achieve a state or condition of total transparency between two separate entities would mean there would be no secrets or disguises, no tension between appearance and reality, and self-deception and hypocrisy would be eliminated from the human scene. So as long as we are in any position to see one another, it is from a distinctly slanted, skewed, and distanced point of view. Fortunately, this universal capacity to see through the glass darkly is precisely what saves us from becoming the equivalent of robots, cyborgs, or clones.

Clones are produced as exact replicas of one another. When you've seen one clone you've seen them all. We could say the process of cloning assures it takes one to know one. In effect, where there is no difference, there can be no distinction—only a uniform and utterly predictable process involving the constant replication or duplication of a set of fully interchangeable parts. Strictly speaking, clones have no separate identity, and there is no way to tell them apart. The one thing the process of cloning eliminates is the possibility of deviation or alteration. In any fully automated process such as an assembly line, every manufactured object is an exact match of every other one. Hence, any one object is fully interchangeable with any other, and any one item can take the place of any other (of the same set or type). Only in fully automated processes can it be said output equals input without convening risk of deviation, error, mistake, modification, or noise.

If human beings interacted in the manner approximated by mechanisms of robotics, automatic writing, technologically perfected cloning processes, or what takes place on a computerized assembly line, then in principal everyone would be able to see themselves as others see them and, as a matter of fact, there would be no way of preventing others from doing so as a matter of course. In other words, there would be no protection or relief from constant exposure to totally transparent forms of self-expression between interdependent sets of separate entities. Moreover, if human beings were constructed like clones, communication would never be a problem because there would be no such thing as noncommunication and no way to envision a state of incommunicability between living creatures like ourselves.

Here the term noncommunication refers to what does not happen or, more strictly, what happens in A's definition of the interaction between A and B that does not occur in B's definition (or the other way around). Here what is on for one is off for another, and one of the two sources is aware that such a condition exists between them. Such a state turns out to be quite a common occurrence in everyday life, as when individual A can see plainly that individual B is not in a position to see A look and watch B walk by (visually distracted) without ever once looking within A's visual field. It is as if B is oblivious to A's presence even though they have just walked by one another. Here A recognizes that a state of noncommunication, at least in a visual sense, can have communicative significance for one person but not another. Here B does not know that A knows that B does not, in fact, know. Likewise, the term incommunicability refers to what can happen in A's definition that, as a matter of principle, cannot be reproduced in B's definition of what transpires between them. For example, A tends to blush when embarrassed, but B, when embarrassed, never does, no matter what.

When human beings directly interact with one another, it is to be expected that none of the respective parties are immune from the impact of what is expressed (by one) but not recognized by the other (noncommunication) and what cannot transpire between them (incommunicability) given the intrinsic boundaries and limits of the existing situation. In other words, what *does* take place and what *can* take place are relative to what does not and what cannot take place between any two or more sources of expressed activity.

The reason that all this matters: the very issue of what does not or cannot take place between human interactants may become the object of conscious reflection and thereby have both indirect and direct effects on whatever registers as having any degree of communicative significance at all. In other words, we can become mindful of the possibilities and the impossibilities of what transpires between ourselves and others in any shared situation. To relinquish the idealized expectation of 'perfect communication' is to prepare oneself to discover anew the uniqueness of each individual as revealed through the uniqueness of every other individual. From this standpoint everyone who engages in face-to-face interaction participates in an encompassing universal drama where each one remains vastly unique and where everything becomes constantly brand new.

THE FALLIBILITY OF ALL THINGS

Human beings have the capacity to display uncanny sensitivity to what each one (1) does or does not expect to occur within the confines of a given situation and also (2) what each one is capable or not capable of doing or becoming (in or out of relation with any other one). What one does is an explicit manifestation of what one is capable of doing or becoming. At the same time what one does not actually feel, think, say, or do in a given situation is not necessarily a strategic indication that one could not have performed such a type of action in another time and place (under similar or foreign circumstances). What qualifies as real acquires definition in relation to what one is presently in the midst of. At the center of individual existence is an enormous capacity to sustain or undermine the possibilities of life and living processes.

So a rule of DO/NOT DO is implicit in all social routines, habits, and practices. Moreover, what one is or is not capable of demonstrating establishes the limits of one's total resources to perform and the limits of one's finite capacities constitute the outer boundaries of what can be communicated (to one source or place to any other) and what cannot have any such value. So the rule of CAN/CANNOT enters the picture as well. In ordinary language use concern for what does or does not take place is central to the implicit meaning of events.

Sensate beings are subject to the interplay of enablements, opportunities, and possibilities in relation to limitations, boundaries, and constraints. Therefore, human beings are quite susceptible to feelings of fulfillment and fallibility in matters where there is some magnitude of discrepancy between what one ought, could, or should feel, think, say, act, or do in shared situations and what one does actually manage to feel, think, say, act, or do. To measure up is to live up to one's capacities, abilities, and skills (performance resources) and to fail to measure up is to leave some things unfulfilled that are well within one's capacity to attain (in some concrete form of social practice). In face-to-face interaction, the complex issue of the relative goodness of fit between one's capacity to perform and one's actual level of performance is never far removed from the center of the action as construed by participants and observers alike.

Every human interactant is an individual in a double sense. There is (1) the inclusive sense of every individual as an absolute source of origin (for the display of lived circumstances) and (2) the more restricted sense of an individual in (or out) of relation with other individuals. Human interchange is contingent on the minimal presumption that one individual is in a position to make a difference in the lived circumstance of someone else or something else. In the inclusive sense an individual is constituted as an *instance* of (the class) individuals, and in the restricted sense an individual is constituted as a *model* of what it means to become an individual for other individuals.

RISK AND CHANGE

Direct interaction with others, by definition and of necessity, poses complex issues of risk and change. When we interact directly with one another, we are prone to use all there is to use, that is, to rely upon whatever personal resources are at our disposal. In the use of complex language we employ the richest and most vital personal resources—material, economic, and symbolic—in concerted efforts designed to insure that our definition of reality, what counts, what matters, what has significance, is taken into full consideration on the part of everyone else. What gets risked in face-to-face interaction is an inclusive measure of one's worldly involvements, commitments, cares, and concerns. Whenever we see, hear, speak, touch, or move in relation to what others see, hear, speak, touch, or move, we participate in the collaborative expenditure of valuable ecological resources—the differentially sensitive appropriation of a finite amount of time, space, energy, and information, surely the most vital of all human resources.

The central question is whether it is worth the effort, the total expenditure of vital resources, to participate in given forms of face-to-face interaction. The costs and rewards, what is lost or gained, for better or worse, include whatever individuals value that is in short supply or unevenly distributed. Moreover, matters of individual risk blend with considerations of shared consequence, intended and unforeseen. Whenever we become what we behold together, we forfeit the pursuit of alternative courses of action that would have been otherwise available.

If the brute fact is life itself, then the real-world conditions at work in face-to-face interaction are those implicating the necessity of personal exposure to the presence of others. The process brings into play varying gradations of tolerance for multiple sources of risk, change, and transformation. Since human events are irreversible and nonduplicable and cannot be, therefore, fully anticipated in advance nor fully recreated later, the central question of whether or how much shared effort and individual striving is worth the effort comes down to the vital issue of whether we are better or worse off than we were before we met or if we end up better or worse than if we had not met at all.

WHY YOU JUST HAD TO BE THERE

Not everything that takes place in one shared situation can be reproduced or reconstructed subsequently in any other one. The first law of human contact is one of localized context and situational dependence. Face-to-face interaction is inevitably bound by the immediate circumstance and the extended historic context of participants construed as living subjects. The initial boundary is the outer horizon of one's immediately affordable sphere of lived circumstance. What we feel, think, say, and do is inevitably bound by time, place, and circumstances. In direct human encounter both source and subject matter are coimplicated in the primordial sense that whatever gets expressed or subsequently interpreted has definitional and directional force for each one who participates in the unfolding construction or destruction of possibilities.

The hypothetical possibility of "total interaction" is undermined in concrete practice by individual and collective considerations: (1) "identical" circumstances, in which what is afforded to 'A & B' is given in exact measure to both A and B as separate entities; (2) "convergent" circumstances, in which what is afforded as given to 'A & B' is subject to identification as more similar than different (by a criterion/value employed by either one); (3) "divergent" circumstances, in which what is afforded as given to 'A & B' are subject to identification as more different than similar (by a criterion/value employed by either one); and (4) "unique" circumstances, in which what is afforded as given to 'A & B' is subject to exclusive forms of identification by one but not the other.

By these standards, the hypothetical possibility of "total interaction" is replaced by the real life necessity that whatever 'A & B' take to be their own shared circumstance is constituted as a creative, evolutionary, and inexhaustible confluence of implicit (mostly unshared) and explicit (mostly shared) influences. This produces an array of definitional features, criterial attributes, and sentient conditions of sense-making practice.

Basic assumption: a theory of what transpires between 'A & B' does not coincide with a theory of A and B as separate entities. The basic unit of analysis remains constant: the relationship between individuals *as* uniquely constituted entities and those same individuals in or out of specified networks of embedded relations with others. In other words, to take individual and collective factors into account, a theoretical conception of the conjoint activity sustained by an 'A & B' is neither to be defined as simply A *plus* B nor A *minus* B. A theory of what is at stake in the mutual engagements of an A and B is to be construed as something *more* and something *less* than a theoretical conception of A and B as separate (actual) entities in a world of (potential) multiple relations between various individuals. Three corollaries follow: (1) a theory of A as a separate entity entails a theory of A as an absolute source of origin (of lived circumstance); (2) a theory of B as a separate entity entails a theory of B as an absolute source of origin (of lived circumstance); (3) a theory of 'A & B' must account for any sense in which 'A & B' become manifest sources of origin for one another.

Because A and B are *absolute* sources of origin, it follows 'A & B' must become *relative* sources of origin *for* one another. This provisional, relational, and restricted sense of human relation is one that does not match or coincide with how each one is constituted as all-inclusive sources of origin (life-world). At all times and in all places an 'A & B' remain (1) an absolute source of origin within an all-inclusive sphere of their own lived circumstance (life-world) and as (2) relative sources of origin for one another (mutual-world). From a phenomenological perspective, what determines mainly the magnitude of the relativity of relation is the ratio of shared to unshared history between the respective parties. Here an entity is a source of origin that is constituted as an organic whole, a bounded yet unified mass of expressive energy, a gestalt field of reference—whether or not it serves as a point of reference for any other source of origin.

The horizon of the immediately affordable situation is central to the process of definition and direction of human relations as sustained across widely extended practices in time and space. Each one is entitled to say to those who missed out or did not show up in time to take into account what actually transpired, you just had to be there. In effect, the meaning of face-to-face interaction is bound by quite specific historical and contextual circumstance acquiring definition and direction at immediate and concrete levels of mutual effort in sense-making practices that change over time even as some issues remain virtually the same. This discovery acquires additional value insofar as individuals find themselves located somewhere within the larger confines of the natural world, some place or site where no one else is around to share the solitude, glory, and sense of wonder and awe that things really are what they are. The following set of six entries examine the sense of communicative practice that resonates in people's lives at times and in places where others are not immediately accessible.

#1 A's view: There have been several times when traveling alone where I experienced moments of serenity or internal peacefulness that, later on, I could not fully relate to another person. An example would be the act of contemplating a sunset at the Grand Canyon or watching a herd of moose feed at a remote site in Yellowstone Park. It is the experience of being alone in a place when there were no other sounds except for the wind causing the brush and leaves to vibrate and perhaps some sounds emanating from the animals. At such times, my thoughts begin with the analysis of what I'm actually seeing before they stray to some completely isolated ideas that linger until something tells me to move on to whatever is next. Later, if I try to explain my experience to another person, it seems impossible to capture the "beauty of the moment" or express the imprecise qualities of personal experience. On one hand this inability to express such feelings to others is frustrating but on the other it makes the moment all the more private and special.

#2 A's view: I went diving in the Bahamas this past summer. On each of my nine dives, I experienced feelings and thoughts that I knew would be nearly impossible to explain to anyone else—even other divers. The idea of seeing or being somewhere where no one else has been is incredible! The vastness, the newness, the total sensual awareness, is very hard to explain in words. The ocean represents miniature worlds within one larger system. To see these "other" worlds and not be able to share the excitement with someone else makes the thrill all the more intense. When I made the dives I saw and felt things that no one had seen or will ever see again! Danger of open water, sharks, and equipment malfunction, etc., tends to keep you on your toes. It's bad enough in familiar water but in unfamiliar water watch out! This constant danger produces ultra-awareness. When I dove in the Bahamas, I had this ultra-awareness. I was confident of my surroundings and felt I was in total control. It was no time or place for any lack of confidence. I was aware of every movement and sound in these potentially dangerous waters. I didn't even try to explain these feelings to anyone after the dives because I felt they'd never understand.

#3 A's view: I had a positive experience of this nature when I jumped out of a plane at 8,000 feet. I know I can explain step by step what happened—I also know that's not the issue. I realize the issue pertains to the feeling behind the experience. I know I cannot fully explain because I can't. No one will know or actually understand what I felt at the time. Four people jumped that day, each for the first time, and we did discuss the experience immediately after. Each of us had a hyped feeling. I sensed it was obvious. The experience produced such an adrenaline pump—it was incredible—a feeling of total excitement. All parts of my body were tingling. It felt as though I had another sense or dimension to my being during free fall. I had some other strange physical experiences. I remember my throat felt as though I had a "V" caught in it. I also felt a strange sensation of what felt like my heart dropping to my stomach within my own body—it started not quite as a pain but a discomfort. I recall thinking if only I could stand the waiting until the ripcord was pulled, I'd be OK and the strange sensations would leave me. After the cord was pulled and I was "chuting," I was in utter awe of my surroundings. I was thousands of feet in the air without a plane. I saw for miles. I felt fresh, invigorating air. My heart had to be beating a thousand miles an hour as I guided the chute. The precise feeling is very difficult to explain because even now I cannot really duplicate the feeling well enough to describe it. I think if I could feel it now I'd be able to describe it better but I can't remember as vividly as I would wish. It was an incredible sensation but I don't know what made it so. Words do not come close to the feelings one goes through when taking a step several thousand feet high. Until you experience a state of free fall you cannot possibly understand the nature of the experience.

#4 A's view: A group of friends and I were hiking in the mountains of Alaska. We saw animals everywhere: polar bears, fox, goats, and sheep. In order not to scare away the sheep we sat behind a little hill and remained quiet while everyone was taking pictures. In the stillness of the moment all I could think was how beautiful a place we were sharing by ourselves. While the goats were walking and running up and down the hills, I kept wondering how the goats manage to stay alive, what they do all day, and other questions were going through my mind. I decided to walk over this enormous hilltop to see what was on the other side. It turned out to be a huge open valley with bright yellow flowers and mountains all around covered with snow. It was the most amazing scene I have ever seen in my life. To run down into the middle of the valley and just look around was so amazing, to see what nature had created. It felt even better because I was all alone and felt as if it was my own world that existed just for me. It was so silent and beautiful and yet I became very sad to think I would have to leave soon and never be able to return. What I witnessed while sitting all alone was a special feeling I do not think I could convey to help any other person understand what it was like at the time.

#5 A's view: Four years ago, I had the fortune of going camping in the Rockies in Glacier National Park. It was an experience I will never forget, but at the same time, the feelings I felt were difficult to understand. Part of the experience dealt with a feeling of intense freedom; way up high looking at the mountains surrounding me and seeing the bluest sky imaginable. Witnessing such a vast wilderness made it difficult to believe there were big cities and other man-made developments so far away. This intense freedom made me feel I could stay up in the mountain peaks forever. It was so peaceful, seeing so many wild animals, like a sanctuary. But along with the freedom, there was fear in me. I'm not sure why but it was tearing me apart, the difference between the dream and the reality. Part of the fear was from being brought up in the big city. I asked myself if it would really be possible to live here. Another issue was the thought of all the material things readily available in the city. This served to call into question my new sense of freedom. Yet this feeling of immense freedom just inspired me so much. It made me feel like the mountains were the greatest thing in the world and so far away from all the bad things in the city and maybe even reality itself would be separated from me. Seeing the warm sun rising over the snowcapped mountains produced a feeling of peace with no comparison.

#6 A's view: While skiing in Colorado I took a chair lift up to the highest point accessible by chair lift in the United States, Arapaho Basin Resort. After getting off the chair lift, we took off our skis and walked two hundred feet up further. When we approached the peak, I felt my body change. All life's worries and problems seemed to disappear into the awesome sight of the vast mountains that surrounded me. I felt like a tiny speck of dust in the universe and yet on top of the world. I felt minute and huge at the same time. It was hard to pull myself away from this incredible feeling but eventually I had to ski down the mountain. It is amazing how many times I've been able to recall that very rare and precious feeling since then. Whenever I feel as though I have problems or the weight of the world is upon me, I remember how I felt at that particular moment. Then, all of a sudden, I feel better and my problems once again seem to disappear.

What one experiences in the solitude *is* the solitude: serenity, peacefulness, and the splendor of the moment. You just had to be there and not here to be in touch with what is so distinctive, pristine, and rare. It is important to watch some things happen for the first time as a unique opportunity to enter into miniature worlds of organic life and natural splendor where personal worries and vexing problems seem to evaporate and disappear. The vastness and acute sensual awareness are greatly intensified in the recognition that the magic is incredible precisely because it occurs all at once and as such can never be fully reclaimed again. It can occur suddenly, unexpectedly, without warning, often when no one else is around. One is transformed by solitude as yet unbroken and things no one else has ever seen nor will ever see again.

The greatest privilege is to be in awe of one's surroundings. One becomes transfixed and spellbound in the miracle of the moment. The splendor of the natural world can take one's breath away: clear sky, fresh air, warm sun, solid ground, signs of life everywhere, the intense freedom, when the world becomes, once again, a sanctuary, a home. There is nothing you can say at a later time and place to even begin to explain what you once saw, heard, said, touched, or moved. It is something you just have to rediscover for yourself on your own. Solitude holds the promise of rebirth, renewal, and rediscovery in the human world.

LOST IN A CROWD

The condition of "solitude" in nature is somewhat analogous to one of anonymity in public settings. In solitude one discovers what one is in relation to all that unfolds within the wider scheme of things. In a state of public anonymity such a discovery can be buried or covered up through personal recognition of states of prolonged inattentiveness and insensitivity on the part of others. In solitude one notices everything, and in anonymity one is noticed by no one in particular. Hence, one's place in the greater scheme of things is reaffirmed by solitude, but undermined or obscured by a state of personal anonymity. Such a condition can unfold when one is in the immediate presence of others just as well as when one is all alone.

In anonymous relationships, one may become acutely sensitive to the acute insensitivity on the part of someone—who usually turns out to be another person. The severity of one's own sense of anonymity is roughly proportionate to the lack of personal recognition, definition, or acknowledgment on the part of others. In such situations one attends to the sheer scope of what is missing or what is left out of the larger communicative equation. Of central concern is what goes unnoticed, unattended, ignored, left unsaid, or what remains suppressed, implicit, or otherwise suspended in partially unarticulated forms of interchange between self and others.

Such conditions introduce paradox: one can be (merely) in the immediate presence of others without being fully present for the others or for the others to be fully present for oneself. One discovers, therefore, it is possible to be located in a shared situation without having any sense of having shared in the collective definition of what transpires. There is rather only the vague sense that one, for all practical purposes, might just as well be someone else, someplace else, or no one in particular at all. To discover that one is lost in a crowd is to become a model of personal anonymity in public settings. Prescription: a source with no name and no acknowledged identity. One goes unnoticed and unrecognized for who and what one's presence makes manifest. Symbols: one's presence makes no difference, no real difference at all. To remain anonymous is to be unable to secure a firm sense of personal identity or to fail to stand out from all the rest. The following set of entries equate a stance of disconnectedness with matters neither lost nor found but rather something located in between.

#7 Individual A gives up drinking for medical reasons. Still, A is a junior in college and wants to keep going to the parties A has always attended. Because A no longer drinks, A begins to see people in a different light. A's friends cannot understand why he doesn't want to get drunk. Although A tells them why, they don't understand the seriousness of A's condition. Others pressure A to drink and then feel uncomfortable when A won't. A realizes one sober person at a party ruins other's sense of "loss of inhibitions." Now A knows others only liked him when he got drunk with them. Individual A can't relate to them when A is sober. He can't explain how it feels to anyone because they are all intoxicated. Individual A remains subdued for the evening and eventually stops going to such parties because he couldn't find a way to relate to anyone else. It's hard to make anyone else understand, especially when you can't account for certain things even to yourself. It's sort of like the feeling of being alone in a crowd of people.

#8 A's view: There have been times when it has been nearly impossible to express my feelings to someone else. I was sitting in the Union with eight to ten people from my dormitory. These are people I consider to be my friends because we always did fun things together. Anyway, I just wasn't having any fun even though I was surrounded by all these people. I really felt alone—maybe I was in a mood or something. I felt it didn't really matter to them if I was there or not. I remember leaving by myself. I didn't go back to the dorm because I really didn't feel like having to confront people. I know they would have asked me what was wrong but I didn't want to talk. I guess I couldn't really say what was wrong exactly, so I just wanted to avoid the situation. I ended up walking around downtown Madison for a few hours. It was late at night and in the middle of the winter! I just wanted to be all by myself. I recall sitting on a bench right in front of the Capitol building—I had to brush the snow off first. I just sat and stared at that impressive building. I guess things can look very different at different times. Sometimes that place looks just like a bunch of bricks. But that night, I can remember how the spotlights pierced through the haze to illuminate the dome. It was almost a religious sensation—really strange. So I just sat there and ended up walking around some more. Being on the streets all alone, I did feel isolated and different from the rest of the world. Going back to my dorm was like admitting I was like everybody else. I asked myself a lot of questions later that night—I don't think any were answered but I did feel a lot better afterward. I realized I am very different from most people and that in itself is a most satisfying feeling for me.

#9 While attending a football game in his hometown, A finds himself feeling very much out of a state of peace with himself. He has brought along two girlfriends and their new husbands and A thinks he is definitely a third wheel. The others are very nice, and they do not make A feel excluded, but somehow he is. Next A takes the group to the old hang out. They take a booth and begin to drink. Well, it isn't the drunk A remembers from high school. So A stares out the window at those who pass by. Not knowing a soul inside or outside the bar makes for a very weird feeling. Individual A begins to think about high school girlfriends who have found God or boyfriends and who will no longer haunt these old establishments with him. A then realizes his current home no longer feels like home either. Everyone has pretty much graduated and moved away. School is only a temporary substitute. The anxiety of not knowing where one will go is awful. A finds himself sitting in the bar thinking (1) My hometown holds great memories but that's all they are, memories of a life never to be the same; (2) My friends have all moved away and are in a different stage of life; (3) Higher education is just another obstacle to further productivity in life; (4) I don't know where I belong; (5) Home has no definition right now, and it's a scary feeling.

#10 A's view: Sometimes when I walk down a busy street, I am struck by the thought we are really all alone in the world. Even though there are millions of people in the human world, we ourselves are single individuals. We come into the world alone and we leave the world alone. This thought does not make me sad however. It just makes me realize I am really on my own. I have friends and family who support me but they are not me and they don't experience my own thoughts and feelings exactly the same way I do. It is so difficult to express this feeling because I can't think of the words to do so. It is almost a spiritual type of feeling that registers deep within my soul.

Anonymity is produced and represented here in three central themes. The first is one in which a participant changes in a certain way others fail to notice. The unrecognized changes are real at two levels, viewpoint and conduct. What goes unattended makes some feel better and others feel worse over vital concerns as yet left unspoken. The second is a shift in the orientation of interaction from largely inclusionary to mainly exclusionary spheres of activity. Appearances of inclusion cover up tacit feelings of exclusion. Moreover, there is a profound sense of being all alone at the very beginning (entrance) and end (exit) of human encounters. Third is the vague sense of being surrounded by the presence of others without being adequately supported and sustained by the personal conduct of the others. It is as if one's presence doesn't matter one way or another. One is left to wander in and out without a firm conception of identity, belonging, or security in the search for a wider sense that one's lived circumstances once again begin to feel like home. Personal anonymity underscores issues of isolation, diversity, and detachment from the rest of the world we share with others.

CULTURE SHOCK

In creating language, we are constantly engaged in the production of a most innovative and constructive activity. The power to create through ordinary language use does not merely involve the use of words or gestures but is constituted rather as a vital medium to act and interact in the human world and to innovatively and creatively undermine the production of any given tradition of creative practices. It is important to remember, therefore, that the creative and constructive use of conventional language may be implemented to undermine, neutralize, or subvert the continuity of any given set of creative routines, rituals, or practices. The linguistic capacity to reproduce diverse elements of tradition and routine conveys a double possibility, either an act of doing or undoing whatever serves to sustain or undermine strategic aspects of what has gone on before the moment is at hand.

Human existence acquires accumulative definition as a specific way of life. One characteristic feature of the way modern people organize an ongoing sense of their day-to-day existence involves each one having a quite specific theory of their own place in the larger scheme of things. This implicit conception of an individual-as-interactant is subject to a reality test at all levels of collaborative activity, in relation to (1) other individuals, (2) other living things, and (3) inanimate conditions in the material world. These factors and forces coalesce sharply when one individual goes through the complex transition from primary reliance on familiar and habituated practices, rituals, and routines to the very strange and foreign circumstances associated with acts of direct personal contact with those who reside in other cultures. The following set of entries trace the limitations of ethnocentric communication against the backdrop of universal or global considerations.

#11 A's view: In the Hispanic culture, a great deal of emphasis is placed on matters of *respect*, much more so than in Anglo culture. This is particularly the case when dealing with the elderly or in certain occasions when a guest receives preferential treatment. It is considered a "sin" for a guest to insult a host. There seems to be a very fine line as to who deserves of the greatest degree of respect, and this usually limits what can or should be said in the company of others. An example of the fine line occurred in a social situation I encountered recently in Mexico. The host of the dinner party was being especially critical of the American "lifestyle" and was using many stereotypes to amuse his guests. Even through it was wrong and offensive, I still did not say anything because he was the host and it would be very disrespectful. At one point, I was asked a question and responded in an offhanded way that the host was amusing but his stereotypes were quite wrong. The host got red in the face and became quite agitated but quickly shifted the conversation to another topic. Later on I was told how disrespectful I had been. Others claimed that living in the United States had made me lose touch with my own culture. There was nothing else I could say.

#12 Individual A goes to Europe for three weeks and tours several countries. A is shocked by the low standard of living and the run-down look. A has traveled quite a bit, but this time when A came home, the feelings A had were just incredible. He noticed billboards, all the American cars, and enjoyed every little thing. When A called home, it was fantastic to hear his mother's voice, and he was overjoyed to see his parents once again. Also, the things A likes the most were all available at home. Individual A loves Fig Newtons, Rocky Rococo Pizza, and Diet Coke—all of which were waiting for him when he got home. All these little things added up to be so wonderful. A tried to share his feelings, but it didn't seem that other persons were experiencing the same set of feelings. A was overjoyed, happy, content, relaxed, patriotic, and other feelings produced such a rush that others could not grasp or comprehend.

#13 Individual A moves to a new city and feels lost and lonely. The worst part is that he cannot tell anyone the way he feels. So A bottles up unspoken feelings and hopes the fear and loneliness will go away. At such times A would feel miserable because it seemed no one else really cared. A would feel as though he was the only man left on earth. The worst part was that A had no one to talk to, and when he did try to tell someone else, the words just would not come out. A would just pretend nothing was wrong and hope no one would find out how messed up he was.

#14 When A first moved to Los Angeles, he experienced what people refer to as "culture shock." Everything seemed quite different from an earlier time when he had visited the area and didn't seem to mind the magnitude of critical differences during short visits. First of all, the sky wasn't blue when there were no clouds—smog created a definite brown haze on the horizon. Then A began to notice a lack of open land and green vegetation. He also began to lose patience in the morning traffic. It took him more than a half hour to drive ten miles. None of these features of the Los Angeles environment seemed intolerable, but put together they became very annoying. A was reluctant to share his feelings with anyone for fear of admitting failure—he had made the wrong decision about moving to Los Angeles. It was only when he described his feelings to a pair of former Peace Corps workers and heard them describe it as "culture shock" (which both of them had experienced) that he began to understand the total impact so much "newness" was having on him, and only then did he start to feel more comfortable with the new surroundings.

#15 Individual A moves to a new city and feels completely alone. It is the first time A has ever moved somewhere without knowing anyone there, and the normal fears accompanying such a move are made even worse by feelings of insecurity about A's potential for success. At this time A receives very little support from family members, who would compliment the apparent courage and extend good wishes without ever once asking how A feels. Since the others all acted as though A should be able to handle everything all alone, A did not feel comfortable admitting how frightened A was or how much A wished one of them would come and help so that A wouldn't feel so lost. Then A decided to show others the "strong" side (one they are used to seeing) while feeling extremely inadequate for not really being that way. Finally, A did express some personal fears to a friend (from the past) who made A feel even worse than A had before. After that one attempt to share such fears, A did not try again for a long time. Instead, A ended up dealing with the problem in A's usual way, being a nervous wreck on the inside while pretending to be extremely confident on the outside—all the while crying late into the night for the first several weeks. It isn't until several months later that A felt sufficiently comfortable with the new surroundings to admit to some new friends how scared and alone A had felt at the beginning. It was only then that A found out others had cried themselves to sleep at night and *they* had envied *her* for being so confident and self-assured.

#16 A's view: Since I had never been separated from my parents since I was a baby, it was not easy to attend school 15,000 miles away from home. When I first came to study in the U.S., the need to stay by myself was a very scary experience. I didn't know anybody when I first came here, nor did I speak the language very well. For the first month I stayed in the apartment all the time. Whenever I went out, I felt very insecure. I didn't have any appetite and lost five pounds. I still don't know how I felt at the time. I couldn't talk to anybody, not even my parents when they called. The feeling was just there: some people called it homesickness. I don't know what I would call it. Whenever it was present I would cry myself to sleep and wake up in the morning feeling like nothing had ever happened.

The emergence of culture shock revolves mainly around unresolved issues of ethnocentrism. At stake is a view of things in which the local community is the central point of reference (close) and everything else (faraway) is scaled and gauged with reference to the immediate landscape. The close-far distinction may be construed in a fluid and open-ended manner or in a rather fixed and rigid way in which what is near or close at hand is taken to be virtuous and superior to what is located far away. Moreover, the standards of the insiders (we) apply to outsiders (them), but not the other way around.

The shock registers in the clash of two or more incompatible sets of cultural demands operating simultaneously. The greatest points of tension occur during movement from one place or cultural milieu to another. The transition from one place to another can be traumatic or transcendent. Either way, respondents struggle to cope and adapt to alternative standards and the absence of familiar signposts and simple pleasures once taken for granted. It is not always easy to be placed in the position of a stranger on someone else's turf or territory while being subjected to such strange customs on the part of the native inhabitants. For some it is a test of divided loyalties and for others an opportunity to explore a whole new world of possibilities or justification to admit defeat associated with the misfortune of being in the wrong place and at the wrong time.

The critical test is whether one can learn to speak a new language without losing touch with the old. Failure to do so is apt to register in a heightened sense of isolation, futility, and powerlessness. Success facilitates opportunity to establish strong ties with others and gain greater access to the necessary resources—symbolic, economic, and material—that permit one not only to survive but to flourish. Once again, the critical import of linguistic competence is underscored most decisively under the very conditions where one travels too far away from home for traditional habits, routines, and practices to be of much use in new, unfamiliar, foreign, or unwelcome surroundings.

FARAWAY PLACES, DISTANT LANDS

The farther one travels away from home, the more reminders there are of the inexhaustible variation in the daily routines of those who live in other communities and tribes. The world, the one we all inhabit, is vast, expansive, inclusive, and all encompassing. We wander, rest, and explore, close or far away from our own local communities with a familiar range of opportunities, boundaries, limits, and constraints and move into a wider set of involvements and opportunities. A spirit of world openness holds out the promise of a rediscovery of who and what we are. To say we are on the move is to admit we are in a common state of constant transition from one set of known circumstances to as yet partially undefined, unknown, uncertain, or unpredictable ones.

#17 A's view: As a senior in high school I had the opportunity to travel to Poland. I had traveled a lot before and since I was on a choir tour I didn't expect to learn much or care much about this country. Warsaw was the first city we visited. I was hyper from actually being there but also exhausted from the flight at the same time. Soon thereafter I found myself listening intently to a tour guide. The guides were telling all about Poland's history—the main feature was World War II. But the guides weren't like others who just rattled off a speech. They were talking totally from the heart. I felt sadness when they told about the massacre of the Jews. I felt despair and desolation as they explained how the entire city was destroyed. I felt the pride the guides showed in pointing out every building that had been restored. Next we visited the tomb of the unknown soldier. There I saw eight urns with soil from every battlefield. I saw the torch that symbolizes the flames that engulfed the city and the crematorium where millions were wrongfully brought to death. I could only picture the bones of some unknown individual but that simply underscored the craziness of the war—millions disappearing. Whose bones are they? Soldiers stand guard twenty-four hours a day in silence amidst freshly picked flowers. They don't move an inch. Only an occasional blink. Nobody said we should be quiet yet it just seemed to be a given. Maybe everyone had a lump in their throat too and not just me. I stood there longer than the rest. It had an impact on my life. My sympathy will always remain (in spirit) encased with those hidden bones.

#18 A's view: I studied abroad for a semester. When I came back I felt isolated from the world here. Although I had expected things to change while I was gone, I was not prepared to admit I too had changed. Everyone asked about my time abroad and I would eagerly start to tell them but after a few minutes they would lose interest and drift off to another subject. It got to the point where I no longer really wanted to talk about the matter because it seemed other people weren't as interested as I had thought and it soon became virtually impossible to explain all the intense feelings. So I stopped talking about the 'most important' subject but continued to answer any direct questions others would ask of me. In the long run this made me feel better because every time I would try to discuss the topic I would either become overwhelmingly frustrated or sad at not being able to relate what mattered most to other beings.

Extended travel opens up the possibility to rediscover who and what we are in relation to one another as distinct individual beings. It is also a reminder that diverse networks of communicative practice can be sustained across immense vistas and landscapes: farms, rivers, lakes, mountains, forests, deserts, oceans, continents, and twenty-four time zones. The globe is becoming rapidly transformed into a well-traveled map of human exploration. In this regard, the personal accounts of the visitors to foreign battlefields are particularly instructive. Here the nexus of connection and disconnection are oriented backward and forward in time and cover many decades and generations as well as matters of interplay in a contemporary world of diverse cultures. For each individual the critical parameters are everywhere pretty much the same. Human beings are civilized predators who happen to be intelligent and forceful as well. We manifest life and death power not only over ourselves and one another but other living creatures as well. Hence the quality of human interaction for each successive generation sets the potential agenda for the next. Between the point of birth and death of every living creature, there is constant and incessant negotiation over the particular conditions in which each one lives and dies. Increasingly, human survival takes place in linguistic and symbolic terms that have decisive symbolic, economic, and material consequences in the long run. Over successive generations the use of words and gestures serves to radicalize the human condition more than ever before.

WHY YOU CAN'T GO HOME AGAIN

#19 A's view: After spending a year of study abroad in Perth, Australia, I returned home to family and friends who asked the same question, "Well, how was it?" It is difficult to sum up the experiences of an entire year in a few short sentences. My mind raced through images: the exhilaration of stepping off the plane to find a huge crowd of people waiting to greet me for the first time; the anxiety of life in a strange country; knowing names in advance but not faces; the joy of being lucky enough to be on Sydney Harbor during the Australian bicentennial, sitting on a boat surrounded by hundreds of other boats all covered with lights, watching beautiful fireworks illuminate the sky in a way too breathtaking for words; the confusion of stepping off the plane back home, surrounded once again with hugs and kisses, knowing I had just closed an important chapter in my life that no one in our country would be able to understand. Whenever others asked the basic question, there was nothing I could say except, "I wish I could tell you but it was simply unbelievable."

#20 A's view: I had just returned from spending a year overseas and getting acquainted once again with life in America. Driving my car, greasy food, and suburbia were discoveries I was making all over again. But I had retained many memories of the Asian land I had left. The country was in me now and no one could see it there. It was so hard for me to tell someone what I had done and how it had changed my outlook. I was sent to Korea while serving in the army. I had not exactly led a sheltered life but this was the first time I had been somewhere so foreign to what I already knew. There was no English language visible anywhere. Streets were dusty and broken with only taxis and busses congesting each of them. Concrete huts and paper shacks layered around each other in the city. Sewage seeped through all the alleys and mixed with the scent of burnt charcoal that was used to heat the homes. These conditions may seem harsh to most Americans but oddly beneath this country's crude exterior it possessed a charming quality. The more time I spent exploring this environment, I became aware of so many simple things that were beautiful. I would walk to the marketplace where anything was sold on any ground available. You could not be a passive consumer in this because you were deluged with peculiar items and a smooth barter would be needed to get out of it. Meals were not just one or two courses and even cheap dining consisted of a sampling of ten different dishes at one sitting. I visited temples in the mountains. They weren't particularly remarkable to look at, yet as you stood there you felt not the humanly constructed structure holding your wonder but all of nature. And mostly what I learned was a language that allowed me to meet many new people. I learned their pride, resourcefulness, and humor and I gradually understood their devotion to their culture. When I came back to the United States, people would ask me, "How was Korea?" All I could reply was, "It was nice." Of course I knew there was more to it than that. Here's a person saturated with trends and amenities and I would try to tell them about something and they would just say, "Oh how nice." I wanted people to be as affected by this mystical greatness as I had. Words are just vehicles for people and they're never really the origin or destination. Gradually these events became less demonstrative and more subtle in how they are conveyed. My travel guide lectures are gone but the feeling still affects my life and actions in many small ways. People cannot readily sense this. When they get to know me better they will become more aware of these things and it's easier to share them. My friends and I are going out to the point for a long picnic . . . I hope they won't mind if I pick up some dried cuttlefish along the way.

#21 Individual A goes to Switzerland for an internship for a summer institute. In July A decides to end the internship early and go down to the valley to stay with some people who had become friends and to learn more about them and their culture. It is a hard time in A's life because A needs to make some decisions about schooling and is becoming aware of some hurts and bitterness left over from the past while struggling in a culture where A cannot speak the language. Individual A ends up staying with a group of women who shower A with love. They leave chocolates on her pillows, flowers in her room, bring gifts, hug her a lot, hide her suitcase so that she couldn't leave and shower her with hospitality such as she has never seen before. Everyone struggled through their English-German dictionaries and ended up realizing that love can bridge any language barriers. What A feels she cannot articulate is the gratitude and thankfulness A had in her heart for them. Just saying "thank you" is not enough as A realized all the healing and restoration that had occurred. There were feelings that were so much more deep, intricate, and close. So A said good-bye to such dear friends knowing A was unable to express what they had done for her. Coming home to the States was also hard—to try to describe to American friends what had happened and how A had changed and felt more "whole" rather than a person who had holes shot in the heart. A realizes that she did not have the ability at the time to articulate the experience, but perhaps through examples her Swiss friends had shown A could pass on that love to others.

#22 A's view: I feel indescribable sensations often, especially when I have an experience that no one else in my communicative network [family] has directly experienced. The first time it was really evident to me was when I was just out of high school and went to France, Portugal, England, and Scotland as well as Cuba with the navy. I not only experienced with my senses, I read and visited, and shopped, took in tours, cultural events, studied the people and their environment. I was just bursting with pictures, events, people, places, adventures, and anecdotes to share with family and friends, coworkers, relatives, neighbors, etc. When I tried to explain I was able to get some interest all right but it wasn't for long and it was one-sided. It felt like I had seen a flying saucer and they hadn't. No matter how much I tried, they could not see all I had witnessed and it was difficult for me to hold their interest. Finally, it helped when I showed them my souvenirs and when my pictures came back developed and printed. But even to this day when I look at my pictures I remember how difficult and frustrating it was to try and tell others how big, how pretty, how many, how exotic, how different, and how alike everything was. Finally, I realized that I had said enough.

The first twenty-two entries in this project give vivid testimony to the relativity of all things. At the center of the action is the expenditure of a great deal of individual and collective energy over the central issue of whether it is worth the effort to share certain portions of our lives with one another. Moreover, the question of how much of this or that type of interaction is at stake (quantities) intersects with deeper considerations of the relative value (qualities) of whether we are better or worse off from having engaged in a particular mode of direct or mediated contact with one another. The entries contribute to our understanding of (1) the limits of human connection and (2) the necessary allowance to be made for elements of disconnection, divergence, and disengagement—the price of admission. The central issue, then, is how much of a risk of communicative failure is considered tolerable in collective negotiation, confrontation, and struggle over the significance of the larger communicative equation per se.

3

The Study of Critical Communication

The purpose of this chapter is to examine complex issues of competence and compatibility in the lived circumstances of various combinations of interactants. So far a number of core themes have been identified in support of such a task. At issue is how commensurate our own personal worlds become at the point of intersection with those of one another. The potential for sharing problematic concerns has been identified, above all else, with the relative goodness of fit in the lived circumstances of separate entities. The term "circumstance" suggests that the meaning of linguistic interchange is appropriated in an environmentally sensitive manner. Language is viewed as a vital human resource and is subject, therefore, to a wide spectrum of use, misuse, and abuse. Therefore, the uneven distribution or scarcity of vital human resources greatly complicates the effort required for diverse sets of interactants to feel safe and secure with one another. These working premises are consistent with a notion of human reality as linguistically constructed. In effect, the public use of words and gestures makes a critical difference in the vitality and survivability of our lives. The critical center of communicative practice invokes human drama with partisans located on all sides.

Our expressive styles reveal not only a way with words but also a way of living in the world. Inclusive levels of concern with communication as a reality-testing mechanism implicate the degree and direction of access into the circumscribed world of one another. Presumably the elaboration of possibilities is subject to multiple levels of reality testing. It is one thing, after all, to make sense of personal conduct within the confines of a situation specific encounter. It is quite another to preserve a sense of connection from one distinctive type of social situation to any another. The continuity of human connection is difficult to nourish and sustain when brief episodes of direct contact are followed by protracted periods of absence and lack of direct or mediated access. Finally, at the highest levels of potential complication, matters of fidelity are transmitted from one decade or generation to another as a means of securing one's position and place among others within the totalizing horizon of the larger scheme of things.

Within this broad perspective one may examine the use of ordinary language to achieve extraordinary ends. Relevant events are difficult to pin down in a neat and tidy way. It is difficult, after all, to know what qualifies as a clear case in point for even a tentative and provisional study of how human beings interact with one another under urgent, decisive, or critical situations. Most striking features implicate conditions of protracted interdependence when it is clear that individual lives are strictly on the line.

The notion of a life-or-death situation is a compelling starting point, but this initial point of reference is not particularly useful because virtually any human interchange is intrinsically valuable—by definition—insofar as each episode serves to affirm or undermine some larger living process. Hence, the decisive issue has to do with the total magnitude of material, economic, and symbolic resources at stake in highly involving and consequential episodes of collaborative action.

At one end of the spectrum of shared possibility is the capacity to affirm, nurture, spare, and preserve the very opportunity to participate in mutually sustained modes of inquiry, exploration, and elaboration. At the other is the capacity to negate, neutralize, block, undermine, subvert, or refuse to sustain, whether by neglect or abuse, shared possibilities in the here and now. In between is the large middle ground—two broad spheres of influence—the imaginative interplay of ordinary and extraordinary effort to create or destroy complex traditions of elaborated language use.

Of greatest relevance in critical communication is whatever each source is capable and willing to be, say, or do to measure up to any severe or highly demanding form of reality testing activity. The intrinsic importance of face-to-face interaction is subject to convincing demonstration in diverse situations where the stakes are quite high, where there is much to gain or lose, and where what gets articulated or left out (by one source or another) can make all the difference in the world in terms of the quality of the lives of the respective parties. It is important, then, to examine the sorts of human encounters that make a decisive or urgent difference in the efficacy and vitality of mutually sustained circumstances.

The strategy here is to examine sequences of critical interchange in a developmental and evolutionary framework. The goal of inquiry is to focus on restrictive and elaborative mechanisms at work in four dynamic spheres of action: birth, living, dying, and death. In each there is a profound and dynamic sense of uncertainty or started unexpectedness. Open systems of critical communication are subject to four pronounced forms of reality testing: (1) procreation—the act of giving birth; (2) dealing with the unforeseen consequences of growing older together; (3) the act of watching someone die; and (4) reactions to the death of others.

PERSONAL CONDUCT IN CRITICAL SITUATIONS

What makes a shared situation "critical" is a sense of collective urgency and total personal involvement: physical, emotional, intellectual, and spiritual. Each individual participates in the symbolic enactment of mutually sustained activities removed from the relatively safe and secure confines of what is familiar, conventional, ordinary, and mundane. Taking the place of the ordinary are a succession of sharpened and intense contact points with what is truly extraordinary, radical, or extreme. Moreover, as incremental sources of risk and change give way to the emergence of a rapid, sudden, and clear-cut set of demand characteristics, there is produced a pervasive sense of "all or nothing" in the affairs of "one among many." Personal involvements in critical situations foster extreme forms of communication that serve to transform ("radicalize") rather than leave individual and collective sensibilities largely intact and relatively unchanged. Thus each source confronts what is worthy of being taken most seriously in the end. It is transformational, after all, not knowing who will live or die as a consequence of the tenor and tone of the type of interaction that takes place.

In critical situations central issues revolve around timeless questions of "who lives" and "who dies" with what "benefit" or "reward" and what "cost" or "expense." Hence, the study of critical interaction may help shed light on the relationship between the heroic and the tragic aspects of the larger human drama. It is highly personal drama, to be sure, an unbelievable spectacle to witness, often in protracted silence. One senses that no one else is experiencing what one is experiencing at the time. There is the pervasive sense of shock and numbness at not knowing exactly what condition the respective parties are in, the nature of the risks being played out, or what the final outcome will be. Most often the heroic is construed as miraculous and transcendent while the traumatic is framed as immediate, concrete, vivid, and specific. Either extreme may be virtually impossible to describe later in its situated entirety.

In critical situations one encounters open-ended opportunity for the fulfillment of the best and the worst human beings offer one another. So many sensations, feelings, and thoughts run through one's mind (a "flash") that the sense of what is unattainable may border on the impossible. An indescribable rush of feelings may sweep over, producing confusion and bewilderment, as the margin of safety narrows and the magnitude of threat or danger increases. An error or miscalculation may prove fatal amidst a flurry of life-or-death decisions. Who is going to take chances? Do we leave one another behind? Is there a source of rescue, relief, and recovery in sight?

Fear of the endangerment of one's own life must be weighed against the value of the total potential for the collective loss of life. Under such circumstances the unfolding drama is transformed into a morality play.

The rate of change and magnitude of risk in critical interaction has a considerable degree of interventional, emancipatory, or transformational power. Still it is not clear whether the heroic or tragic aspects of the encompassing drama will bring out the best or worst that human beings can afford one another. In any case critical situations provide a severe and vivid reality test of the capacity and willingness of various individuals to take into account the diverse strivings and yearnings of one another. Thus, the rate, diversity, and salience of change in personal conduct intensifies dramatically in the following types of critical situations: work in an emergency ward of a hospital, a near-miss air collision, electrical shock, a tornado, near-drowning, auto accidents, and a severe form of miscommunication during a deep sea dive.

#23 While working in a hospital, one often encounters the life-or-death situation of another human being. Individual A witnesses this miracle or tragedy as an experience in itself. Person A works at University Hospital and often runs into one or both of these types of events. It is the sort of experience to be explained in part to others, but to actually witness it is truly unbelievable. It is almost impossible to put into words the many different thoughts that run through your mind and the rapid successions of extreme mood swings. You feel happy or sad one minute, and yet something happens the next to change completely how you feel.

#24 A's view: It was the frightening experience of a near-miss air collision at O'Hare. Having been on a "hold" pattern due to dense fog, we were finally scheduled to land. The sky was completely black. While flying in circles above Chicago, we approached a dark red-orange glow—then foggy, hazy light about 300 feet below. Suddenly, the plane made an abrupt thrust toward the sky. Everyone was thrown back into their seats. Silence prevailed after an "oh-ug" voice vibration occurred. It was a "hang-on" situation. I squeezed the hand and arm of my seatmates and was rendered speechless. My heart was pounding while feeling I should say my prayers and briefly I did. The shock of not knowing the specific conditions we were in prevented any real thought—just a body numbness. I tried to explain such numbness to my seatmates but it was impossible. To explain my "feelings" several days after landing was quite different. It was just a brief "we had a nearmiss and everyone was frightened." What happened was unexplainable. I cannot convey the empty feeling of being so frightened. I did not have a "thought" and that in itself could not be expressed to anyone else at the time.

#25 A's view: About four years ago A was the victim of a very unusual accident. Person A was near death and in the depths of a sort of personal trauma experienced as a dream or vision that was virtually impossible to describe in its emotional totality. The word "exorcism" is probably the closest description, but it pales (as one-dimensional) in comparison with the full magnitude of physical and emotional involvement.

#26 A's view: The thought of "death" to a young child qualifies. When I was nine years old, I was electrocuted. Two days later I went to a doctor who said if the shock had lasted five or ten seconds longer—for a total of twenty seconds—I surely would have died. The thought of death to someone so young is so unattainable, almost bordering on the impossible. Needless to say, it threw me. Virginia Woolf called this the "gap of language."

#27 A's view: When I was thirteen, my family's house was destroyed by tornado. I was in the house when the tornado hit. The fear was something I have never experienced before or since. I can't fully explain how I felt at the moment—not knowing if I would live or die. It is an experience to be understood only by those who actually live through one.

#28 A's view: As a child I spent much personal time in fantasy. As early as age five I remember "turning off" immediate sensory input and "turning on" to my own controllable private world. Most fantasies could not be explained to anyone else. As an adult such modes of behavior still operate during highly intense or traumatic times. While sailing one afternoon I fell overboard. I was out of sight of land and the boat was moving quite fast out of sight, despite my most vigorous crawl. I clearly remember treading water and assessing the totality of the situation. There was nothing rational or reasonable to be done. I started swimming but eventually became tired and drifted off into the fantasy world of my childhood. Also, there was a special place in my personal fantasies. It was green, covered with mosses, violets, and huge trees, very shady, and a little scary. There was a small stream moving slowly through the center of my vision, from left to right. Small rocks stuck out of the water and caused little whirlpools and other wonderful patterns as it moved so slowly and made gurgling sounds if you listened hard enough. By the time the gurgle could be heard, the other background noise, which was a ringing sound, could be heard. There was dim awareness the sounds were from the outside world and not to be listened to for detail but rather for their total harmonic quality. They would raise and lower in pitch and intensity. Anyway, I was no longer swimming aimlessly in the Gulf of Mexico but rather laying in the cool green mosses and trying to smell violets. It seemed strange that I could not smell them. I wondered if I had ever smelled them and leaned back against one of the great trees that didn't feel threatened at the moment. It seemed important not to doze off to sleep. It was one important rule about this place. I could *never* sleep here. I stared into space and could barely hear human voices in the distance. They were far away and sounded excited but I just looked out at the stream, the little rocks, and smiled at the pattern of swirls behind the rocks. The voices grew louder, more clear, and definitely excited. I stared at the water. The trees moved and startled me. While I struggled to get up I turned around and saw a woman's face and a man's too! There were two people, a man and a woman, pawing and talking to me. I focused and realized I had just been pulled out of the water. I had been rescued and had missed it. At that exact moment I finally realized I was in shock and took measures to deal with it. The couple took me to a marina just as it was getting dark. My friends were in a panic and relieved to see me. This is the first time I've had an opportunity to tell this story.

#29 Individual A was involved in a serious car accident. A had a fractured back and endured surgery that fused A's back with inserted rods. Complications developed, and A was paralyzed from the waist down. A's first emotional reaction was a kind of numbness. The only thing A could think of was to be strong. So A shed no tears and could show no deep emotions. If A should ever cry during such a crisis, it would be an admission that he might not ever walk again. During the whole ordeal A had one particular thought constantly in the back of his mind: if he wasn't going to be able to walk again he would kill himself. Individual A didn't want to be a burden to his family. It would ruin his parents' plans to travel together when they retired. He would be a liability who would only hinder others. After a long period of recovery, A looks back and feels shallow for having had such morbid thoughts.

#30 A's view: One particular time comes to mind while on vacation in Cozumel, Mexico. I had been diving for six years now, but it seems no two dives are ever the same. No matter where you go or what you do, even if you are revisiting a former dive site, things always seem different. The waves and motion of the water constantly bury and uncover things so secret that what surfaces one day may be hidden the next. One particular dive sticks out in my mind that will never be repeated. The cruise was to last all day. The boat left shore at 9:00 A.M. and we were to return about 5:00 P.M. The trip consisted of two dives: one to a depth of about eighty feet and a second to a more shallow forty feet. It is necessary to schedule dives in this manner because nitrogen tends to collect in the bloodstream when you dive. Because you absorb more nitrogen the deeper you go, and because nitrogen collecting in the bloodstream can lead to an ailment called "the bends," it is important that you carefully monitor the amount of time spent underwater and depth of descent. An error or miscalculation in either matter can prove fatal. When the boat finally reached our first dive site, the divers were instructed to "gear up." Because my girlfriend was not licensed to dive, I was forced to pair up with another diver. My dive partner ended up being a New Yorker. He was about thirty and a salesman back in New York. He told me he had been diving for about fifteen years and had been to Cozumel several times. This, however, was his first dive at this particular location. After we reached the bottom we followed our dive master to the point where our dive was really to begin. We were in about fifty feet of water when the dive master stopped, motioned us to follow, then began swimming toward a ledge. As we swam up to the ledge I suddenly realized where I was. The ledge was not a ledge at all, but a sheer wall falling 3,000 feet to the floor of the ocean. What had appeared to be a ledge was in fact the edge of the continental shelf! As we swam past the lip of the continent the wall dropped below us. As the water grew deeper it turned a dark blue so I could not see where the wall ended. While swimming over the edge I noticed a strong current that ran along the wall at such a speed it was not necessary to swim. Of course, this same current also made it hard to stop and impossible to swim back into it. This is what is called a "drift" dive that permits you to see a great deal of ocean life while conserving your air supply. It turned out to be a bit more than that. As the group descended along the wall we began to spread out. Our depth was 84 feet. At this depth we could safely stay down for about forty minutes. Any longer and we would have to postpone our second dive because of the large amount of nitrogen that would build up in our blood. As we drifted along I kept an eye on my partner. Every few minutes I would monitor my own air supply, via a pressure gauge, and then motion for him to do the same. When he looked at this I would also turn the gauge toward me so that I would know how much air he had left. Everyone starts the dive with about 2,700 pounds of pressure; roughly the amount of air in a public phone booth. After reaching our maximum depth of 84 feet, my partner had about 1,800 pounds and I had 2,100. We drifted along the wall for several minutes, enjoying the colorful and exotic marine life before members of the group began to stop, swimming against the current so they could get a better look at some plant or animal. My partner began to drift away from me, and it was at this point I became concerned. It is a rule in diving you never leave your buddy's side. You should never be more than an arm's length away since a sudden loss of visibility due to sediment or a swift current can quickly separate you. My buddy and I were a bit behind the group and he was constantly stopping. I was having trouble stopping in time to stay next to him since the current was moving so quickly. I was also unable to read his pressure gauge. My own gauge read 1,500 so he had less than I did. It is another rule of diving that you begin to ascend when your pressure reads 600–700 pounds. This is to provide a margin of error, should your gauge be inaccurate. By heading to the surface at that point, it is safe to assume you will have enough air to reach the top. After another quick check of my air (I was down to 1,300), I finally was able to meet up with my partner. When I reached him, he was blowing bubbles like crazy while pointing to a hole in the wall. After getting much closer I was able to see it was actually a cave that had formed in the wall. We both struggled against the current and I was motioning for us to join the rest of the group when my partner suddenly swam head first into the cave. I shouted into my mouthpiece for him to stop but he did not hear me. He turned toward me, motioning me to follow, then swam around the corner of the cave. I turned toward the direction of the rest of the group, who were quickly drifting away, hoping someone else had seen my partner go into the cave. No one had seen him and three pairs of divers were already beginning their ascent to the surface.

My gauge read 1,000 pounds. I was gripping a section of coral attempting to hold my place against the wall. I didn't want to enter the cave for fear of getting lost, swept into some tight cavern, or God knows what else. For all I knew that cave could have been a chimney or a chute that runs straight to the bottom of the ocean floor. If it were, there would be a tremendous current moving through it, one I would never be able to fight. I looked around, hoping someone had seen what happened and would come and help me. I was afraid to enter the cave for fear of endangering my own life but I felt that I should somehow try to help my partner. Without knowing what I should do, I pulled myself into the opening of the cave. Once inside the mouth of the cave I pulled my knife from its sheath. I banged it against my metal air tank to create a loud noise. Since water is more dense than air it carries sound faster and further. I hoped my banging would provide a signal to my partner to swim toward. My gauge red 900. After banging on my tank for several minutes I remembered a small flashlight I had stuck in my pocket. It was a small light, using the smallest size AAA batteries, but it was a light. I had brought it down with me to see if it was really waterproof. As I twisted the lens to turn it on, a small beam of light shot against the cave wall. It really was waterproof. I swam a few feet into the cave so that I would be able to look around a corner. Once around the corner I could see only another corner heading to my left. I looked at my gauge, saw that it read 800, and made a decision I hoped I would never have to make. I carefully backed up to the mouth of the cave. I knew I didn't have enough air or the equipment to go into a cave, which is one of the most dangerous places to dive. I decided I would have to leave my partner behind in hopes of getting to the dive master in time for us to do something. As I swam out of the cave and into the current, an indescribable rush of feelings swept over me. I knew that my decision would most likely lead to another person losing his life, but I felt that to risk my own as well would only be foolish. I felt fear and guilt and remorse pour over me as I swam toward my dive master. As I swam I looked at my gauge: 700 pounds. Only a few divers were left down now; most had already ascended toward the top. I swam toward the dive master wondering how I could be able to express what had happened and how we would ever be able to rescue my partner in time. I knew it was going to happen. I knew it when he began to break the rules. I swam blindly, my mind running back over the events of the last few minutes, replaying the scene with a different ending—with me stopping my partner before he had a chance to enter the cave. Suddenly I felt a pull on my fin. I turned quickly, startled because I was so deep in thought. To be honest, I have to say that as I turned, I half expected to see a shark or something, since I realized I had not seen anything as I swam thinking about that cave. When I did turn, my heart nearly stopped. It was my partner, with a smile on his face, but confusion and bewilderment in his eyes. I immediately grabbed his gauge to check his pressure—500. I pointed to the surface, this time making sure I grabbed his arm as I climbed. When we got back on the boat, he explained to me the cave was only a tunnel and that it had come out about 20 feet from me and downstream about 50 feet. My partner said he had waited for me to come out the other end when he finally gave up and swam toward the group. He couldn't understand why I hadn't come through. I never said anything to him in front of the rest of the divers but on the second dive I paired up with the dive master. I wasn't going to take any chances. I will never be able to explain how I felt while looking back into the cave, just before swimming back out into the current. It was so unexpected. The relaxing, mellowing atmosphere of Mexico, with the nightly fiestas and the slow, warm days had not prepared me for the dive. It was something I will never be able to describe and never be able to forget.

Such radical forms of critical communication transform the respective parties rather than merely leave them in much the same condition as they were before they met. It is transformational, after all, not knowing who will live or die, the nature of the risks, or whether the heroic and tragic aspects of the encompassing drama will bring out the best or the worst human beings afford one another. Critical situations provide a severe and intense reality test of the capacity and willingness of the respective parties to take into full account the various strivings and yearnings of one another.

Respondent accounts underscore a number of central themes. First is an aura of disbelief associated with what is witnessed firsthand. There is the full spectrum of interpersonal sensitivities: expressions of love, joy, surprise, interest, excitement, and negative or unwelcome displays of anger, fear, and sadness. The shock of not knowing what is about to happen can produce gradations of body numbness and a blur of sensations from frightening experiences that prevent any "thought" from being explained to any other source.

Personal trauma: near-death "dreams" and "visions" are nearly impossible to describe in their full range of emotional totality or sheer magnitude of physical and emotional involvements. In the case of a near-fatal electrocution, for example, one's thoughts may border on the impossible. To witness one's home being destroyed by a tornado and not knowing whether one will live or die is an experience to be understood only by those who live through one. Take the case of nearly drowning: turning one's immediate sensory inputs off and turning on to the more controllable world of personal fantasy, a highly intense and traumatic time when there is absolutely nothing rational or reasonable to be done as one becomes more and more tired before drifting off into a world of childhood fantasy, a special place. Also, a serious car accident: paralyzed from the waist down, an ordeal, total numbness. To give in to the urge to cry out would be to admit defeat. There is the thought of killing oneself should it turn out to be impossible to walk again. After all, no one wants to be a burden on others.

In the case of deep sea diving the margin of error becomes very small. One feels fear of getting lost in the darkness and being unable to fight the tremendous currents. The basic fear is of endangering one's own life and, at a moment of not knowing what one should do, having to decide to leave one's partner behind—a decision most likely to lead to another person losing his life. Later, one finds the other party just in time to be able to return safely together to the bright surface, never again to be able to describe precisely what transpired and yet never to be able to forget.

THE ACT OF GIVING BIRTH

It is useful to compare those types of shared situations where individual lives are in jeopardy with those involving the act of giving birth. It is in the nature of "beginning," Hannah Arendt (1958) writes:

[T]hat something new is started which cannot be expected from whatever may have happened before. This character of startled unexpectedness is inherent in all beginnings and in all origins. The new always happens against the overwhelming odds of statistical laws and their probability, which for all practical, everyday purposes amounts to certainty; the new therefore always appears in the guise of a miracle. (pp. 177–178)

Relevant accounts of what it is like to have a baby are as complex and varied as the lived circumstances that give rise to them. One woman recalls labor with curtains wide open and with her legs exposed. It didn't bother her because she was in another world. It was as if no one else was really there. She was staring out of the window in a daze as a way to shut off the pain. It was really neat, a feeling she would like to feel over again. Another woman finds the birth of a firstborn child to be a big surprise, arriving one month early and leaving the mother unprepared for such a premature entrance into the world. The newborn baby turns out to be a source of joy, a living miracle, an experience beyond words. The joy transcends anything one might be able to express in a verbal mode.

Still another gives birth to a baby with Down's syndrome. The woman does not want to believe the news and prays it is just a great mistake. The mother does not want to see the newborn baby. She does not want the baby and wishes it would die but cannot bring herself to say so. Over a period of several months inexpressible feelings turn to love just before the point where the baby develops a devastating infection and dies. Once again, the mother feels powerful emotions too deep and complex to share with anyone else. Likewise, after the birth of a fourth child, another respondent falls into a deep depression, which progresses as the weeks go by. The woman in question cannot eat or sleep or do the chores. The easiest task becomes a mountain. All she wants to do is stay in bed and hide these feelings without sounding as if she is feeling sorry for herself. After considerable effort to keep away from family and friends, the woman agrees to see a doctor, who labels the illness manic depression. She finds it comforting to put a name on this strange illness which in her case has been treated successfully now for the past twenty years.

In these four cases the drama of giving birth involves intense struggle to adapt and accommodate to a severe set of demand characteristics and treated with utmost seriousness, care, and concern. It is highly personalized drama where heroic and tragic aspects of human exchange are implicit in the privilege of one source of life to be a source of origin for a new source of life. At stake in the developmental process of birth, growth, development, and renewal of possibilities is the anticipation of all that must be eventually relinquished, surrendered, or otherwise taken away.

THE PRIVILEGE OF GROWING OLDER TOGETHER

Alfred Schutz (1967) once defined communication as the privilege of "growing older together." This key insight of Schutz can be interpreted in the following terms (taken from Mortensen, 1987): Every source of life bears witness to manifest relations between the living and the dying. All life-death issues are therefore issues manifested in living-dying flesh. In human terms this means everyone who is alive in the world is a living symbol (model) of what it means to be alive in the world. Every manifestation of life alters the cumulative definition of life. Every living person is a living symbol of what it means to be a living symbol maker. Everyone who lives affords lived expression to the way of life they live. A symbol maker symbolizes a way of making symbols in a manner that has never been revealed before or again by any other symbol maker. The symbolic constructions of the symbol maker are nonduplicative and nonreplicable from the point of origin (birth) to the point of destination (death). The very act of birth thrusts the one who is born into lived activities, and the gradual ascendancy and erosion in the range of those lived activities culminates in movement toward death. Thus, the conditions of life, living, dying, and death are implicit in all birth, origin, and beginning.

We symbolize to one another what it means for each of us to be alive and to live in the midst of a living universe that sustains diverse and divergent sources of life and living who are constantly threatened by the possibility of dying or premature death on all sides. We symbolize to one another what it means to each one of us to be living his or her own way of life, living in this particular time and place and not some other time and place, constrained by the horizons of this here and now instead of some other imagined here and now, and interpreted from within this perspective and not from any other. We symbolize what it means to grow older together and alone. We symbolize the particular conditions granted to a given way of living a life that ultimately slips through one's grasp. We also symbolize to one another what it means not to be able to grow older indefinitely, eternally.

Life cannot be sustained in isolation from other life. Life is both sustained and threatened by life forms located on all sides. We are dependent on one another for survival from the very first moment of life to the very last. The idea that what we express to one another does not finally establish our position and place in the human world is an arrogant illusion. So is the glib notion that words and gestures are cheap and therefore have no real life or death implications. In point of fact, we remain dependent on one another to tell us who and what we are—and how much it does or does not matter that we live or die—from the beginning and ending of all our beginnings and endings with one another. My symbolic universe is what I create/destroy whenever I am in the immediate presence or absence of others, what I cannot escape, and what I drag around with me from one human contact to another. Such a legacy constitutes a living definition of life incarnate.

DEATH AS INEXPLICABLE

Arnold Metzger (1973) identifies the following points of relevance (cited verbatim, pp. 7, 172, 179). In the act of dying we discover what life is. We always understand ourselves from the standpoint of the limit. When we speak of the disintegration of existence, we mean that existence loses its self-awareness. The moment becomes speechless. The senses grow mute. Life is the countermove against oblivion. Human existence, aware of itself, is a dialogue with death. The process of downfall, of being extinguished, the dissolution and destruction is inherent in the creation of the existent. Every existent, according to its kind, partakes of self destruction. One's power is always wrestled from ultimate impotence, capacity from noncapacity. Experience consumes both the process of experience and that which is experienced. We do not seek nothingness. We seek the One. We stand in the world, that is, we continuously confront the task of humanizing the inexhaustible matter of the world: of creating unity in the human community.

The task of promoting unity in the human community is severely tested each time some member strives to preserve unity despite the threat of the premature loss of some other member. Particularly instructive are reported sequences of interaction between those who live with those who suddenly die. They indicate just how important our individual lives actually become to one another and what is required to dredge up the courage and conviction to say and do what must be said and done while there is still time. Finally, each is a model of shared struggle to affirm life among the living and to delay, postpone, or prevent premature deterioration and decay. At the very moment someone dies, those who remain discover the full measure of the communicative urge, despite what appears to be inexplicable. The following sets of entries include interactions implicating suicide, accidents, and fatal illnesses.

#31 A's view: About seven years ago I saw an older man die before my eyes. My family and I were spending time at Walt Disney World on a hot August day. We were standing in a long line waiting to get on a water ride. The sun was so bright I stared down at the sidewalk. Then I heard a deathly scream of a woman when my eyes focused on fresh, flowing blood on the sidewalk about ten feet in front of me. I looked up to see a man cry for help. At this point I kept staring at the blood-stained sidewalk, unable to move. I had the urge to reach out, help the man, and release him from pain but there was not a single thing I was qualified to do. While the crowd gathered to let the man have space, my eyes were literally planted in the sidewalk. I didn't want to leave his side, hoping he would sit up. Paramedics arrived and strolled him into the ambulance. I glanced at his eyes, glossy and stagnate, they stared through the sky. He was obviously dead within a matter of seconds. This was the first time I ever witnessed or experienced a person die. As I look back, there was a good possibility I was in shock. Not only could I not move physically but mentally I felt time had stopped. My thoughts were not racing or confusing but directed toward the man's condition. I felt I was in a trance until the ambulance was totally out of sight. It was then I focused on his wife, realizing she was now a widow. How awful to die in the middle of a crowd at a place that is designed for pure amusement. I found it terribly disturbing how the crowd just got back in line, not even responding to the event that had just occurred. This played on the negative side of my personality—how people can be so uncaring. It also opened my eyes to the meaninglessness of life—how it could be over so quickly. This moment disturbed me the entire day, wondering constantly if the man even had a chance to be revived. After we got off the ride, janitors were mopping up the stained blood from the sidewalk. I felt sick. His eyes were so vacant. To this day I still wonder about his wife, hoping she is happy.

#32 A's view: Yes, there was a moment where I couldn't express myself to anyone. I'm alone. I'm surrounded by a plush bedroom furnished with a canopy bed, an ivory colored bedroom set with golden handles and flowered wallpaper—everything a little girl could dream of and more. Looks can be deceiving. I had everything I would ever want and more, material-wise, but what I really wanted I had no control over. My stuffed animals didn't matter, my Holly Hobby collection didn't matter, not even my cat who loved me mattered. I heard yelling downstairs as I hugged my knees to my frail body. I heard it many, many times before but this night it was particularly bad. How could you call someone such names if you're married to them? I was catatonic. I couldn't move a muscle. There was a familiar noise of a diesel engine in the garage. Why did it run so long? Isn't mom going to leave the claws of my dad by running away? I somehow unglued my knees from my chest. I remember opening our garage door and becoming overwhelmed with the smell of carbon monoxide. Ugh!! My small body could barely withstand even a few minutes of the awful poison. There was mom, sprawled out in the front seat sleeping. Of course my instincts told me something was wrong, although I was too young to know that carbon monoxide can kill if inhaled long enough. The doors on the car were locked—it figures. They were always locked when she did this. I frantically pounded on the window of the big yellow beast. By this time I was nauseous and ready to join my mother in the endless slumber. She wearily woke up and looked up at me with droopy, beet red rimmed eyes. She saw her only daughter, her pride and joy, her life. She unlocked the door and let me pull her out of the jaws of death. I resented her once again. The same questions laid heavily on my heart: Why didn't my dad rescue her? The same desire rang in my head and tears rolled down my cheeks as I sat rocking my mom in the crook of my arms—all I wanted was a mom and dad who loved each other.

#33 A and B are friends until B, despite apparently having everything going for him, commits suicide during high school. This takes a dramatic toll on the family and affects A in unusual ways that leave her deeply afraid to discuss the matter because the feelings were so strange. For several months A goes to sleep with her light on every night. She becomes afraid of the darkness because darkness seems like death to her. At times during the night she scares herself terribly, thinking someday she is going to die and will be put into a casket forever. A dwells on the fact she would never have the chance to live again but only lie in that casket forever. After the suicide, A becomes afraid to go to the bedroom because it hurts and scares her so. She is afraid she will see B alive in his room. She is also afraid to go into the downstairs kitchen where B died because she can somehow picture B's body lying there in that spot where the tragedy took place. She is even afraid to pass the living room on the way to the bathroom because just by looking into the living room she could see B's picture, his carrot red hair and nice smile, the way he was when he was here with us. So A runs past that picture and tries not to look at it. She can never tell anyone of the fears she has. She doesn't know if anyone would understand her fears or if they would think of them as stupid. Today she can talk about them, but it still hurts so much to think about B. Her fears have subsided a little, but in some ways they are also still present. Darkness still scares her, and she doesn't know whether that nameless fear will ever go away.

#34 A's friend is discovered after she hanged herself in her dorm. Individual A leaves town to escape the pressure, stress, and strain. A's friend had taken her gift of friendship away, and A doesn't even know why. A's last memory of her friend putting her arms around A and saying everything that was happening in the world that A thought was bad or unfair really did have a larger meaning or lesson behind it. That night A remembers asking herself, "OK, Ann, what the hell kind of lesson are you trying to teach me now?" Throughout the next couple of weeks, people would come in and want A to talk about A's feelings. A wonders, "How are we supposed to feel anything?" A felt her heart was frozen like a block of ice. For a time

A did not want to care, love, or have the friendship of another person because A would not know who else would do the same thing to A that Ann did. A hated Ann and for the world of things that were happening in A's life. The only way she could cope at that point was just not to feel anything or express her feelings at all for that matter. It took A a long time before she could even tell someone how she felt, but it helped to talk about her feelings instead of keeping them bottled up inside.

#35 A's cousin (B) and A were rock climbing. B was leading. A was relaying him. When B got up about seventy feet, he slipped and fell. Watching a person you've known and loved for so long die is an intensely personal experience. So many thoughts and feelings run through your head that are virtually unexplainable or unrecognizable.

#36 Recently A had a close friend who was killed in an auto accident in which a train hit the side of the car. She went home to the wake and funeral to pay respects to the family and last respects to her friend. They had been as close a set of friends as there ever could have been back at a time when they did almost everything together and talked about everything. Gradually they began to grow apart, and when they talked, it always seemed to just scratch the surface and be sort of shallow—"How have you been?" "How are your parents?" They never had the in-depth discussions they had before. When her friend passed away, A felt there was no one she could turn to who would understand her feelings. She felt that the two of them had never reconciled their differences and that she had left this world without giving her a chance to really talk to her. A now feels like the only person in the world who would really understand her feelings if it had happened the other way around. When A thinks of the things leading up to her friend's death, she is very sad, almost as if she owes her friend an apology for the times they never talked or never called. Since she is no longer here, it is frustrating. No one is here to explain the emptiness felt inside. A wishes she could do it over again and change things and make them right. Others don't understand, because she hears so many people say, "I'll just remember her for the last time I saw her (happy)." When people say, "That is just the way life is," A can't accept or understand.

#37 A's view: When I was a sophomore in college a friend of mine from high school was killed by a drunk driver on a visit home. All I could think of was how easily it could have been me. I was scared, sad and I felt guilt because I should have called more and made more of an effort. The absolute worst feeling occurred when I went to visit my friend's father in the hospital. Out of three people in the car, he was the only one to survive. They taped her funeral so he could watch it later. When he saw me, he grabbed my hand and started to cry even though his eyes were swollen shut. He told me how much she liked me and what a good friend I had been. He told me how much I reminded him of her. That hurt the worst. I couldn't understand why she and not me. Everyone told me it was stupid for me to feel this way but the feelings were very real and no one seemed to understand.

#38 After the unexpected death of a family member, A has difficulty talking to others about it. Individual A lies to keep others from knowing. A blames himself for the death of the family member and thinks that if only A had been with the person who died, it might not have happened. Death by suicide is a taboo subject. A feels empty without the other perso... A thinks about how life might have been different if the other person had not died. A hides the reality of such a painful experience. A does not want to discuss such a private issue and lose the friendship of others as soon as they come to know A's deepest secret and pain.

#39 A's view: My mom died when I was in the seventh grade. She died of lung cancer. I had always tried to get her to quit smoking, telling her that she would get cancer. Five years later, she did get it. It was hard for me to deal with her death. I mostly pretended it never happened. I talked to my friends more than my family members. This also caused me to face death at an early age and now I am terrified of it. My friends and I talk about it once in a while—usually when we're drunk or something—when we're secure and our inhibitions are down. We get pretty deep about it but I can never really express how deep this fear is for me.

#40 A's view: My best friend died in a car accident when I was seventeen. When she died I had a lot of feelings inside that I could not explain. First I felt the normal pain and loss you feel when someone close dies. But ever since then I have had a much more negative outlook on my future and the future of the people I love. In a way it is good because I now realize and make an effort not to waste time fighting with others. We only have one life to live and we should live it to the fullest. I now realize we can be taken out of this world at anytime and I am very afraid that either myself or someone else I love will be taken out of this world. If I think about this reality too much, I become very emotional. I have a hard time explaining how this idea makes me feel. I want all the people I love to know how I feel. I want them to live life to the fullest but I don't know how to explain this without sounding like someone who is obsessed with death or even socially deviant.

#41 A's view: When my father passed away, it was when I was a lot younger and not very mature and not really sufficiently well educated to understand truly what was going on. It was something I did not expect and it came as a total shock to me. At first I felt very much like I was looking at it from outside of myself. I was so confused at the time that I didn't really know what to say or feel. I didn't know exactly what words to use so people could truly understand what was going on with me at that time. I was too young to have this kind of responsibility put on me. I then found it very difficult to tell anyone else and help them to understand my mixed emotions and not think I was just a kid. Now, as a young man, I notice it can be very hard with close relationships to express exactly how you feel toward the other person. You both think you have to be so cool and not let on that you are actually giving some of your ego. It is so hard to break down and let them see the real you—unguarded with your big block down and really talk. As much as it is hard to talk to your partner, it is just as hard to tell your closest friends. You don't want them to think you're being weak and falling for someone else. It makes you feel like the less dominant one and that you are being all mushy and stupid. It seems like no one truly knows that particular person like you do. Although they may seem like a jerk or asshole to someone else, they can be an entirely different person to you.

#42 A's view: My grandmother was diagnosed with cancer six months before she died. She was a grandmother I was not very close to and never really did much for other than writing thank you notes back to her for birthday money. When I found out she had cancer I started to do more. She enjoyed the fact that I was taking a German course and could speak with her in German. So because of that I started writing letters to her in German, telling her how much she meant to me and the family. Now it would be easy to say what I did was to make her feel better but instead I did it to make sure I said things I needed to say to her—in my own mind—so I did it to make myself feel better. But one strange thing, even though some of the later letters were received but not responded to (because of her condition), when I went to the funeral I felt so much closer to her even though I didn't really find out anything more about her as a person through my letters. I felt this happened because I shared with Grandma a part of me rarely shared with anyone else.

#43 A and B are brothers who love one another deeply. Suddenly B dies. A has feelings inside of great love, great memories, and mostly great secrets they had shared. A holds these feelings inside and will not share them with others. A assumes such enjoyable secrets were made in such a way that no one else could experience them. A feels joy and would love to share his affections with others and let them know how great and how much fun A's brother was, but A assumes that no one would be able to capture this special range of feelings that were shared between them. Still, A recognizes it is foolish not to convey his feelings because A is not the only one with memories that do not have the same initial effect as the time when they were first created.

#44 A's view: On occasion, I get a complete sense for just a fleeting moment of what it means to die and cease to exist forever. This sense is so real to me that I get frightened and my heart pounds and my breathing quickens and I often find the urge to run and move around and affirm my "aliveness." I cannot express this to anyone else because (1) it is hard to explain just how intensely real death becomes to me in such a moment and I feel like no one would understand my reaction to it unless they could understand how horrible it is and (2) it is embarrassing. I find it hard to believe anyone could understand how I feel and what I experience. I'm afraid people will think I'm losing my grip on reality.

#45 A's view: Stop for a moment and imagine what it would be like to sit in a chair with nothing around you and just hang out. You couldn't move and you couldn't do anything but think. The only catch is that you would be there forever. You could never leave. There would be nothing to look forward to and you would have to do that forever. The idea of "nothing forever" is the strangest concept to imagine. Also, I often feel that no matter what I say I could never convey the actual way I feel. People say they understand but I know they don't. It's an empty, helpless feeling with nothing to look forward to but nothing and it never ends.

There is a point where the communicative capacities of human beings are tested to the very limit. It is not so much a point of no return as a state or condition of utter finality. It no longer matters what one feels, thinks, says, or does because one has reached the limit of one's ability to intervene and make any further difference in the course of events. There is nothing further to be gained. All that remains is what lingers as inexplicable.

The value of life is severely tested in those shared situations in which one discovers the open-ended privilege of growing older together cannot be expected to be continued indefinitely into the future. It is not the sort of presumption to be taken for granted on a continuous basis. This is what makes human life so precious. One may imagine the "eternal" renewal of human possibilities (faith), or one may instead imagine the impossibility of any further engagement in any form of face-to-face interaction with any other person (finitude). Each time one talks directly to someone else, there is at least an outside possibility that one will never meet or ever be in a position to greet the other person again. This is, as Heidegger says, the one possibility that is not to be outstripped.

The purest case of "radical incommunicability" in human relations occurs every time one individual is in a position to observe the death of someone else firsthand. What one experiences is the final end of the opportunity to engage someone else in a succession of direct, face-to-face encounters. Death is inexplicable because it does not reveal any of its secrets. One may see, hear, speak, touch, or move in relation to someone who is no longer in a position to see, hear, speak, touch, or move toward or away from anything or anyone in any particular manner, shape, or form. For the first time there is lived expression without the possibility of a reply. One may speak to someone who no longer is able to answer back. In the aftermath of unexpected death, one may discover the sheer magnitude of what is lost and at least some measure of what cannot be expressed, reclaimed, or replaced.

What is inexplicable about the sudden death of others has an impact on the communicative practices of the survivors. First are tacit defensive implications that register when one source lives while another dies: (1) not feeling anything in particular at all, reacting as if nothing ever happened, or wanting to run away and escape from reality operating well beyond one's power to control; (2) struggling with the urge to hide the pain behind a mask, lying to keep others from knowing, and hoping the memories go away; (3) refusing to discuss private and sensitive issues and thereby risk the loss of friendship of others as they come to know one's deepest secret and pain; and (5) repressing a lot of feelings and forcing oneself not to think about what is grim. Second are variations on themes of guilt and anxiety: (1) blaming oneself for the demise of another and (2) maintaining a taboo over some unspeakable subject. Third are various expressions of care and affection amidst mutual efforts to keep alive tender, loving secrets, much private joy, and comfort. Finally there is a deep sense of loss or emptiness, together with a profound sense of speechlessness.

When an individual blocks out others, serious misunderstandings are apt to occur. Often verbal modes of exchange diminish and nonverbal cues must carry the entire load of implicit personal striving. Initial acts of denial and withdrawal are compelling forces. Death puzzles us in so many ways— the ultimate in unanswerable questions. When people lose contact with an important part of their world, they are also severed from a larger understanding of their own unique position and place in the human world.

Ordinarily everything is done to render the subject null and void. Nonverbal cues convey or elicit a sense of overall uneasiness. At the same time there are various efforts of those closest to the deceased to cope with the loss together and thereby spread the pain and suffering around—in rituals of bearing one another's burdens through personal displays of the strength and courage to come to grips with death as a mechanism for a new lease on life. Words of consolation compensate for the massive lack of understanding. Those who remain confess, through gestures of grief and mourning, unspoken measures of loss and the search for a restoration of communal ties. Initial withdrawal from others gives way to private meditation. Self-oriented reflection intermingles with negative emotions that occur less frequently over time, and positive emotions are allowed once again to come to light.

Closely related are images of the deceased. These take the form of a set of imaginary conversations that refer to what was missing or lacking in some actual sequences of conversations from the past. Quite striking is the realization of what the gift of friendship really means once it has been taken away without one ever knowing why. One respondent feels closer to a friend who had just died by thinking of letters that had been received, but without sufficient time for the other person to respond. Another reflects upon the urge to extend a belated apology for the times the two friends never talked or neither one of them ever called. Here there is a desire to do it all over again and change things for the better, so that the one left behind doesn't feel so empty and alone. Still another laments the fact that it will no longer be possible to say hello and good-bye or give the other person a hug or a kiss. It is natural to think of how future interaction could have been so different if only the other person had not died. It is a matter of sheer spirit, perhaps, that prompts one woman to go to the grave of her beloved mother and share everything that takes place in her life—whispering things that can't be told to anyone else while preserving the sense that the deceased is still a living part of the one who remains.

In the aftermath, there are personal and mostly private realizations. The news hits home—any individual can leave the human world at any time. It makes one realize how vulnerable each human being really is. It also makes some things more difficult to grasp, particularly when one wants so badly to figure out what is to be believed without being sure at all. There is no reason to reveal to others what one doesn't understand by oneself, not knowing what it all means and realizing one would not be able to say anything anyway. It is an opportunity for some to take stock, accept death, and come to terms with it or, on the other hand, to feel even more vulnerable over the thought of one's own mortality—the meaninglessness of life and how it can be over so quickly. One respondent describes the lingering mood as "a shadow over me—the darkness." Others react more actively by striving to work through the pressure, stress, and strain and somehow finding the urge to run and move around, affirm one's own sense of aliveness, and thereby reaffirm a larger sense of connectedness with others in the surrounding human community. The final realization: there is only one life to live, and each one must strive to live to the very fullest to the very end.

As memories of the aftermath fade over time, those who remain are relieved of the burden of any further engagement in the sorts of conversations for which human beings are not usually well prepared. There is a need to rediscover how to talk about one's deepest, unspoken feelings instead of keeping them bottled up inside. There is also the urge to reach out and touch, hug, or embrace those who remain—perhaps as a means of achieving reassurance that those of us who remain are still quite alive. One respondent describes the transition as one of coming back from where you have no clue as to what to say or how to say it and where you don't seem to be quite so sure anymore how you really do feel.

Some observers experience considerable difficulty in relearning how to talk to others about the fading images. One source refers to not knowing whether the nameless fear will ever go away. There is also some comfort in the realization that no one is ever really completely alone. Sooner or later, virtually everyone is placed in the position of striving to recover from a sense of impending devastation or permanent loss. With the passage of time, one may become more able to talk about the incident in question and account for more of what has taken place. There is additional relief in the discovery that every other individual has similar sorts of memories that also lack the same effect as when they were first created.

The restoration of communal ties is accompanied by recovery from primordial wounds. As for what remains as yet still unspoken, some can only hope eventually to express unresolved or unspoken issues gradually over time, a process not necessarily to be eagerly anticipated, but something that should and must be achieved for the greater welfare of those who remain and still care.

THE WEB OF SIGNIFICANCE

The task of humanizing the world is achieved largely through a succession of sustained communicative practices. On the strength of the mutual display of words and gestures in a series of critical situations, we discover what it means to be a model of a human being. The universal task of creating and maintaining a spirit of unity in the human community is a collective burden. When we talk with great care about the meaning of life, we incorporate tacit elements about the implications of dying and death. This is the eternal price of admission. Each time a person dies, those who remain may search and find common support and assurance that together each one may be able to work through the personal consequences of someone else's death.

The heroic and tragic aspects of language use bear witness to individual resilience and collaborative vulnerability at the same time. To be human is to be in a position to care about the living, but to aspire to be humane is to care also for those who are no longer or not yet alive but yet somehow live in the spirit of those who remain. No one can prevent the inevitability of personal death, but everyone can strive to be a living model of what it means to resist the perpetuation of the very conditions that reproduce a spirit of premature death or resignation on the part of those who remain.

Every individual runs up against the inevitable boundaries, limits, constraints, and source of restraint implicit in the desire for wider participation in an all-inclusive spirit of world openness. This stance presupposes a framework of receptivity and willingness to affirm the movement toward a sense of oneness, unity, and unification within the surrounding community. It is a domain in which each event in each day of every life is discovered to be infinitely sacred, and individual lives are presumed to be precious and unconditionally worthy of consideration as kindred spirits.

REFERENCES

Arendt, H. (1958). The human condition. Chicago: University of Chicago Press.

Heidegger, M. (1962). Being and time. (Trans. J. Macquarrie and E. Robinson.) New York: Harper and Row.

Metzger, A. (1973). Freedom and death. (Trans. R. Manheim.) London: Human Context Books.

Mortensen, C. D. (1987). Violence and communication. Landham, MD: University Press of America.

Schutz, A. (1967). The Phenomenology of the Social World. (Trans. G. Walsh, F. Lehnert.) Evanston, IL: Northwestern University Press.

4

The Construction of
Interpersonal Boundaries

It takes only one source of expressed activity to produce discourse, but two or more to construct dialogue. Creative interplay between these two sets of interactive forces gives rise to a certain degree of dialogical tension. The introduction of friction, strife, and strain serves to monitor and regulate the ebb and flow or back-and-forth motion of face-to-face interaction. What emerges is an unspecified margin of opportunity to preserve existing boundary lines or dissolve them. This is accomplished largely by transforming constraints into enablements or vice versa. In an action-oriented perspective, it is important to separate the effects of intrinsic constraints from largely manufactured or fabricated boundary conditions.

THE EMERGENCE OF EXCLUSIONARY BOUNDARIES

Every interactant participates in the construction of interpersonal boundaries. A boundary is created insofar as a given source places some limitation, restraint, or constraint on the degree of direct access to be granted to any other. Face-to-face interaction unfolds as a structured array of enabling (accessible) and constraining (inaccessible) conditions with open-ended opportunity for various sets of individuals to explore multiple lines of action within the context of their tangible (immediate) and intangible (unforeseen) consequences. A state of interdependence requires the respective parties be in a position to surrender some measure of psychological freedom and autonomy to one another for the sheer sake of preserving a spirit of give-and-take.

The very fact that each party must yield, submit, and share in the distribution of scarce conversational resources is a strategic indication that free association may be far less free than what appears to be the case at first glance. In effect, the notion of "psychological freedom" presumes that each individual has some measure of control to grant or deny others permission to engage in a direct personal encounter. Personal invitations may not always be welcomed nor well received. As with any creative enterprise, just about everything registers in the rhythm and the timing.

Human relations acquire definition and direction through the use of a personal logic based on principles of inclusion and exclusion. It is the sort of living logic that regulates concerns and cares over who is in or close (center), who is out or far away (periphery), and what difference it makes (involvement). Since the potential for direct human encounter is so much greater than the actual rate of occurrence, complex gradations of psychological need and desire are implicit in how and why any one source strives to chart a course that moves away from some individuals and closer to others.

Exclusionary and inclusionary principles operate on a small (micro) scale and large (macro) scale. On a micro level, relevant considerations center around issues of personal authority, legitimation, power, influence, and control (toward/away) in negotiated and complementary relation to accompanying matters of affection and concern (for/against). On a macro level, important issues affect the collective distribution of scarce resources throughout the social fabric. At both levels the process of dialogue resonates in matters affecting complex issues of who controls what and how the respective parties feel about their respective place in the encompassing social hierarchy and, more remotely, the larger scheme of things.

Of initial interest, at the micro level, are tacit assumptions involved when taking the personal conduct of any other person into account. The central issue: How much room must one allow for inclusionary and exclusionary activity on the part of self and other? The primary assumption is that any set of interactants ('A↔B') operate within the reality of the absolute present tense and possibilities that unfold within the immediacy of the here and now.

Specifically, public knowledge involves tacit interpretive procedures that generate the basic ground rules used to grasp and comprehend the explicit, manifest features of human action (Berger & Luchmann, 1967; Fararo, 1989; Schutz, 1967). Communicative practices are ordered intentionally and strategically across space and time in recursively generative forms (Giddens, 1984; Platt, 1989) of reality (re)construction so as to reproduce the complementary, typified, habituated, and routinized conditions that sustain them. As Verhoeven (1985) states, "to reach others in face-to-face relations, a stock of knowledge is given, and to the extent we are remote from others, we use a stock of knowledge equipped with idealizations, i.e., types of what the others want to do. These are expressed in linguistic typifications and recipes for behaviour that are given to us by our predecessors" (p. 83). This is the generalized domain of problematic issues and concerns that apply *equally* to anyone who is in a position to *be* someone to someone else.

The basic assumption is that every individual who participates in a constructive definition of individual relations imposes a tacit set of presumptions about what is manifest in those particular relations. This is a universal and preliminary burden imposed on any given set of individuals as constituted within a larger context of their multiple involvements with other sources (life-world). In other words, both actual and potential considerations between 'A & B' are at stake at implicit and covert as well as explicit and overt levels of sensation, perception, and conception. From this perspective it seems futile to strive for a narrow definition of what constitutes an individual in utter isolation from coimplicated relations with other individuals. To be an individual is not only to be a source of origin, a center or sphere of experiential reference, but also to be considered worthy of being publicly construed as an agent. To be an individual is, as Harris (1989) notes, "to be a 'somebody' who authors conduct construed as action" (p. 602).

Interpersonal boundaries are reflections of the sum total of relational considerations in the personal conduct of the respective parties. What or how certain matters get included or excluded from expressed consideration is a global measure of mutual integration or interrelatedness: the immediate relation of 'A & B' construed not only in reference to all possible and actual connections and disconnections with other A's and B's but also the more inclusive material resources that give rise to such expressed strivings in the first place. Such a holistic conception includes the individuals, relations among them, relations with environmental factors, and relations between these factors and the individuals as agents (Mathien, 1988; Saegert & Winkel, 1990).

Limitations and constraints are intrinsic features of face-to-face interaction. Salient demand characteristics are routinely introduced and reproduced in communicative practice through principles of repetition, substitution, and alternation in the form and content of expressive acts. Multiple networks of interpersonal encounter are fluid and subject to all manner of substitution, displacement, alternation, and rearrangement of one feature, attribute, entity, word, or thing for any other. Furthermore, personal boundaries and constraints are made apparent, acquire definition and direction, within the all-inclusive horizon of fused relations with other potential A's and B's who also serve to define and differentiate given spheres of shared activities.

In a minimal way, 'A & B' are entities who (1) can place one another at a distance, close or far way, at the center or the periphery, and/or (2) can take the place of someone else or something else at least in a tentative or provisional way. This principle of partial "intersubstitution" suggests how each member in a community of individuals is identical to every other member in the global sense that each one is subject to risk and change because of personal exposure to an array of intrinsic and invariant features of any shared situation. Hence, any set of 'A & B' will be in a position to bear witness to a multiplicity of identical, similar, different, and unique definitional features in the personal conduct of one another.

An important exclusionary consideration is embodied in the urge to move away from what the presence of some individual affords to the observer. The urge to turn away involves avoidance tendencies associated mainly with the failure to measure up or live up to the expectations of someone on behalf of someone else or something else. The urge to move away, change focus, withdraw, escape, or explore alternative possibilities culminates here in one or more of three broad classes of exchange in noncommunicative types of social settings: (1) denial of access (as typified by modes of escapism, xenophobia, indifference, alienation, malaise, shyness, emptiness, or isolation), in which one ends up with no one to turn to; (2) missed opportunity for future interaction (as typified by missing out or falling short and lapses into states of isolation or loneliness), in which one ends up with no one to talk to; and (3) substitution or partial replication of vicarious or imaginary modes of conversation for actual human encounter (as typified by personal secrets, dreams, fantasies, lies, illusions, episodes of withdrawal into fictitious worlds, and the steadfast refusal or unwillingness to express any explicit intent), in which one ends up with no one to confide in over extended time periods. This broad spectrum of exclusionary conditions serves to underscore important aspects in the personal conduct of those who are prone to be construed as relatively noncommunicative individuals while operating in unfavorable situations or highly demanding living environments. Each instance shows how the decision to participate in a particular set of communicative episodes effectively rules out a host of alternative courses of action.

ESCAPISM: THE URGE TO RUN AWAY AND HIDE

The desire to escape arises early in life. It is quite common, therefore, among those who are young, small, weak, poor, unskilled, vulnerable, fragile, or disadvantaged. It is often basically a matter of what the strong do to the weak, the old to the young, and the rich to the poor. Presumably the urge would be much weaker if the human drama would be played out on a more level playing field. In fact, the deck is stacked mainly in favor of those who are firmly entrenched in positions of social dominance over those who are subordinated and marginalized. Escapism is usually attributed to inclusive forms of pressure, strain, struggle, and strife induced from the top (above) of the invisible social hierarchy upon the bottom (below), from those who are in (center) upon those who are out (periphery), and from the haves (privileged) upon the have nots (unprivileged). Hence, dialogical tensions are manifest in terms of imbalances of power, control, domination, and authority over the appropriation and distribution of scarce ecological resources, symbolic, economic, and material. In this broad theoretical framework human relations acquire definition and direction both toward and away from some source of limit, boundary, constraint, or resistance that is construed in relation to a highly valued aspect of someone else's room to move or total margin of expressive freedom.

Consider what adults do to prompt children to want to run away and hide. Here the reported conduct of children is mainly under the control of adults who teach them how to feel, think, talk, listen, touch, and move about and then proceed to spell out relevant assumptions, rules, guidelines, and unspoken mandates about conventional or normative practice along with attendant threats, sanctions, reprisals, and unspoken implications or consequences of not fulfilling a particular duty or obligation soon enough or well enough.

Ordinary adult-child interaction is replete of praise and blame, threat and promise, and changing latitudes of permission and obligation over resolute or shifting parameters of what adults presume to be the case about the respective capacities, willingness, and limitations of various children to live up to the desires, expectations, and intentions of their elders. Interaction between parents and young children is rarely free of the risk of the sort of developmental damage that accrues either as the result of too much attention (getting too close) or not enough (getting too far away) for protracted periods during the first three years of life. Consequently, the childlike desire to run away and hide is frequently associated with a diverse array of shared circumstance that coalesce around four central themes: (1) sexual violations, (2) language systems based on diverse methods of physical domination, verbal abuse, and victimization, (3) faulty interaction patterns associated with the disintegration of family ties, and (4) destabilizing social networks.

On the matter of sexual abuse, respondent reports of incest range in age from five to fifteen and for periods lasting up to ten or more years of repeated abuse. Ordinarily the adult offender uses seductive language as a principal means of assault. The act of penetration and violation is shrouded in a ruthlessly imposed vow of silence and secrecy designed to cut off all contact with the outside world. No one else must ever know what takes place behind closed doors. A five-year-old girl is told by her uncle not to say anything, or else *he* would be in big trouble. The child is far too young to realize that what *he* was doing was wrong. By the time the young girl is old enough to realize *he* was wrong, it's too late. The damage is done. The child does not think that anyone else would believe her, so she just blocks it out. A decade later the uncle still does not remember that one grown woman can now remember full well what she was once forced to forget. It is a hard issue to talk about because she is prone even now to feel it *was* all her fault.

In the act of incest, language is used to control, dominate, and oppress in a primitive form of violence against a small, helpless, and innocent child. Language thus serves as a defense for violence against those who are willing but unable to defend themselves against repeated violations of their body boundaries or expressed will. Consider a grandfather who sexually molests several granddaughters. Each child is too young to know it is wrong because the very same thing is happening to *all* the other sisters as well. Each child is forced to take turns in episodes of "cool" violence during periods of protracted silence. Everyone else pretends not to notice what is taking place under lock and key. No one says a word. It is useless for the young children to cry out for help. As the young girls get older and begin to defend against further attacks, each one remains utterly alone, isolated, and steadfastly silent. Striking back is futile and does not stop the abuse from occurring anyway. It just goes on and on and on, and still no one says a thing. Finally, an older sister tells her mom, and the whole family finds out. Each victim understands what no one outside the family will ever understand. To this day the very thought of talking about such an unspeakable subject is merely a mute possibility because the perpetrator still refuses to acknowledge the validity of the respective claims of younger kin, flesh and blood, violated as a matter of whim.

The urge to escape and run away and hide is most pronounced in those family settings permeated with destabilizing patterns of attempted suicide, repeated physical abuse, intense fighting, verbal conflict, or a pervasive atmosphere of agonistic relations. One father repeatedly hit his young son throughout grade school in an escalating series of unprovoked violent outbursts punctuated with stern warnings never to say anything to anyone else. This brutal treatment caused the son to be terrified of ever being left alone with his father, particularly during episodes that forced him to hide or leave home so that his enraged father would not take it out on him anymore. The son soon learned to say nothing and ask no questions so as not to be hit or start to cry again. After six years of verbal torment and physical abuse, the son decided to tell another adult who, it turned out, refused to believe him. Thereafter, the son decided not ever to mention such matters to anyone except close friends. His invisible wounds remain to this day a closely guarded secret.

Alcoholism and chemical dependency enter in. Children who want to yell at parents to stop using drugs or alcohol may shrink back out of fear of angry reprisal or the sight of a clenched fist. Such issues are not mentioned outside the immediate family context largely because of the widespread assumption that no one could help the situation and therefore would only make matters worse. Soon the children learn not to rock the boat and to endure their respective burdens in protracted episodes of enforced silence. When young children are forced to watch parents engage in terrible fights, they are prone to feel massively guilty themselves. One salient presumption is that the children *must* have done something wrong.

A code of silence often protects family secrets of chemical dependency. In alcoholic families, what does not and is not allowed to happen is precisely what matters most in the long run. First there is the awkwardness of not being able to have friends over and the vague sense of having to miss out on relevant outside events. The world inside the front door is closed from the source of ultimate cure—intervention from the outside world. Eventually it becomes important to realize, in the midst of so much pain and denial, the unhealthiness of one's own family life and to be lucky or clever enough to spend a great deal of time somewhere else with someone else. Only then can one begin to tell the secret and find reassurance that it really was not one's own fault, but beyond the realm of personal control. Still fears too great to bear linger while at the same time not being allowed to do anything. When family members fight with one another until they become practically strangers, each one creates a disturbing space, a gap so great that nothing personal can be discussed, thereby preserving the sense of an invisible wall between each member.

Faulty interaction is at the very core of the urge to escape and run away. The issues addressed by the respondents are as complex as the family legacy itself. At the heart of the matter is an imbalance of collective resources to control, regulate, and appease certain patterns of behavior that exhibit extremely unpredictable or unstable levels of personal affection, support, and mutual regard. The theme of too much control in the presence of too little affection is critical. When one individual controls the overt responses of another person without preserving a spirit of acceptance, regard, and self-worth (despite the threat of disagreement and misunderstanding), something important is bound to be missing. What is lacking is usually an adequate supply of affectionate resources required to tolerate or withstand various efforts to control and dominate or else the necessary resources required to resist the imposition.

Ordinarily, implicit friction, strife, and discord help to define who is in control of whom and at what price—for or against. Here "strong" equates with "power over" and "weak" equates with being an "object" of someone else's power. Likewise, affection equates with a movement toward (like or love), and disaffection equates with a movement away from (dislike or hate) further contact. Such face-to-face interactions serve to regulate the distribution of conversational resources—material, economic, and symbolic—in a host of matters where issues of 'power' and 'affection' are subject to considerable definitional and directional confrontation, struggle and strain. Faulty interaction occurs when the distribution of scarce resources leaves some family members in a state of scarcity and others in a relative surplus condition of linguistic appropriation, application, and use.

On the control side, age differences create barriers, an inability to talk on the same level that prompts some children to give in to the urge to go it alone. When parents, because of age differences, leave their children with the impression that there is no way to understand what their children are trying to share with them, family talk (about what matters most) is apt to stop. The severe risk of parental disapproval prompts some children to stay quiet and say nothing important at all. When parents seem to want to hear only good news, but no mention of personal troubles, children quickly learn how not to share what really counts, what is most bothersome, because it would, after all, make them feel too naked. As objects of massive degrees of control from such superior sources of authority and influence, children who are not allowed to do things freely may feel devastated, put up a fuss to no avail, and go through brief outbursts of rage between periods of total withdrawal and silent isolation. Such conditions produce children who, once grown, may want to leave home as quickly as possible and not say good-bye or ever look back again.

Parents control through demand, injunction, prohibition, or command over what the offspring shall do or not do and can and ought not do. Implicit in this guidance and instruction is the power of sanction and potential withdrawal of available resources. One father is relentlessly demanding each time his grown son returns home to visit. The father has a list of jobs to be completed quickly and with great care. The mere act of giving out the list means that everything is to be done precisely and right away. The son owes a lot for all the father has done, but since age eighteen the son has been on his own with little help from home. It really burns him when a list is waiting as soon as he walks in the door. For this reason, he tends not to go home very often anymore. His father likes to watch over him to make sure every little thing is done exactly the right way. The rub is that the son sees himself as a very responsible and mechanically inclined person. It hurts to feel so unacceptable in his father's eyes while completing mechanical tasks for the one person who apparently does everything better. The son feels belittled in his father's eyes, and this leads to even more distance and isolation. It is too bad, really. Even though his father drives him away, the son would like to spend more time at home.

In the endless power struggle, the parent's way is often the only right way. When children are treated in a ruthless, authoritarian manner, some grow up feeling very bitter. On the affection side of the equation, the worst part is when the parents fail to show signs of love and affection for one another. Under such conditions, a teenage son or daughter may fall in and out of depression, concerned solely about personal well-being, feel increasingly pressured, out of control, and desperately want to talk to someone outside the family network but know it is strictly taboo and then feel crazed, numbed, and lacking in vitality and a sense of aliveness. At such times, one may even think of suicide if the pressure should become too great to bear.

What one can't relate through the tears is the desire to be away from everything because of the vague sense that the only difference between being just barely alive and not actually being dead is just the absence of a pulse. Such periods of despair register in not having the faintest idea of how to acquire an inner sense of power over one's own life and the presumption that those who are around don't have it either. Under such conditions it is difficult to convey what "power" and "self-esteem" mean to those who are unaware of the possibility of feeling either one.

Parents as well may feel the urge to escape and run away. When one family goes through a difficult period, things begin to catch up and pressures start to build. Soon one member feels bogged down, quite depressed, and frustrated with self and others. The desire to run away and hide is permeated with fear that such a feeling, if expressed, would not be taken seriously or would simply be dismissed. So, instead of talking, the respondent in question withdraws from whatever situations are most conducive to the things that cause problems. As a consequence, the source feels lonely and hostile toward the very people with whom should be the easiest to converse. In unfavorable situations, the person may not be in a position to explain what is wrong or why, the feeling of being so trapped, and want to run away while knowing it is quite impossible. Therefore, one can't explain why, but only the desire to get away from it all.

When children grow up in troubled families, it becomes progressively harder, if not impossible, to sustain a state of undistorted communication among the various members. Under adverse conditions, some siblings become allies against their parents so that they don't feel so alone. When expected to obey every command, feeling the grip become even stronger, they may be tempted to run away from the family mayhem and just hang out more with close friends. Reasoning with messed-up parents only makes matters worse. Such parents are prone to take out their own problems on their kids. Here talk only makes matters worse. No matter where the kids go for outside sources of support and sympathy, it is hard to express what is really going on within. All along, a cloud of deceit hangs over the head of each family member. It is enough to tear one in half knowing this particular cloud was neither necessary nor normal. Even today, it is still hard to explain why one respondent felt so divided way back when.

Prolonged faulty interactions often lead to the disintegration of family ties. Respondent response to issues of divorce are many and quite varied. Generally, the urge to escape arises when parents split up and leave those who remain to struggle to hold the rest of the family together. Oldest children have the greatest responsibility but cannot lay their problems on younger siblings who are preoccupied with their own. Where there is much uncertainty over why such splits occur in the first place, some young people may refuse to tell others anything, particularly if they have always looked up to their own family as a model of the "perfect" little family unit. In any case those who remain are left to hide the truth from everyone else. When parents have protracted marital problems, it may be hard to admit to anyone, the tip of an iceberg, usually what one does not even want to admit privately to oneself. Feeling there is no one to turn to, hiding all the feelings and frustrations inside, a respondent may keep everyone else from realizing what one is going through. Eventually the huge secret that one respondent has been hiding for so long comes out.

Distorted family interaction is a reflection of the magnitude of social support that is lacking within the surrounding community at large. It does little good to escape and run away from immediate family members into a wider array of situations no better than those one left behind. Here the most relevant theme has to do with the destabilizing effects of being moved around too much as a young child. When parents move around from one city to another, one six-year-old child is left feeling (1) isolated (no one is experiencing this situation quite the way I am); (2) overwhelmed (by a situation so enormous that it defies description); (3) embarrassed (over not measuring up to some imagined standard or not being able to cope with a difficult situation); (4) afraid (no one around can understand what I am going through); and (5) of not being well understood (over the feeling the family has just moved to the far corner of the earth). It takes a great deal of determination to keep such volatile feelings all locked up inside.

FAILURE TO LIVE UP TO THE EXPECTATIONS OF OTHERS

Face-to-face interactions differ widely in degree of self-reflexivity. What takes place at an explicit, overt level is subject not only to mutual forms of perspective taking from multiple and shifting points of view but also to alternative and reconstituted viewpoints about the shifting alignments, positions, line of orientation, slant, and skew. As a rule, what gets expressed and interpreted is subject to various degrees of interpretive revision and reconstruction. Conversational activity moves forward through expectations and anticipations of what will come next or is yet to be and backward through reflections over what once was the case but will never be quite the same again. Moreover, remnants or traces of previously constituted segments of conversation may infiltrate the actual course of subsequent interactions. These recursive or reflexive elements greatly complicate matters but also add a depth dimension to enable, sustain, and enrich each participant one way or another.

It is also possible to have imaginary conversations with ourselves (private discourse) about the course of our actual conversations with one another (public dialogue). Moreover, we can maintain certain access with segments of our imaginary conversations almost any time we want, either before, during, or after the actual ones that take place. We can imagine the way it was or the way it will be. We can envision this or that, more or less, one thing or another, getting closer together or staying farther apart, and encounters getting better or getting worse. In other words, when we go public, we drag unresolved aspects of our private realities around with us. Here what is private is simply the affordance of some self-reflexive aspects of discourse to be supported and sustained within the lived circumstance of any one interactant but denied to every other. The sound that comes from talking with others does not rule out the possibility that we may continue to talk intermittently in silence with our own selves.

At issue is how well one measures up to the array of self-reflexive expectations and reflections of everyone else and how well others measure up to one's own personal standards, logic, criteria, and valuation. One may imagine that who or what one is or does is subject to a reality test in the reflexive and recursive evaluations and judgments that are rendered by others. The evaluative and judicatory aspects of direct human encounter are necessary and inevitable, the price of admission into whatever types of communicative practices can be sustained within the surrounding community at large.

Of interest are the lived circumstances, conditions, and contingencies that generate imagined conversations with boundaries and limitations in the degree and magnitude of personal access. Here the first prototype is a shared situation in which one interactant produces segments of private dialogue based on the presumption that one has not or will not measure up to the expectations of someone else. This leads to an even greater sense of discrepancy between what is and what ought, could, should, or would be the case if only things were somehow different. Presumably this possibility applies to modes of personal conduct most subject to close scrutiny.

One may or may not be in a position to take the expectations of other individuals into full account. Here there is a dual set of possibilities: one can see that others don't measure up, and one can see that one doesn't measure up to what others expect. One wonders how one source can observe something happen and think nothing of it while someone else may think everything about the same matter. There is also the type of situation in which seemingly everyone claims that everything will be all right to someone who knows it most certainly will not be all right. Furthermore, personal interests and vested interests may not coincide, as when no one else cares about the very thing that matters most to someone else. It can be even more vexing to be in a position in which one does not know how or what to do or be to measure up, particularly in situations where one is just average and everyone else is better in some decisive or critical way.

As a case in point, it hurts to be in the position of being an average achiever with above-average expectations. Here to not live up is a personal invitation to becoming upset to hear others claim one is feeling sorry for oneself or should not let something become bothersome. No matter what one may say or do, to show it *is* bothersome and upsetting and hence a source of self-pity that others don't understand; but it sure would help if they did. Likewise it can make matters even worse to be totally immersed in highly competitive sports and not be treated as equally talented as one's best friend who eventually receives all-conference honors. It comes down to working very hard every day for several years to win the golden ring and then ending up with nothing to show for all that one has invested. At each award ceremony it feels as though someone else is shutting one out of much-coveted recognition, glory, and honor.

Similar pressures accompany family life where high standards of academic thought and personal conduct are required of every member. In such highly academic families excellence is expected, as well as the individual ability to be well liked and admired by everyone else. Coupled with this intense pressure is the strong religious need of one respondent to be morally above reproach and witness to one's faith in every aspect of life. The respondent in question describes this pressure as the need to be "on" all the time and never to be honest about disappointments, fears, or insecurities. In such a pressure cooker situation, it is almost as if you didn't talk about any personal concerns because the mere act of talking would sanction or legitimate sensitive personal issues that were supposed to be under such perfect control. One is supposed to be a totally genuine witness (twenty-four hours a day) instead of someone who is floundering most of the time. The crux of the issue is that one is not regarded as OK without appearing to be perfect, and no one can keep up such an exalted front forever.

Personal disappointments may be repeatedly manufactured, fabricated, or reintroduced into the subsequent course of human events. It turns out that personal expectations are often both an opportunity and a risk—to measure up or to fail to measure up. One may feel "more" toward what someone else feels "less." The fear of failure runs deep in shared situations in which no one else lives up to one's own expectations of self. Violated expectations may stem from not getting out what one puts in. Consider a case in which one individual causes problems for another individual over a long period of time. Each time individual B tries to tell individual A how much it bothers B, it turns out that B can see that A does not see what A is doing and therefore cannot comprehend the consequences of A's own actions. Since individual A is very vindictive, it would be useless to retaliate. Individual A cannot see how his actions hurt others and how much inconvenience he imposes on everyone else. Individual B does not think that individual A would listen and feels a sense of total futility from having to constantly deal with the situation without a solution.

Suddenly, in another instance, there is an unexpected change in plans between best friends. Individual A calls individual B on a Monday night, and the two friends agree that A will visit B from another city over the weekend. The next Thursday night B calls A to confirm the plan. Individual A then informs B that A has decided instead to go to another city to spend the weekend with someone else. Now B becomes upset with A but does not tell A how B feels about the outcome of the entire situation. Soon individual A becomes just another friend to B. Individual B is lead to this conclusion through a long sequence of similar incidents.

There are situations in which one source of expressed activity engages in the sorts of thoughts and feelings that others would only find embarrassing. One may not be able to deny such feelings but still be ashamed to tell someone who might laugh or think one is being shallow. At such times one's mind may wander and think about things that no one else knows what I am feeling right now. Such feelings may be too ludicrous to be expressed to anyone else and may even be denied to oneself. What can't be disclosed is mainly over fear of the possible reactions of others to self. One may assume that telling others one's real feelings will cause them to laugh and say, "God, what an asshole!!!"

There are also situations in which personal feelings lead one individual to assume or expect a certain response and yet is still not able or willing to accept the responses that are actually given. Here one respondent's expectations may have been too high; that is, the person was expected to internalize the feelings, quickly get to the nitty gritty, and yet be apprehensive about subsequent reactions of others. Perhaps others can't identify with one's problems because of their uniqueness and would not be of much help. One may also realize that part of the value of sharing personal experience is not necessarily the particular advice to be given but the relief that comes in sharing something that is bothersome or draining of one's energy.

When one is a capable, intelligent person, it affects one greatly to achieve less or come up short. It is difficult to accept failure or defeat. One respondent meets the woman of his dreams and repeatedly attempts to get her to like him, but all to no avail. The man is routinely shut down and feels hurt, rejected, and defeated. He is not sure whether the pressure is self-induced or inflicted by some outside force, but either way he still has to try to perform. Feelings of failure may eat away at the source. You did your very best, but your very best was not good enough. Such an individual may be inclined to blame others for his own problems and still not be able to comprehend the full impact of his actions on the personal conduct of others. When someone fails to show up in time or deliver the goods and services as promised, someone else is left to bear the burden alone.

Moreover, one may not be able to express oneself to anyone out of fear of failure. It turns out that respondent A gives great effort but does not get back anticipated results. Individual A thinks his own life has been cursed with bad luck, and no matter what, he never will get back what he has put into things. He never expresses this feeling to anyone else because he does not want others to claim he is a failure or that life is not fair because he knows already. Individual A is afraid his good efforts in life will not get him very far. He longs to talk to someone about this deep personal fear but does not think there is much anyone else could do to help. This is how life is, and he better start getting used to it because it probably only gets worse. When one does not live up to the expectations of others, knowing on the inside, not letting it show on the outside, one may not get another chance to think it over because one has already been disgraced in the eyes of others.

ALIENATION: HAVING NO ONE TO TURN TO

#46 It occurs when one is alienated from one's own body. Individual A has a health problem (eating disorder). A assumes no one else knows. A can't talk about the problem to anyone else. A feels alone, alienated, depressed, and helpless. A doesn't think A can do anything about A's condition. Yet while others start to notice, A continues to deny the problem. A does not want to admit anything is wrong. A is afraid to tell anyone else. A is also reluctant to share any personal thoughts and feelings with others. Then, suddenly, another person forces A to go to a clinic. At the clinic A finds it more difficult to talk about A's problem. A begins to feel increasingly afraid and isolated. A thinks staff members at the clinic are ridiculing her. Then A becomes even more angry at the others for making her talk about her problem. Finally other people suggest that she do something. Yet the more others talk, the more A resists because she does not want to be treated like a guinea pig or used for other people's purposes. Still A cannot admit the problem but somehow knows inwardly what must be done to solve the matter without additional help from others.

Entry number 46 is an exemplar of a protracted sequence of problematic encounters that produce or generate more alienation rather than less. Here face-to-face interaction involves the reproduction or perpetuation of a spirit of personal alienation that is manufactured in the manner of an all-inclusive, all-encompassing fabrication. Basic moods and textures coalesce around several important features of a partial or fragmented state of articulation: discontinuity in relations of feeling, thinking, saying, acting, and doing; the inability and unwillingness to make sense, to discriminate and decipher, to sustain with others a continuous sense of meaningfulness through the interchange of verbal and nonverbal forms of distinction and discrimination; self-censorship—a radical and extreme set of sensibilities intent on exploring the full magnitude of what one ought not or should not express in any form to anyone else; the presumption that no one else feels the way I do; the state of feeling overwhelmed with the sheer multiplicity of possible meanings; fatalism—anything one can or would do surely would make no actual difference to anyone else; a concealed sense of helplessness amidst protracted struggle to make one's lived circumstance clear and explicit to others and remain articulate about what one's presence makes manifest to them. Kierkegaard might well have characterized such highly guarded forms of self-presentation to be prototypic or ideal instances of a profound state of 'shutupness.'

Here alienation from self and others has no single cause, no absolute point of origin, and no simple point of beginning, middle, or end in an imagined or real feedback loop. It is, therefore, not apt to be confined or located within a specific site, modality, or location. There is, for example, no necessary sense of insides refusing to spill out, as it were, to the outsides of one's body boundaries. Rather, everything that counts for anything is somehow taken as foreign, strange, or otherwise undecipherable. Usually what is at stake is some real or imagined lack of personal access to some vital human resource: food, the presence of others as caretakers, talk that sustains rather than threatens existing circumstances, or silence as refuge from the noise, clatter, and din. Such an inclusive sense of personal isolation registers both inwardly and outwardly in relation to the dialectical tensions of having to be a part of others and apart from others at the same time.

What one does not feel, think, say, act, or do may lead to resolute convictions regarding the magnitude of what one does not appear able to feel, think, say, act, or do. In matters of personal efficacy, vitality, and spirit, one may dwell or focus on what one has not yet become or what one can never be. So instead one becomes aimless and adrift in denial, fear, and reluctance to share and make manifest what one is to other human beings.

Take the case in which the more others talk, the more one resists any further discussion of the condition of one's own body. One struggles vainly to overcome an unexplainable urge. One may be scared as hell that to acknowledge the problem might provoke loved ones to do something drastic. If others ask why one binges and then throws up the food, it would not be possible to give a sensible answer. The whole ordeal is so overwhelming that no one knows where to begin. It just piles more on the list of things that one cannot tell anyone else. What must be covered up is the all-encompassing sense of personal vulnerability, lack of confidence and control rather than what one tries to portray to others. One fears what others might say. What is crucial is not to let loved ones know and do everything possible not to let them ever find out. Three representative instances follow.

#47 A's view: Through experience I've learned how powerful the mind can be when you allow a situation to go too far. I am a male who for the last two years has been anorectic. If people were to look at me, they wouldn't be able to tell the difference between me and a normal twenty-year-old male. During the first stages of this situation, lasting at least a year and a half, I wasn't able to talk to anyone for fear of being the object of ridicule or criticism. The worst thing was to hear someone tell me I was wrong or that I should just stop what I was doing. No one could understand what I was going through. I'm not sure whether it was stress or just the world we live in (being so weight conscious) that forced me into such a risky habit. I was afraid to tell anyone close to me what I was doing because I felt inside like I was a failure. I was given a normal, healthy body and now I was trying to "improve" it. (I see now I was ruining it instead). In our family two older sisters also had serious eating disorders. This made it even harder for me to tell someone else how I was feeling because I didn't want to be treated as my sisters were. What was hardest to admit was that I had a problem. I didn't want to be classified as having a problem and have others see me in a different light. I was most *scared* of what others would think of me. I am still going through the after effects and rely on the same new-found medicine to help me through the bad days. The talking medicine.

#48 A's view: At the end of my freshman year in college, I became bulimic. I did not know why I was doing what I was doing and was so ashamed I had sunk to such a low level. Since I was having trouble identifying my own feelings, there was no way that I could even begin to express such matters to anyone else. The next summer my behavior continued until I joined a weight control group, followed the rules to the letter, and got my behavior under control. I was so proud to have solved my problem on my own—but no one knew what I had been like before so I couldn't share my total success with anyone. Unfortunately, when I got back to school in the fall, history repeated itself and I was right back where I started from—only worse this time because I had spent the entire summer getting back on the right track. I didn't know what prompted my behavior but my feelings of guilt and shame involved issues that could not be explained to anyone else no matter how many times I swore I would get help. When I finally shared my problem with two friends—I felt they didn't really understand what I was going through. In fact I assumed that sharing my problem somehow made it unimportant because others claimed that if I followed the proper steps in the right order, I would get better and that would be the end to it. I faced a similar barrier when trying to speak to a counselor. I felt the counselor was looking beyond what I was saying and trying to make it fit her picture of a typical bulimic instead of seeing my own feelings as part of me as a unique individual. This happened again when I told my parents—I still haven't been able to talk to them about it, even now, a year after recovery.

#49 A's view: I had an eating disorder and felt very alone with my problem. It started last year and I wasn't even sure I could admit it to myself, let alone anyone else. I went for several months without saying anything to anyone. I held my emotions, my anger, my frustrations, and my problem as far inside of myself as possible. Then one day a friend called from high school and she cried over her eating problem. She was looking to *me* for support and advice. Of course I was able to listen. I was filled with all sorts of helpful advice for her but was still unable to admit that I too felt the same way. Meanwhile I was running to the bathroom after each meal and desperately trying to remove those awful calories and boxed-in emotions. I was purging out my internal worries rather than communicating with someone about them. I felt gross. Who could I tell and not be looked down upon? There wasn't a *soul* I could imagine telling. Because to me, everything was just *fine*. I could go on and on about the difficulties of discussing all the garbage I had been holding inside for years. It is unbelievable the degree of difference that good, clear communication has made in my life recently. I'm finally starting to feel my inner feelings are in sync with my external emotions. It feels good.

Here the forms of talk that can be heard but not listened to are mainly speech acts designed to facilitate the future incorporation of manna: food, nourishment, sustenance, and life-affirming rituals, ceremonies, and routines. Moreover, one who is alienated by so much unwelcome talk is estranged from what could quite literally save one's own life if only one would permit the full force of the affordable supply of words and gestures to restore a more integrated sense of community with other living creatures. Here a state of personal alienation is subjected to a highly symbolic reality test where the ultimate goal is one of liberation from what Tillich once described as "bondage to the given." The linkage between symbolic acts and the material circumstances are conspicuous when there is deprivation in eating that matches up so precisely with what is absent in the talk. The direction of cure lies in relearning how to eat and what to say about the taste of food in the presence of so much renewed opportunity for participation in the world of words and gesture.

In other relevant entries, the *alien* conditions coincide with circumstances that one's own presence makes manifest to others regardless of what is revealed to oneself. Technically speaking, alienation is not so much a question of the lived circumstances one happens to inhabit but rather the sedimented burden of unresolved issues one drags around with oneself from one situation to another. So no matter what the lived circumstances of others appear to be, one's own lived circumstances manage to preserve the sense that whatever one is in the midst of is somehow alien, foreign, and strange. Common themes: the *expectation* that others will not be in a position to grasp what one is going through or what one has to say. One is inclined to feel *as if* no one in the world has the same problem and could not possibly relate to what is actually taking place at the time. The problem feels so massive and overwhelming in the presumption that no other solitary individual could ever feel so completely isolated and alone.

The most severe forms of exclusionary activity involve those issues that deny direct access to everyone and grant permission to no one. All potential sources of direct encounter may be equally ruled out and everyone is thereby kept out of reach. Often it turns out that protracted intolerance of another's presence leads eventually to unlimited tolerance of another's absence. Irony: the same spirit of radical exclusion may apply somewhat even during episodes of direct encounter. Those who are not denied direct access may still, nonetheless, be excluded as much as possible *within* the inclusionary conditions that are afforded in any given shared situation.

The basic constraining condition is predicated on the assumption that there is no one who is capable or willing to be attentive and receptive to what one has to say. Words and gestures, after all, count for little or nothing if they should fall on deaf ears or flash before eyes that do not see the one who produces the talk. Therefore, one may imagine the urge to produce a litany of words and gestures under conditions where there is no one around to take them into personal account. Two relevant instances follow:

#50 It occurs when one is afraid that no one else will be able to relate to the feelings you are experiencing at the time. You feel as if no one in the world has the same problem, and no one could possibly relate to what you are going through. The problem feels so massive in your mind that either (1) someone else finds out or (2) you break down in stress and confide in someone who understands totally because they have had the very same type of personal experience. What is so frightening is the overwhelming possibility that one is all alone. Once you have company, such problems turn out to be much more easy to handle.

#51 It occurs when one is under a lot of stress, things are strained at home, and one is under heavy time pressure at work. Individual A feels it is all too much, and that she is in over her head with obligations and commitments. Person A has a friend (B) who has nothing to do in the evenings, so after work B would call A and want to talk every night for at least an hour. The simple truth is that A can't spare that much time everyday and doesn't have that much to say. So individual A starts to avoid personal contact and has one of her friends, C, traffic phone calls and get her only if things are very important. Well, eventually C and B start to talk every night for an hour or more. It gets to the point where C would get the phone and talk endlessly to B, hang up, and then tell A that B says hi. Needless to say, A now feels very hurt. As time goes by, B and C start going out to lunch and shopping and doing just about everything together. Suddenly A feels left out. Even when A has time to spend with B and C, A feels like A doesn't belong. This leads to many fights. Persons B and C accuse A of pushing them away, avoiding contact, and not wanting to be friends. Individual A feels hurt and rejected. A's two friends are now the best of friends, and A is left out. This is what has always constituted A's worst fear. A tries to explain over and over again such fears of rejection and subsequent loneliness. Person A thinks that B and C never do really understand the depth of emptiness and betrayal she feels at being left out. A has no idea how many arguments this has caused. So A runs in circles, and the situation gets worse, and she feels even more rejected each time A watches B and C get closer together and even more pitted against her.

DENIED ACCESS: HAVING NO ONE TO TALK TO

One may inhabit a world with individuals who are potentially available and accessible to one another but not on the basis of any anticipated forms of future interaction. The production of such relatively inaccessible conditions may take any number of forms. Several are reconstructed here in outline form.

XENOPHOBIA: FEAR OF TALKING TO STRANGERS

The logic of discursive exclusion applies most directly to those who appear as strangers to one another. In the sea of faces one may experience xenophobia as a fear of interacting with those one does not know. The issue is how one can talk in light of the sheer magnitude of what is unshared or the totality of what is lost and can never be reclaimed. The first impression is not that talk per se is ruled out but rather that the matter of talking openly is simply out of the question. One may not know what to talk about or how much to say. It can be quite disconcerting to know that one can be outgoing with those who are well known and yet when dealing with strangers, feel they might laugh, ridicule, or make fun. It is difficult to know why one is able to talk and talk and talk about the deepest subjects with well-known friends and yet still be able to say practically nothing to those whose very presence is taken to be a symbolic manifestation of the fact that what initially matters most is the sheer magnitude of what is, as yet, unshared, unknown, uncertain, and undetermined. Here the most vivid descriptions of xenophobic situations underscore an underlying sense of feeling trapped from within *and* without by the severe limits of one's own communicative abilities and by the sheer magnitude of what is unknown about the demand characteristics of the existing situation.

INDIFFERENCE: WHEN NO ONE ELSE SEEMS TO CARE

One who is indifferent to what the immediate presence of other individuals makes manifest is either apt to be (1) out of a position to make a difference or (2) in a position to make a difference but somehow fail to do so. Moreover, one may find oneself in the midst of those sources whose own desires, intentions, interpretations, involvements, and personal concerns are directed elsewhere, toward someone else or something else. Here one is indifferent toward what matters least or not at all. As a consequence, to be the object of indifference is to find oneself excluded from precisely what is included within a given sphere, scope, or focal point of concern and care on the part of others. So instead of discovering others as fully present, one construes them as merely present. For every source of indifference there must be at least one object of inattentiveness and nonreceptivity.

Young children are especially vulnerable to the sense that others regard their bodily presence as a mere object of indifference or dislike. One eighth grader considers killing herself to prove that no one else really cares. She thinks that if she kills herself, no one would notice. The way she expresses her deepest fears is through a diary. Each night she writes about depression and loneliness and how interesting the idea of suicide has become. Yet something in the back of the mind never allows her to go through with it. At the time it does not occur to her that many other people are feeling the same way. Likewise, a sense of personal insufficiency enters in:

#52 It occurs during times of major change when one feels inadequate and a loss of self-confidence. Under such circumstances anyone else would feel the same way. Not knowing whom to trust, only the desire to tell just one person who does not disclose the matter to anyone else. One feels the need to keep such matters to oneself. There is no solid reasoning behind the emotional instability over major changes. One might not be able to bear to think how one might look to others. One does not want to seem weak in any way. It is a terrible experience, as if a part of oneself has just died. One is speechless and cannot find the words to say what would explain what one was feeling then and there. It hurts so much, not being able to tell anyone what one is feeling because one does not understand it oneself. It is something to cling to while one portrays a wonderfully false image. No one suspects the sadness one feels at the time.

MALAISE: FEELING SOMEWHAT DISCONNECTED

It is often experienced as a vague desire or yearning to make meaningful connections with other individuals only to be subjected to varying degrees and gradations of disconnection and misconnection. It is as if given sets of individuals are trying to locate one another during late-night fog or early-morning mist. Various individuals call out to one another, and each one strives to make solid connections without ever being able to establish a mutual sense of commonality or common ground. At the level of meaning, malaise implies that what matters most to one matters least or not at all to someone else. Hence, the disconnection registers in the lack of personal alignment of the shifting involvements and concerns of the respective parties. In critical situations there may be a lack of integration in the hierarchy of personal valuations. What is privileged as most salient and relevant to the lived circumstances of any one individual may rank as mere preference or whim to those of any other.

#53 It occurs when an individual is afraid of losing control of one's life. Individual A appears to be composed on the surface and acts decisively, as if A knows exactly where A is going in life. A can't explain this feeling to anyone because it is frightening, and A does not want to appear vulnerable. Sometimes A gets very tired of having to be together. Constantly A acts like a woman of the world who doesn't need help with anything when in truth A is as scared and needy as anyone else. Sometimes A just wants to curl up in the corner and have someone take care of her, but she can't. Something inside will not let A show this side of herself. A does not know why. A knows there are people in her life who care about her and would take care of her, but she still can't reach out to them and feels totally unable to express the way she feels to other people.

#54 It occurs when one feels that no one else has ever felt this way before. You are alone in all of this, and if you tell anyone, they probably would just laugh, and you couldn't take it because it would hurt more than the original pain. But even if you could find someone who might not laugh, would they really understand? Or would they sympathize and be glad someone had shared a secret with them? If they say they understand, would they really? How would they know what you are going through? Oh, sure, they might have experienced a similar situation, but they would not be feeling what you would be feeling at this particular moment. To be realistic, you can't expect another person to understand you totally and completely. To find someone who can lend an ear or shoulder is enough. The situation is yours and yours alone, and you know that no one else will ever know. Eventually a sense of vitality returns as do the joy and happiness of life. The pain becomes a memory to be felt often in the future, but much more dull as time goes by.

SHYNESS: MISSING OUT ON A LOT OF WHAT TRANSPIRES

In the construction of interpersonal boundaries, shyness, reticence, and apprehension over personal engagement in various imagined forms of face-to-face interaction become a major theme. Shyness is an exemplar of inhibiting influences interacting with distorting influences. In effect the urge to move toward more direct contact with others is inverted and transformed incrementally into a compulsion to move away from them. The individual who becomes shy or reticent prefers the unknown risk of noninteraction to the known risk of interaction (as previously constituted).

Imaginary conversations play a major role in the perpetuation of a spirit of shyness. One imagines what would happen in future or anticipated conversations based on composite recollections of prior (and often faulty) interactions. In effect, what one imagines to have happened or what might well happen (in a faulty manner) becomes a self-fulfilling prophecy that serves to guard against the potential from being realized all over again in a new form. The more that shyness becomes a dominant aspect of one's life, the less one is able to figure it out or explain matters clearly to others. When one feels safe and secure in environments shared with others, one may blab on endlessly. Other times, however, when one does not feel safe or secure with one's circumstances or immediate surroundings, one may be prone to fall into lapses that prevent one from being able to figure out why one is so quiet or reserved.

It turns out that shyness is closely related to the magnitude of one's own sense of insecurity. One is apt to become most reticent about various urges, feelings, sensations, thoughts, reflections, or expectations formed when unsure of the effects their expression would have on others. It is particularly hard when dealing with someone whose affection and loyalty is so conditional or otherwise at issue or in question. One is apt to feel least able to express oneself when unsure of the effects such possible expressions would have on others and even more so whenever one *cares* deeply about the effects such expressions might have on others. This is particularly apt to be the case when one has so many complex feelings and sensations simultaneously that one doesn't quite know how to give coherent expression to the complex array of sensations and feelings that unfold within a very short span of time and space. Shyness is often experienced as if one were encased within a large invisible bubble or clear plastic shield between oneself and every other person. One hears a question that cannot be answered because of the magnitude of the fear that no matter what or how one may speak, it will be taken the wrong way. So one is resigned mostly to say nothing at all.

Extreme shyness is equated most often with a totalizing sense of personal helplessness at not being able to reach out to those who care. The feeling arises from extreme sensitivity to the *possible* reactions of self to other and other to self. The imagined talk would only hurt the other's feelings. Moreover, when moving through a difficult or unfamiliar setting, one is apt to feel that the only one who does not know what to be or do is one's own self. One shy individual admits to becoming really scared because of the inability to know how to ask anyone for help with even the small, simple things. Such an individual thinks that others would think she or he was being a bother or, even worse, that they would laugh. It is better to not say anything at all than to be laughed at for what one does manage to say in one way or another.

#55 It occurs in any circumstances where individual A would prefer silence than risk revealing an inner thought or feeling. This has been conditioned into individual A and is due in part to A's innately shy nature as well as the troublesome environment in which A grew up. Being shy and living with two alcoholic parents traumatized A's self-concept (but enhanced A's coping and survival strategies). Research literature about alcoholism indicates that certain patterns develop in children from these homes (Black, 1981). Put simply, these are the hard and fast rules that are learned: Don't talk. Don't trust. Don't feel. Silence even becomes safer after a verbal put down by one's father at age twelve (A can still relive the whole damned scene). Unfortunately, A's silence was interpreted as aloofness during high school, and this definitely limited A's interactive skills. Individual A talked very little but smiled a lot, and this got A by. Individual A got by outwardly but was tormented inwardly. A wanted to be drawn out and to communicate effectively. A needs to add here that A has a voice like Minnie Mouse, so A always avoided phone contact, such as making appointments or calling to inquire about something. A thought people would think they were just talking to a kid. It's hard to sound assertive when you have a voice like a mouse. The incident with A's dad caused A to be very cautious in interactions with male members of the species. A tends to stereotype men as being verbally competent and emotionally controlled. A hesitates to reveal a thought or an emotion in the presence of a male. Basically A doesn't feel safe. So, A hesitates to express personal thoughts very often, especially when in the presence of men. It makes relationships most difficult. However, smiling and sex get A by in important relationships. Nonetheless, there is so much of a sense of hurt and helplessness inside.

THE VOID: FEELING FULL OF EMPTINESS

Some exclusionary boundaries give rise to a heightened sense of paradox and contradiction. It is not just a matter of one interactant expressing something that contradicts what someone else has said or done. It is rather a situation in which given sets of individuals adopt positions and take multiple perspectives that are somewhat contradictory or unresolvable with one another. In other words, what each one expresses is in complete opposition to what another intends, interprets, or expresses. When interactants become a source of such expressed or interpreted contradiction to one another, they may be said to produce a paradoxical relation.

One irksome interactive paradox occurs where the interaction between two or more parties gives rise to one or more of them feeling as though they were operating in a void. While human life, *existence*, may be said to be protean, that is, as always full of this or that as opposed to absolutely nothing at all (death), one may gravitate into a position where one is full of an amorphous sense that no one thing stands out over any other, as in being full of a vague sense of nothing in particular. Any given set of interactants can easily manufacture such a sense of being in a void in a manner that is roughly akin to a state of hunger, in which one's stomach feels completely empty. In such a situation one is apt to become aware of what is missing or lacking. Something similar holds when something takes one's breath away or in a case of exhaustion, in which one lacks the physical strength to carry on. Hence, a void need not imply a total vacuum, but rather an intense longing for what is lacking or missing in the sense of what is not yet the case or what can never be the case again. Thereby one may be full of a sense of what is excluded by whatever is fully included within some designated sphere of mutually sustained activity. A void is a primordial acknowledgment of what is lacking or missing in relation to the existing scheme of things.

First is the primitive sense of what is lost, discarded, misplaced, and can never be reclaimed in any given interactive situation. One individual associates feeling full of emptiness with a personal lament over the loss of the one person in the whole wide world who matters the most of all. Insofar as the memory of the loss may be completely blocked out, one is left feeling nothing more than a huge void or empty space. As long as one is alive, one is full of existence, but the very definition and direction of one's journey can still appear as though it is being totally undermined or subverted at any point along the way.

Second, one may have to make a crucial choice in one's life and yet feel completely blank or empty about the matter. This is most apt to occur in the sorts of shared encounters in which one of the respective participants has little or no control over the outcome of the total situation. Others may offer all the support possible and still be utterly useless and ineffectual in the end. This in itself may compound the feeling of being all alone with no place to turn. As time passes, one just goes through the minimum number of necessary actions to get through the course of a single day but eventually musters up the courage to seek out those who are in the best position to help make the best possible decision. Another individual describes the void as if a part of self has slipped from personal reality, so that one is no longer in full control of one's own life. It is a terrifying experience to feel so hollow and empty. Not being able to express one's own confusion and turmoil only leads to more confusion and turmoil. In such circumstances some feel increasingly more isolated, alone, and prone to fake it or just pretend.

Finally, the sense of living in an interpersonal void is closely associated with what is lost or misplaced in the manner of a profound personal betrayal. It is most apt to occur when given individuals are completely overwhelmed and think the whole world is out to get them. These are times when one feels there is no one to talk to and even if someone were available, one wouldn't admit how one really feels. Others keep insisting that it will be all right. No one else knows what it is like to go through a period of crisis when one thinks others do not really care because no one listens to what one has to say. Three representative instances follow:

#56 A's view: I went out with a guy for seven years. We met at the lake where both his and my parents have a cottage. After seven years of a relationship with him, he broke up with me. The breakup was very hard. The hardest part was a time when I was at my cottage all alone. It was at night and dark with the street lights on. Mark, my old boyfriend, was seeing a girl named Kitty at the corner from my cottage. The first time I saw them together, having fun and enjoying each other, was the night I was alone at the cottage. I can't tell you how much I hurt inside when I saw Mark and Kitty under the street light in front of her cottage laughing and having fun. My stomach felt so empty! I've never felt so empty. I was so alone. Not only was I alone because I was not with Mark but also because no one was around me to talk to and get comfort from. I felt so sickened inside, but somehow I stood and watched them until they walked away into his cottage. All I could do was cry, cry, cry. I felt so alone and disheartened. The only consolation for me was that I didn't have to hold in my feelings. I decided to cry out loud and really wanted to because I was the only one around.

#57 A and B become intimate. Yet A has an sense of emptiness she could never explain or express to anyone else. She starts to feel that she has no reason to live. The pain is excruciating. A feels that no one really cares. She had always been content before getting involved with B. Person B makes A think that the world revolves around him. She is enveloped in whatever he says. He turns out to be the most possessive man she has ever known. Individual B wants to run A's life, and she lets him do it. He continues to manipulate her until she gets ready to leave him. She had been trapped beneath someone's hand for so long that she never realized she could have such freedom. No one knows the turmoil she has been through for three years. Sometimes she tries to explain, but it only seems like a scary fairy tale.

#58 A feels empty yet full. When A is betrayed by A's best friend (B), A cannot express his sense of loss to anyone. Words couldn't match the pain. The pain he feels is like the void you feel when someone you love dies, but it's 1,000 times more intense because the pain is intentional. A grew up with B. A trusted her with his secrets, and one day B decided to use that information to hurt him. It was like falling dominoes. He wasn't kicked in the teeth just once. Every time A remembered something he had told B that she could use to hurt him, A felt a fresh blow. He tried to tell others but couldn't. Even if A could have expressed it, he wouldn't have wanted to subject others to the pain. So A feels empty and yet somehow still full of anger.

ISOLATION: FEELING VERY DIFFERENT THAN EVERYONE ELSE

A sense of isolation occurs insofar as one loses sight of all the ways that other people are subjected to identical or highly similar conditions or contingencies as oneself and yet still manages to attend only to the ways in which they are different or unique. The more one focuses exclusively on matters of individual uniqueness and distinction, the more one is apt to feel removed, detached, and different from everyone else. It may occur in something as simple as the sense of excitement and satisfaction one gets from a job that not even close friends understand, even when they work at the very same job. Interaction over such subtle matters may intensify the feeling that others could not possibly grasp the situation as one does because they minimize, maximize, or diminish the true meaning of the situation. One may become totally aware of what others do not grasp, comprehend, acknowledge, or recognize.

#59 It occurs when an individual has an idea or feeling about things that may be understood intuitively without knowing exactly how to put them into words. Individual A often feels that words can't explain what A wants to share. There is also the sense that even if words could express things clearly, no one would understand what A is trying to say. At such times A feels frustrated and not sure of how to say what he intends. The strongest feeling at these times is utter isolation— no one else is with me or understands what I attempt to express or convey.

#60 It occurs when a strange sensation overcomes those who feel that they are somehow not part of this earth. Individual A gets this type of sensation once in a while of feeling almost alien—as if A doesn't belong here. This doesn't happen when A is lonely, so A doesn't think it is loneliness. It is more of a metaphysical experience where A gets set completely apart from the immediate environment A is in at the time.

#61 It occurs when an individual feels so deliciously unique. Individual A felt a sense of euphoria that no one on earth was feeling at the time. A had even convinced A's self that never again would A have such a physical and mental intensity that brought such strong emotion to A's being. The memory would last for a long time to come. What was so special for five short minutes was that the person closest to A wanted so badly for A to be able to disclose the feelings, but they could not be explained because they were so fresh and new.

HAVING NO ONE TO CONFIDE IN

One may have others to turn to and talk to but not to confide in. Here the most relevant boundary consideration is the outer limit in the number of alternative sources who are available for exchange over highly personal, sensitive, or intimate matters. At one end of the spectrum are personal concerns that exist in somewhat inarticulate or unresolved form. Under such circumstances one may well lack the capacity or willingness to express the complex mix of unspoken feelings, sensations, and thoughts welling up inside. One may start to focus on what is going on and still be unable to find the right way to express one's present condition. Moreover, one individual may want desperately to be in a position to confide in others and yet still end up feeling unsuccessful, ineffectual, and defeated and therefore risk becoming increasingly isolated and cut off from others. Here one is full of the sense that everything that matters is left unresolved. Often such conditions are attributed to the sorts of personal weaknesses and vulnerabilities that prevent one from allowing others to know how one really feels within the confines of a given situation.

THE EXPERIENCE OF LONELINESS

A radical extension of exclusionary practice is manifest in the experience of loneliness. Here individuals underscore how far away other people seem to be and how far away one seems to be from them. Loneliness covers devastating loss. One case of immense emotionality produces extreme sadness and anger over the fact that the source in question does not tell another person how much he matters until it is too late, and then the sadness returns over and over again. Moreover, there is also the sort of loneliness where the newness of one's entire living situation begins to wear off. It occurs at a time when other people are establishing close friendships and wider groups of friends and associations, and suddenly one finds oneself feeling all alone and completely left out. It comes at a time when one does not feel close enough to anyone to share deep feelings from within. Everyone else may be under the impression that everything is going great because one has spoken so highly of certain things just to cover a deeper realization that one is too far away from home to escape the misery of the existing situation.

Loneliness is also visualized in fleeting and transitory terms. One respondent moves to a new city and feels lost, lonely, and unable to tell others what or how he is feeling. The tendency is to bottle up personal feelings and hope the fear and loneliness will just go away. No one else seems to care one way or another. Such lived circumstances produce the sense that you are the only human being left on earth. The worst part is either having no one to talk to—or when someone else is around, it turns out the words just will not come out. One just pretends nothing is wrong or hopes no one else will discover how messed up one really is. In a similar tone, times of chronic depression consume another respondent in self-pity. At other moments the source in question is determined to cheer up and get a move on in life. The hurt can never be expressed, so the source just tries to hold it all in.

There is also the sort of loneliness that does not go away. It consists of the urge and need to share sensitive matters with others amidst the acute fear of their adverse reactions. If others should ever learn of some deep personal secret, they surely would only think less of the source. There is also the larger fear of putting other individuals in situations in which they simply do not know how to respond or else would feel quite uncomfortable and distressed with the subject at hand. Other people may insist they understand without one's being convinced they really do. So one ends up with "thanks for your help" and leaves the interaction just as lonely as before the conversation first began.

Loneliness can become extremely frightening to one who grows up seeing oneself and being seen by others as abnormal. From grade school on it becomes obvious how cruel other people can be. Many judge others by their physical appearance. Those who reveal the source of their abnormality in a highly visible area of the face may well feel like outcasts or even something lower on the imaginary scale. Under such severe and demanding circumstances it seems best not even to try to meet new people except those who say something first. Such fearful doses of loneliness may leave one feeling as if no one else in the world has the same grave personal problems.

One respondent offers the following allegory: Picture yourself standing ALL ALONE in a desert during the middle of the day when the sun is the hottest. There is no one around, and yet you have no idea where to go. Soon you sweat profusely and begin to feel a little faint. You become so scared that you can't imagine the feeling is ever going to end. You are trapped. Then you fall asleep and later awake to find others there to comfort you. You tell them your story and yet because they did not go through the same sequence of events, you find yourself unable to convey to others what transpired. Moreover, because the others cannot relate to your (story) situation, they cannot follow you and drift off. This only escalates frustration and the fear that nobody has ever felt the same way that you do. You start to feel your own feelings aren't real and maybe you aren't real either.

Loneliness is terrifying when construed in terms of personal suffocation. For one respondent there is considerable conflict between not wanting to feel so suffocated when no one else is around and yet knowing the condition is inevitable. Such an individual begins to analyze and question his own existence, an action that in turn further decreases the ability to communicate with others. The process of withdrawal grows deeper until the source can't get out; nor can anyone else get in. Fortunately, over a period of several months, someone else is able to penetrate the shell, and the source is released.

Another case in point is where one individual has all the friends and close relatives in the world who really care and still feels lonely and all alone. Such periods of isolation occur for one respondent who becomes so frightened and humiliated without being able to talk to anyone about a crucial matter. The source in question now becomes even more terrified over who is going to know than what is going to happen while having to appear normal to everyone else. The source does not want others to know the truth because the source hates the truth of what one has done. Surely everyone else would too.

EXCLUSIONARY-INCLUSIONARY TENSIONS

So far we have examined individual constructions of exclusionary logic that serves to ostracize, circumvent, delay, avoid, undermine, or prevent any possible future interaction between potential interactants from actually taking place. Often this involves intense periods of introspection over what was missing, absent, or lacking in some previous human interchange, and then the implications are projected forward as a range of possibilities to be avoided at all costs. It is also important to see how exclusionary principles serve to regulate the frequency, duration, or magnitude of personal involvements that accumulate over longtime frames.

SECRETS/DREAMS/FANTASIES

Face-to-face interaction may be viewed as a reality testing ritual in which certain themes, textures, and moods are produced in the manner of a secret, dream, or fantasy. Here it is not always possible to distinguish clearly between the vicarious and the real because during problematic phases of face-to-face interaction the lines can become distorted or blurred. Here what is included within the immediate grasp of one interactant is precisely what is excluded from the sphere of conscious awareness of any other. One individual refers to feelings and sensations that produce the sense that you are watching the movie of your life and exist outside the film as a viewer of your own conduct. Another reflects on episodes where you know how you feel, and others know how they feel, but we can never prove we feel the same way because feelings are so intangible. Still another has a strong desire and deep longing to know certain persons whom one has never met but nonetheless *knows* to exist. One day such an individual actually meets certain people who fill the bill and quickly feels the urge to give the others the impression (which still cannot be pinned down) they are already soulmates even though they have never actually met one another before. This involves extraordinary empathy—one person's self in other persons' bodies, much like a secret club that one seeks to welcome newcomers as one would instantly recognize the sight of kindred spirits. Another notices that everyone has some things that they try to keep from other people. It is not a good idea, perhaps, to list one's little secrets but rather quite often not to tell others what is really going on in one's life. After all, it is for the best. Telling others everything is not always smart.

Sexual secrets abound. Abortion ranks number one in frequency of mention. One individual (A) has the hardest time keeping to herself all of the pain associated with having an abortion. It's tough not to be able to tell even closest friends about the cramps that last twenty-four hours straight. Instead one lies and says that one might have ovarian cancer in order to justify going to the doctor and throwing up. Besides the excruciating pain is the realization that one has just become another statistic. One more minority teenager got pregnant and had an abortion. Under such circumstances one couldn't come close to explaining this magnitude of frustration with anyone. Individual A has come a long way since that time. A's self-confidence was at an all-time low but is now happy and shining. Individual A's abortion has had a big impact on who A is today. But what is more important to note is that A dealt with it on A's own terms without anyone else knowing. Now A tries not to remember what A did and how it felt. Such a tactic works most of the time, but now and then it still haunts A who really does *want* to talk about it. So A takes a deep breath and realizes that A's biggest secret will be with A till the day A dies.

Secrets over abortion affect second parties as well. One of A's friends (B) had an abortion last year. Individual A did not know about it until after the fact, but when B needed to confide in someone about the matter, she told A. Individual B indicated that the act of telling somehow gave B a sense of security and confidence. Individual A was willing and open to listen to her, and the two friends expressed feelings and fears that had never been voiced between them before. However, after a while, B became very hostile toward A. She began to talk behind A's back, become angry, and would try to start disputes. Individual A felt B did this because they had become too close before, and A knew too much about B. By acting this way, B pushed A away as fast as she had drawn her close. Individual A could not express the situation to anyone else without violating A's own pledge not to tell the secret. Such secret covenants become a burden to everyone who is concerned. In a similar vein, another individual (A) gets drunk with some friends and ends up cheating on A's boyfriend (B) with someone else (C). Though A and C swore to keep it a secret, eventually B finds out and breaks up with A. It was the most guilt-ridden six months of A's life. Others would ask A what was wrong, and A would always say "Nothing." To this day A does not think that A can ever tell loved ones the truth.

There is considerable tension in semisecret messages that appear more open than closed. It is possible, after all, to maintain an open secret from another person, a third party, or an entire community. In alcoholic families, it is frequently the case that every member is aware of the alcoholism and exchanges covert messages about its effects. The family's coded messages are a semisecret way of maintaining family integrity despite the pain of each of its members. To openly divulge the secret would, in all probability, produce second-order (radical) change in which the rules of family integration and family boundaries would be in jeopardy.

Some semisecret messages are also those that are purely malicious in intent and design and depend on the thorough knowledge of the other's way of making meaning. In this type, the very fact of semisecrecy is itself a lethal or toxic message. It suggests the secretholder knows something of importance to the other but will not share that valuable information. In so doing, the secretholder's victim has no knowledge of the extent to which, if at all, withheld information has dire implications for her or his safety or well-being. It can be terribly destructive, a form of symbolic violence. Such semisecrecy is also a secret bearer's way of holding the recipient hostage to threats inherent in the implied meaning of the act itself. Allowing partial disclosure conveys to the recipient a power imbalance in which they are controlled by the person in possession of the rest of the information.

Semisecret messages generate considerable ambiguity, which, in turn, generates anxiety. To know that one doesn't know, and to know also that one may need to know for real or metaphoric survival, often triggers a futile context for anxiety, fear, and, at times, panic. This quality of semisecret messages may also play into the secret bearer's sadomasochism. Sadism is self-evident in the pain maliciously inflicted on the recipient. Masochism is extant in the secret bearer's awareness of the recipient's ill feelings toward him or her. Hence, acts of semidisclosure produce not only anxiety and fear in the recipient, but also a form of loathing for the bearer's manipulation and control of the recipient's feelings.

There is another aspect of semisecret messages beyond those just discussed. If they are shared in a conspiratorial manner, they can serve to create a collusionary bond between those sharing the experience. It may be impossible for source A to inform B of the totality of a given secret. But if A can allow B access to partial information, they may experience a type of comradeship or kinship. This is exemplified in alliances and insider trades.

Semisecrecy is a type of exchange that may require total disclosure within one relational context but partial secrecy in another. This is certainly the case for family secrets. Family members often keep the reality of sexual abuse totally secret from one another. Yet, one or more members may reveal the hidden truth with a therapist, friend, or extended family member. Moreover, there is a related form of semisecrecy, and that is one for which two parties, A and B, interact with C while exchanging secret information in C's presence. Person C may believe he/she knows exactly what is being conveyed at a literal level. But C may not be aware that A and B are using highly coded language and metalanguage to connect with one another over issues or matters that they do not want C to apprehend. In effect, the use of highly metacommunicative language preserves one set of boundaries while eliminating others. Much depends on which side of the line one happens to be located.

Some secrets remain utterly inexplicable, particularly if manifest in the form of a dream. Various remnants and traces of the sight, sound, and touch of other people encountered during the daytime hours register in sedimented and diffuse form at night. In sleep the light is transformed by the darkness. Dreaming is a form of second-order communication—a diffuse and highly condensed expression of what is left over from the sights, sounds, and textures of daylight reality. The starkest nighttime secret is of course the nightmare. One individual describes nighttime terror in the following terms: "The dream is strange, usually very terrifying. Everyone around me is bloating and I am becoming suffocated. Strange sensations cause my body to become numb and shiver in the darkness. I wake up, body shaking, in a cold sweat. The strangest part is not being able to figure out what is 'dream' and what is 'real.' It is all so lifelike that I can't actually tell if it was a dream or not." The essential implications are captured by a small child.

#62 A's view: When I was in the second grade I woke up in the middle of a dream. I went into my parent's bedroom to speak to them about it because I was unsure of the content of my dream. I wasn't able to explain my dream because I couldn't verbalize any of my thoughts. To the present day I still can't explain my dream. From my education I am able to surmise that my dream has something to do with existentialism. To try to explain, my dream let's me know that I can only be truly aware of my own existence but I could not deny the existence of others. I knew that if I wanted to raise my own hand, all I had to do was to wish it to happen. I could not raise other people's hands by a simple wish. There is something stopping one from existing within the domain of another entity or in any other human body. I guess I thought or realized that I was not able to "be in two places at once." My existence is very limited to me and my own body boundaries. I cannot feel what others feel in the identical manner that they do. I can only think I feel what they feel and I have to perform this 'feeling' from my own body. I guess I wished I could feel someone else's feelings from their own subjective point of view. I have times where I don't know for sure whether things actually happen or if it was all just a dream. Many time I think I have had a certain experience when it was only a dream. And when it comes to reality, it doesn't happen that way—my dream was better or more perfect than reality itself.

LIES AND ILLUSIONS

#63 A's view: A and B are intimately involved with one another. After two months of dating, A discovers evidence that B's supposedly new diaphragm had in fact seen some use prior to their relationship. Person A thinks he has been lied to about a very personal and important matter by someone with whom he thought he shared mutual respect, trust, and love. The discovery took place while moving her things to his place where they were to live together. A feels betrayed, used, hurt, sad, and angry at the same time. He cannot think of a time where he has ever been so overwhelmed with such mixed emotions. He confronts her by asking why she would lie to him. She is caught and she knows it. In a very uncomfortable and tearful talk, she explains that she didn't want him to know about one of her past boyfriends and that it shouldn't matter that much. She adds that she had not slept with her most recent boyfriend. She admits to misleading him and tells him she is sorry, asking if he could ever forgive her. Over the next week she tells him her entire dating history in what he perceives as an honest effort to regain trust. He is in love with her, but once he is lied to, it is very difficult to regain trust for her. He finds himself questioning (mostly to himself) many things she has told him. He is especially concerned about her being on the rebound. This turns into a spiral situation in which she perceives him questioning things that make her more defensive, and her defensiveness only makes him feel more isolated, hurt, and suspicious. Eventually A and B hardly communicate at all, but the external circumstances force them to remain living together for the time being. The relationship is doomed as it was from the beginning. During this conflict A professes to want to work things out but sees her as appearing less willing. He thinks she has all the power in the relationship, something he resents. She also resents him for questioning her. The feelings of resentment, betrayal, hurt, jealousy, and being used are mixed with very real feelings of love and friendship. The fact that A and B like one another leads to an emotional upheaval the likes of which A has never felt before. Needless to say, the relationship ends.

The presumption of a lie or illusion changes everything else, of course. Here there are considerable discursive and dialogical tensions, stress, strain, and resistance to strict adherence to a standard of transparency, clarity, articulation, and sensitivity in all matters of translation and interpretation. Expressive and interpretive tensions emerge in the dislocation and discontinuity between what one takes for granted or calls into question at the level of the voracity and the efficacy of a given succession of expressive acts. Where telling the truth is the standard of observation, the act of falling short of the (intentional or goal-oriented) mark is instantiated as a matter of tacit or explicit compromise in the capacity and willingness to be as clear, articulate, and transparent as possible (within one's power) given the limitations and enablements in the immediate situation.

There is a certain amount of inertia in the decision to tell a lie. As a course of least resistance, lying is easier than telling the truth in situations in which one chooses to lie. Dredging up the courage to tell the brutal truth is often harder than taking the easy way out. The rationale dissolves into rationalization. The persons in question take into account their own sensibilities—how am I going to be affected by my lie? Imagination then takes over as one presupposes how someone else would handle the truth. Since we lack full access to the private reflections of others, we may take it upon ourselves to presume what others can ultimately handle. When one source determines someone else could not possibly deal with our own version of the truth, it is usually just a matter of guessing without direct knowledge of the actual response. Tacit appeal to mitigating circumstance may be used to justify the act of telling a lie. This gives such interactants an *out* to their lying and an *in* to taking on the public appearance of the idealized person they so desperately aspire to be.

Interpersonal compromise registers and resonates in ingenious patterns of accounts. Many leave the most important considerations out of the dialogue altogether. There is deliberate imprecision, rough approximation, and "guesstimation." Misinformation generates a set of crucial omissions: shortsightedness—not identifying what really matters most, taking discursive shortcuts, evasions, magic tricks, taking refuge in ambiguity, misleading advertising, maps, or direction, taking too much or too little for granted, talking around the subject, stammering, stuttering, stalling, ignoring the question, stalling for more time or for a better opportunity, running off at the mouth, putting your foot in your mouth, eating your words, bullshitting, jiving, jockeying for position, putting someone off or being utterly determined to remain silent at all costs.

There are many good reasons for not telling the truth, the whole truth, and nothing but the truth to self or other. Others will look down on me; others will think I am stupid; I must lie to keep my ego intact; to tell the truth would be too much—it would be so degrading; expressed lies may be necessary so that loved ones will not feel upset, betrayed, used, hurt, sad, or angry at the same time; it shouldn't matter so much; the truth makes some people feel so uncomfortable and causes so much pain and emotional upheaval; just ignore the problem, and it will go away; sometimes it is necessary to cover up one's true feelings and concerns with sarcasm and cynicism; tell the truth and set yourself up to be taken for granted; tell the truth and reveal too much. Sometimes the expressed truth turns out to be too communicative for the participant or observer to handle, grasp, comprehend. Suppose you tell a lie, and someone else believes the lie. The lie is then incorporated into the lived history of the other person. At this point the lie lives on in the personal reality of another being.

Five rejoinders: (1) One who lies may be discovered to be a liar, and at this point the lie is exposed for what it is and is of no further use. (2) Give people the benefit of the DOUBT even if it means you must ignore your own feelings. (3) The decision to refuse to tell the truth can have detrimental effects on the one who lies. (4) One may wish one had spoken out and known the truth rather than living in the private domain of what-ifs. (5) Hindsight is always 20/20, but in the process one needs to know that searching for answers is troublesome until one can focus clearly.

WITHDRAWAL INTO FICTITIOUS WORLDS

#64 A's view: The way I felt was the end product of a long process of introversion. No one, unless they too had been a party to the long process, could make the connection, or understand how I felt that day. I had conditioned myself into a state of emotional deadness and isolation throughout the last month and had become terribly self-involved in fictitious worlds. Nothing other than completely woven fantasies could even slightly stimulate my mind and eventually drew me into a totally fictitious life. I had lost touch with reality within myself. It took that day's events to bring me so low that I truly believed I could never feel so awful in my life. Everything I ever feared would be found out, all my private thoughts could be uncovered, all I ever feared was uncovered and blatantly thrown at me in harsh blunt words. Each word cut into my crumbling pride and finally I fell to the lowest point I could ever fall to; I felt like I wanted to lie dead even more than before. But no one would have understood because they didn't hear past the harsh words into their meaning. How could I begin to express adequately or even remotely what I was feeling to anyone? It was hard enough to admit what I felt to myself.

#65 A's view: There are times when A's emotions and feelings are so deep that A has had problems expressing them to anyone. The first thing that A does is to cut off all communication with anyone who is close or important. Individual A then withdraws into a little imaginary world. It is as if A is in a vacuum and sees no way that any individual could possibly be able to interpret or understand A's most inner feelings. A uses A's own little world to escape the frustration of being unable to express A's feelings to anyone. Silence helps A escape from the realities that surround.

REFUSALS: THE UNWILLINGNESS TO COMMUNICATE

So far the expressive urge has been described as a movement toward the transformation of tacit and covert definitional features into explicit and overt (observable) form. By such a standard, a nonexpressive urge would work the other way around, that is, to render what is observable (to one source) back into some private, inaccessible, or inarticulate form. Here ambivalence translates into the dualistic urge to uncover (reveal) and cover up (conceal) at the same time.

One may struggle for or against the fulfillment of an expressive urge. On a larger scale, the force of conversation can be supported and sustained or subverted and undermined. In descriptions of faulty interaction patterns among relatively noncommunicative family members, several themes stand out. Hinting is important where indirect modes of self-expression prevail. Here members rely heavily on context and situation to convey unspoken desires, urges, intentions, lines of action, strategies, and goals. Individual members may be reluctant to spell out the hidden agenda in any explicit verbal form. Each individual is supposed to be instantly aware of what transpires without benefit of explicit acknowledgment. Indirection and misdirection outweigh direction. Cases in point: (1) presuming that others can read your mind without your having to say a thing; (2) taking matters of care and affection for granted without ever being able to say to someone "Your life is precious" or "I love you"; (3) deception: feeling suppressed hostility, anxiety, or aggression (within) while denying such a condition (at the surface); (4) unspoken forms of duplicity and the imposition of double standards; and finally (5) the tendency to project or transfer (in disguised form) unfavorable aspects of one's own lived circumstances onto those of others and thereby make the others responsible for fictions they are not in a position to know or ascertain.

Logophobia may be understood in terms of the fear of using words and gestures to maximize the efficacy of mutual efforts in sense-making practice. A number of considerations enter in: reticence, shyness, avoidance tendencies, communicative apprehension, and tacit discomfort over what self and others feel, think, say, act, or do. Such psychological resistance may culminate in various states or conditions of refusal in which the expressive urge (in one source) is ignored, undermined, or circumvented (by another). Hence, individual achievement of communicative competence is no assurance of mutual compatibility.

The noncommunicative styles of interaction demonstrate a spirit of intolerance and devaluation of expressive freedom. Instead of encouragement and support for one to speak up and spit it out, there is rather collaborative discouragement, unresponsiveness, and trained insensitivity. From such a radical perspective, some respondents must go through extraordinary efforts just to break through into shared situations where there is no option to walk away, no matter how bad others make one feel or how badly one allows the others to make one feel. The urge to push back may well up as compensation for loss of confidence, feelings of rejection, and an utter sense of uselessness when surrounded by other equally mute family members.

Some find it easier just to give up than to have the brass ring constantly dangled in front of the nose in the manner of a tease. Making excuses can become a way of life and an all-purpose crutch. There is considerable pretext in the text: say one thing but mean another. Do not bother to figure out what is going on because in the end clarity or confusion is all the same. Some grow up with poor communicative skills and resources and suffer extensively throughout adulthood before those who respond with indifference (so what?). Interactive stress, strain, struggle, and futility may intensify without any explicit or manifest acknowledgment on the part of one source or another. The silence becomes overpowering. Personal neutrality is the unspoken rule. Mandate: keep conversations short, brief, truncated, understated, and quite terse. Better to be on the safe side and express too little than too much. Let others fill in the blanks. The ears are hollow. The eyes grow dim. The senses become numb in due course. Hereby kindred spirits pursue the illusion of becoming strangers to one another once more.

REFERENCES

Berger, P. & Luchmann, T. (1967). *The social construction of reality*. New York: Doubleday-Anchor.

Black, C. (1981). *It will never happen to me*. Denver: Mac.

Fararo, T. J. (1989). *The meaning of general theoretical sociology: Tradition and formalization*. New York: Cambridge University Press.

Giddens, A. (1984). *The constitution of society: Outline of the theory of structuration*. Berkeley: University of California Press.

Harris, G. G. (1989). Concepts of individual, self, and person in description and analysis. *American Anthropologist, 91*, 599–612.

Mathien, T. (1988). Network analysis and methodological individualism. *Journal of Philosophy of Social Science, 18*, 1–20.

Platt, R. (1989). Reflexivity, recursion, and social life: Elements for a postmodern sociology. *The Sociological Review, 37,* 636–667.

Saegert, S. & Winkel, G. H. (1990). Environmental Psychology. *Annual Review of Psychology, 41,* 441–477.

Schutz, A. (1967). *The phenomenology of the social world.* (Trans. G. Walsh & F. Lehnert). Evanston: Northwestern University Press.

Verhoeven, J. (1985). Goffman's frame analysis and modern micro-sociological paradigms. In H. J. Helle & S. H. Eisenstadt (Eds.) *Micro-sociological theory: Perspectives on sociological theory,* Vol. 1, (pp. 71–100). Beverly Hills: Sage.

5

Silence, Discourse, and Dialogue

The distinction between "communication" and "interaction" is critical in the study of human problematics. The opportunity to engage in face-to-face interaction gives rise to communicative possibility but does not insure its fulfillment. The minimum threshold is reached at the point of making sense of what transpires. Whatever interferes with the achievement of the ideal—clear, transparent sense—is presumed to qualify as a potential problem or problematic in interaction. In nonproblematic interchanges, the sense of things is presumptive, taken for granted, or merely given. In problematic exchanges, what matters most decisively is the sheer magnitude of what remains undefined, unsettled, or otherwise at issue. Relevant empirical boundaries include whatever one is in a position to see, hear, say, touch, or move. Sometimes the interplay of various modes of sensory activation is at issue or in question. The purpose here is to focus on relations within verbal, visual, auditory, and kinetic modes of misalignment or disconnection. Of specific interest is what registers at the intersection of complication and silence.

SIGHT, SOUND, AND SILENCE

Silence registers in discourse, and silence resonates in dialogue, but the two are not one in the same. The silence that registers in discourse is embedded within larger considerations of when, how, or why any one source produces a given sequence of (filled) sound or decides to remain silent. In contrast, the silence that resonates in dialogue is an inclusive reflection of the totality of expressed options accorded to participant and observer alike. We wrap ourselves and one another, as Buber once said, in layers and layers of silence.

A preliminary distinction entails the complementarity of the two forms. Discursive silence coincides with the absence of filled sound while dialogical silence involves the synchrony of sound and silence as sustained by alternative sources of reference engaged in multiple forms of meaning-endowed activity. Sight, touch, and movement overlap and enrich the mix. We observe the transition from sound to silence, the synchrony of turn taking, and the goodness of fit between the two.

Discursive silence is digital (ON/OFF) and complementary in construction. The transition from speech to silence implies not just the absence of sound but also the refusal or unwillingness to talk. We can think of silence, as Ehrenhaus (1988) notes, as a transition into a state in which one is rendered momentarily incapable of making productive use of verbal constructs. The unspoken involves not just what is missing or lacking but also what interferes with the flow of talk to the point where the "interpretation of experience is problematic" (p. 43).

One speaks and listens to others through the interiors and exteriors of one's own body boundaries. Sound permeates exteriors and penetrates interiors, while silence punctuates strategic aspects of sequence and meaning. Bateson (1972) speaks fondly of conversations having an outline in which the form, shape, and contour of sound and silence are an unfolding measure of the depth and magnitude of what is turned on or off in any designated sphere of relevance. If speech acts signal implicit urge, desire, intention, direction, and personal orientation, so also do acts of silence—whether welcomed and supported or resisted and disrupted. In this equation silence interupts the stream of talk even while being sustained within the larger process. Moreover, sound-silence patterns are inhabited, indwelled, and transformed in a holistic manner. Participant and observer take in the silence in direct proportion to their capacity and willingness to take out (defer) the production of talk. Within the immediacy of the encompassing silence are located the cumulative burdens of all that is left unsaid.

One may be filled with the sound of one's own voice or else with an implicit sense of what the absence of such sound brings to light. Either way, there is much to be discovered inside or outside the edges of the silence, what Ihde (1976) calls "the other side of sound" (p. 112). We live (indwell) within the sounds of our own voices in relation to what we decide to leave unspoken—what can no longer or not as yet be reclaimed in any audible form. The spiral of silence unfolds in relation to the actual spectrum of sound. One who cannot tolerate the silence is not apt to thrive in the production of talk.

"Dialogical silence" is an analogical (either/and/or) construction. It involves the interdependence of sound and silence of any one source in transitional states of anticipation and response to the audible or silent activity of any other. My decision to be silent provides renewed opportunity for you to fill the air with the sound of your own voice or else make the decision not to say anything further about the matter at hand. Our collective sense of sight, sound, and silence provides a succession of open-ended opportunity to verify what is seen in relation to whatever else is felt, thought, said, or done.

As a mode of encounter, silence provides opportunity for self-reflexivity and contemplation—what one can do or know without speaking that enriches the personal significance of relationships. In "remaining silent we speak," as Scott (1972, p. 146) notes, because the decision to say something is a choice not to say anything else. The copresence of word and gesture assures that "what is said always carries with it what is present as unsaid" (Ihde, 1976, p. 151). The voice that silence speaks is indeterminate and richly implicative. Despite all we may attribute to it, the silence encountered within dialogue cannot tell us what it means or signifies to the one who produces it (Brummett, 1980, p. 289). In the words of Merleau-Ponty (1973), we consider speech in relation to the ground of silence "which precedes it, which never ceases to accompany it, and without which it would say nothing" (pp. 45–46). In effect, the horizon of silence "surrounds" the field of sensory activation (Ihde, 1976).

Face-to-face interaction gives rise to an ever-changing mix of communicative styles. The sequencing and asymmetry of the respective styles is a strategic indication of complex matters of competence and compatibility. Here style coincides with the formal manner of personal presentation. By this standard, one's communicative style acquires definition through a structured sequence of engagements in responsive and anticipative modes of coordinated action. What qualifies as one's sense of experience coincides with what one is in a position to grasp through one sense modality or another. Of central interest is the dialectical relationship between what is seen, said, and heard and the wider domain of inclusive silence.

The purpose of this chapter is to explore the communicative significance of silence across diverse systems of communication. Resultant complications become problematic for all the complex and subtle ways that serve to bring participants closer together and yet still manage to keep them somewhat apart over widely extended courses of concerted action. Of relevance is how various individuals use words and gestures to come together (in one sense) and yet move apart (in another sense) at the same time. Sometimes even mundane episodes of conversation can become unexpectedly complicated, encumbered, and weighted down with a multiplicity of possibilities acted out against a wider backdrop of constraints and obligations. Moreover, this condition may be encountered at the very point where one's own communicative resources run the risk of being a liability to someone else. Such heavily weighted forms of face-to-face interaction tend to be problematic insofar as they serve to radicalize, or render more extreme, the succession of stances and positions to be assumed by the respective parties. What is most decisive is how various combinations of interactants signify their way toward the utter extremes of tolerance or forbearance.

What follows is a typography of silence, discourse, and dialogue. It is taken from the point of view of those who observe in silence what the immediate presence of other interactants makes manifest. In each instance someone adapts an unspoken perspective toward what the sight, sound, and silence of someone else brings to light. At work are both the communicative significance of silence and uncertain complications associated with the consequences of what is left unsaid.

Thirteen scenarios are arranged thematically as a means of exploring the communicative significance of what the depths of silence reveal in manifest form: (1) intrusiveness, in which noise, interference, clamor, and din disrupt the intention of someone to remain silent and say nothing further to anyone else; (2) solitude, in which silence is chosen as the best alternative; (3) reflections over why some things are better left unsaid; (4) rationale for not saying what might scare others away; (5) protracted silence as a means of self-protection; (6) a case for waiting in silence; (7) the code of silence as a loyalty oath; (8) the sense of feeling trapped inside the silence; (9) the state of enforced or imposed silence; (10) the urge to break out of the silence; (11) appeasement, in which shared silence is a turn-taking opportunity; (12) silence as a refuge or sanctuary; and (13) silence as a source of wonder and awe that things really are what they are.

INTRUSIVENESS: NOISE, DISRUPTION, AND OUTSIDE INTERFERENCE

#66 A's view: A and B meet for the first time. A views B as obnoxious from the start. A views B as the sort of person who would make A feel like being rude. B makes lots of noise and much disturbance while A is trying to concentrate on a task. B asks A for information. A gives B information. B starts cussing and bitching about the situation. B asks A for more information, so A provides B with added information. Individual B continues to complain but eventually tries to apologize to A. At this point A becomes mad (angry). At the end of the encounter A views B as not having B's act together and for blaming others for B's own problems. Suddenly individual B leaves the scene while completely unaware of A's view of the real cause of B's difficulties.

#67 A's view: Very recently I had an experience that was nearly impossible to explain to anyone. I was sitting in the Memorial Union one rainy afternoon. I was sitting in a back booth alone, working on a paper. I had been there for four hours. Out of nowhere, a man with a red beard, a torn sweater, and a lit joint came over and sat across from me. I was completely taken off guard and sat stunned and silent. The man proceeded to ask questions about what I was studying and my nationality! I wanted him to leave but I was nervous, embarrassed, and did not know what or how to do so. He continued to talk to me for the next hour and a half! He discussed art and technology, the Roman empire, German founders of Wisconsin, and the plight of our jaded world. However, by far the topic that caught my attention most vividly was his discussion of the loss of innocence once a person loses his or her first love. The topic was timely as the previous evening I had broken up with my boyfriend of four years. I wondered if for some reason I was supposed to listen to this man. (Looking back, I don't think so). Finally, after saying no more than twenty words in all that time—I got up and left.

#68 A's view: I lived with a woman named Adele. Adele was a woman of true "character." She aspired to be a clown—as a career. This career choice stemmed from her true personality. She was a clown at heart—at work, at school, at play. Imagine life with a clown. The situation was inexpressible mainly because anyone who came to visit was extremely charmed by her. "Sure, she is animated, sure she's vivacious—what a great person" was all I would hear. No one could understand the anxiety and frustration caused by living with her day by day. She followed me around nonstop from the moment I walked into the door to the moment I fell asleep. She had so much energy. She never stopped and I, working my first eight to four job, was the epitome of the walking dead by six p.m. for the first couple of months. Imagine my excitement at each and every offer to run down to the lake, meet her "juggling buddies," or go biking. Everyone else thought this hyperactivity sounded wonderful but because I was just starting out in my career and had yet to learn to balance my personal and professional life, the mere act of having someone who never relaxed and always hanging around was a personally tormenting situation that no one else could understand.

#69 A's view: It happens when one is able to blab on endlessly in one situation but have absolutely nothing to say in the next.

#70 A's view: There are special moments that I have wanted to keep to myself and times when things were going bad and I couldn't open up to anyone else. From the positive side, people usually think that if you are feeling pretty good you want to share it with someone. This is not always the case with me. At this point in my life I am extremely focused and my philosophy of life is getting better. Before I was feeling blue and it was 'kind of dark' outside. I want to live this life because it is the only one I will ever have. This is just as hard for me to express as it is for you to comprehend my point. Maybe this is why I keep such matters to myself.

In entries 66 to 70 the respondents who inhabit silence as a preferred mode of operation share much in common. At the outset each one is situated in a stance of introspection or solitude, which is then broken by the noisy and disruptive action of someone else. Here personal actions are construed as 'noisy' with a double meaning. What registers in the auditory stream of the observer is mainly invasive, asymmetrical, mistimed, and disproportionate—it quickly exceeds tolerable limits in the continuity of the unspoken. What resonates in the stream of consciousness is the sight, sound, and diffuse sense of unwelcomed modes of personal conduct—unsettled, busy, compulsive, self-preoccupied, insensitive, prolonged, excessive, and extreme. Corresponding modes of silence are relinquished, overcome, broken, and eclipsed. In the process each one sees and hears far more than what can or is explicitly stated. What matters most is precisely what is left unspoken. Because the other person insists on filling the air with so much talk and idle chatter, the very possibility of mutual dialogue is construed to be null and void. After all, nonstop talk on the part of one undermines or prevents genuine give-and-take among all the rest.

Imbalances in the flow of sound and silence introduce translational and interpretive conundrums, contradictions, and quandaries. Most noticeable is the lack of parity in the distribution of expressive constraints and interpretive enablements. Participant and observer express and interpret their way into a stance of fixed positions from which one does the talking while the other the listening. Overt restrictions (by one) open up (for both) a margin of opportunity for reflection and implication over unsettled definitional conditions. The silence of each one enlarges the opportunity for talk on the part of every other one. Hence, the pattern of turn taking is a reflection of how sound and silence are subject to negotiation and distribution as coequal resources. All of this is grounded in the realization that it usually does not work very well for two or more sources to try and talk at once for very long and still make sense of successive forms of personal conduct.

When the quietest member does attempt to say something, the words are mostly brushed aside, dismissed, or ruled out. Talk here is mostly impatient, frantic, hectic, and demanding. Moreover, the producers of the rhythms of dialogue are quite out of sync—the more one talks, the less the others have opportunities to speak. In the uneasy balance, talk is the main mechanism of interpersonal control while silence functions more like a receding line of access to a linguistic court of last resort. Finally, after all the intrusive talk is completed, one member returns to the encompassing silence from whence the episode began while the others move away, immune from the discovery that what was left unsaid was precisely what the noisy party most needed to hear but could not bring him or herself to recognize and respond.

Oddly, what little face-to-face interaction does occur is mostly a symbolic cover-up of private realizations rendered mute as having no distinct expressive or communicative value. What gets ruled out is the very possibility for mutual discovery and recognition that one member cannot grasp the adverse effects of his or her own behavior on others nor see what the others can see and hear but never say.

WHY SOME THINGS ARE BETTER LEFT UNSAID

Sometimes silence is a preference rather than a burden or a dire necessity. Personal choices measure the magnitude of one's sense of obligation to others. The decision to say nothing at all is an alternative to telling others everything they want to hear. After all, the whole truth may be too much to admit, particularly if one has failed someone else, feels totally ashamed, and yet is unable to acknowledge what is being felt about some unspoken aspect of the past. Unresolved issues that trouble one may bother others even more; at such times it is often best that only one person knows for sure. The risk of keeping silent may be less than the risk of engagement in any further forms of personal disclosure. During periods of great uncertainty, pain, or loss, silence may spare one from the disturbing reactions of others to self and/or self to others. One woman refuses to believe that her husband, after disclosure of a secret marital affair, would walk out on a wife and four children after twenty years. Feeling totally devastated and unable to share the crisis with anyone living outside the family, the woman says nothing to her children on the grounds that "silence seemed to be the best alternative."

Sometimes preference for silence is created during complicated or vexing episodes of conversation. It happens when one individual goes through a period of great personal change. Eager to discuss the radical nature of the change, the individual in question starts out quite eager to share the news, only to discover after a few minutes that others lose interest and drift off to other subjects. It gets to the point where the individual no longer wants to talk about what matters most because no one else is as interested as he had first thought. Under such strained circumstances, he stops any further discussion on grounds that it can be so overwhelmingly frustrating to share in bits and pieces and saddening to acknowledge privately that one cannot relate the totality of one's personal interests and concerns to anyone else. Others prefer silence rather than risk the revelation of deeply intimate thoughts or feelings in troublesome situations when nothing that is ever said really gets through. Moreover, silence may seem better than dialogue in situations in which one party does not seem safe or secure.

#71 A's view: It seems that everyone has something they try to keep from other people. I'm no exception. Although I don't want to list my little "secrets," I admit that quite often I don't tell people what is going on. Although I am a very open person, when it comes to expressing various feelings or moods, there are times of depression or possibly even sheer joy which don't seem appropriate. Perhaps I'm not right in keeping things to myself but I think it is for the better. Telling people everything is not always smart.

#72 A's view: It happens when one doesn't feel the need or desire to open up. One is left to oneself and must keep the problem in question strictly private. It happens when the expression of one's true feelings would have not helped to change the definition of the immediate situation. It happens when one may want to express what one is feeling but does not know how to appropriate the means to do so. It's not that we don't want to express what we feel, because we all do within the confines of a 'certain' type of shared situation but rather that emotions are often tied to unrecognized motivations which may further complicate the accompanying modes of expression. What one expresses may reveal too much about one's inner self that one does not want others to come to know.

ON NOT SAYING WHAT WOULD ONLY SCARE OTHERS AWAY

#73 A's view: I find myself continually holding back in initial interactions. I have a fear of alienating the other person. I am always wondering what is going on in the mind of the other person and how will they react to what I say, rather than just saying it. It seems no matter how much I love or risk I still long for a sense of security. I just don't want to chase anyone away by offending them or challenging them too much when I'm just getting to know them. Yet I hate to hold back sometimes feeling I could learn more from another if we could just let loose and speak our minds. Mistakes are made so easily and to correct them takes such a huge amount of effort but to me it is worth it. From the pain and the mistakes I want to learn and grow and the knowledge will come to me by efforts other than my own. I must learn to be patient and wait to ask some of my biggest questions or give some of my deepest comments because then when my moment arises it will be feel all the better.

#74 A's view: It happens when one chooses to remain silent rather than speak out and risk the possibility that others will laugh and make fun of the fact that one is just being oneself. In such situations one may be insecure about what to talk about and how to talk about it, regardless of what the topic of conversation happens to be. Moreover, it may also happen at a time when one prefers to say nothing rather than risk the revelation of some inner thought or feeling in a troublesome situation. Prolonged silence may be safer than constant exposure to verbal put-downs. Finally, it may happen when one is a very private person who feels no need to express personal feelings out of a fear of letting too much be shown to others. When one shares such feelings it is easy to get hurt or be taken advantage of. It is necessary to struggle to live one's life as one pleases regardless of what others may think.

#75 A's view: There have been many times when A has engaged in thoughts or feelings that were quite embarrassing. A can't deny feeling that way but is ashamed because if A told someone else they might laugh or think A was shallow. At times A's mind wanders and A thinks about things and thinks no one else knows what A is feeling. There are also times when even A knows that what A is thinking and feeling is ludicrous so A wouldn't express it to anyone and may even deny the feelings to A's self. The main point is that A can't express to anyone what he sometimes thinks and feels mainly because of fear of the other's reactions and A's own. A lot of difficulty stems from being scared of what the other person is going to feel and of scaring the other by letting out one's own true feelings.

#76 A's view: It happens over personal problems that cannot be talked about. One searches for the meaning of what it is like to be alone, alienated, depressed, helpless, isolated. Key assumption: One can't do anything about it. One is apt to engage in self-denial. One doesn't want to admit that something is wrong. It turns out that one is afraid and finds it difficult to talk to anyone else. One becomes increasingly reluctant to share feelings and thoughts with others and to see oneself as just another object of public ridicule.

#77 A's view: When I know anything I say will hurt or injure the feelings of other people, I feel caught. It is the feeling that I am stuck or trapped in what I know about the impact of my words on those I care about. The only thing left to do is to say nothing at all.

One central theme in these entries is replayed over and over again. There are many variations but the most striking are those that link silent anticipation of future interaction with fear or apprehension over what would happen if X said Y to Z. Three types of unspoken fears enter the picture. Most inclusive are personal concerns that seem to engulf every aspect of one's being: the fear of admitting the full magnitude or urgency of one's existing situation; pressing issues and insistent demands, not wanting to open up or let on, facing up to feelings of personal turmoil, vulnerability, helplessness, or death anxiety; resistance to unwanted or unwelcome change, unknown fears about future possibilities, not knowing where to turn or how to ask for help, vague discomfort at the *thought* of telling others how frightened one is or the inability to take the steps required to make the necessary changes in one's own life.

Also relevant are the imagined consequences associated with unspoken fears over disquieting but nameless, uncertain, or unknown factors and forces in someone's life. Some individuals struggle over what they cannot define or articulate—what lingers as nonconveyable, inexplicable, or strange bodily discomforts without a clue as to cause, rhyme, or reason. Such problematic conditions prompt recognition that we all wear masks and at many times may be afraid to reveal who we are and what we think of life. One individual describes these sorts of conditions as fear of an "unbearable" load of "unknowns." Finally, there is common acknowledgment of individual difficulty in the search for the truth about one's life, admitting finally the truth to others, and living with the consequences. This involves fear of saying something that *forces* one to admit the truth about oneself and the reluctance to give up what prevents the truth from being fully shared. Of greatest relevance is an underlying fear that all of one's pent-up thoughts and feelings will come pouring out some day in waves of sentiment and passion so that everything one has struggled so long to keep private is finally manifest for all to see.

The second class of personal concerns are framed as interpersonal fears or relational implications. One individual stands out as a working model. Day after day the person in question feels deeply afraid to call someone up who happens to matter very much and yet refuses steadfastly to answer the phone out of fear of announcing or hearing any more bad news. Instead, the participants at both ends of the line are left to suffer in silence over what neither party seems capable or willing to penetrate.

Central here is the difficult search for underlying aspects of personal responsibility and interpersonal accountability. On the self-oriented side of the ledger are a long succession of what-ifs: what would happen during imagined interaction if one would finally disclose one's own personal problems and own up to the possibility of being judged wrong, bad, or at fault and also admit to fear of failure or negative aspects of a self-picture or a bruised ego. Often personal tensions implicate small things too. There is fear of appearing silly, foolish, or embarrassed at one end or else covering up the full intensity of one's anger or breaking down and crying at the other. On the other side of the relational slate are an assortment of unspoken fears over what others might or will feel, expect, think, say, or do in response to an imagined set of possibilities.

Mostly aversive anticipations are implicated: fear of hearing unfavorable reactions, letting out true feelings, getting hurt, being taken advantage of, or being the object of someone else's anger, indignation, abuse, or rage. There are also complex fears over concerns that others can't help, won't be able to relate, or would only make one's situation worse, whether they would laugh, make fun, or watch one play the role of fool. In matters of unspoken warmth and affection, there is also the fear of saying "I love you" and not hearing the same words back or hearing something completely wrong or otherwise out of place. This involves the risk of not being liked, the risk of rejection, or putting others in a situation in which they don't know how to respond to the subject matter at hand. Most of these imaginary possibilities reflect an underlying fear of criticism, harsh judgment, unbridled evaluation, or devaluation. Most troublesome is the prospect of not being taken seriously as an individual who is just being oneself in difficult situations that give rise to a mix of fear and guilt over what makes others feel worse for having to deal with one's own problems, perhaps even hurting the other's feelings in the process.

The third sort of unarticulated concerns coalesce around communicative implications of anticipated or imagined forms of direct encounter. Here one archriding theme stands out—fear of not being able to make sense of one's experience while being in the presence of others. There is fear of revealing too little or too much, fear of not being able to express personal feelings or clarify thoughts properly, but mostly fear of being misinterpreted or misunderstood. This is, in fact, the basic logocentric fear of all. It is not a matter of one's capacity to deal with the full range of individual stylistic differences or likely disagreements but rather a more fundamental substratum of misunderstanding that always seems to stand in the way of mutual effort to grasp and comprehend. Here again we see a variation of the central theme—how complications in lived circumstances can undermine efforts at mutual influence over the definition and direction of relations and thereby produce a succession of disagreements and misunderstandings, imagined and real, unspoken assumptive burdens to be endured or tolerated in silence.

These varied apprehensions are a reminder that what and how we think about our direct encounters with others can be a powerful catalyst for further physiological reaction and response. We feel what we think as well as how we act. In the silent experience of the emergence of our own tacit or unstated urges, desires, intentions, expectations, and reflections, we form an implicit vision of imagined communication about the types of reality testing exercises that are manifest within the entire range of explicit communicative activities and practices we maintain with one another. The silence that registers within a given sequence of communication is supplemented by what each participant discovers by living through the encompassing silence that endures before and after the expressive use of words and gestures actually begin and end.

SILENCE AS A PROTECTIVE BARRIER

Unquestioned silence provides comfort and protection from unwanted or unwelcome talk or chatter. Within the production of discourse and the maintenance of dialogue there must be room for each participant to move fluidly from one state or mood to any other. As one starts to speak, silence is broken. As one ceases to speak, silence is restored. The movement toward silence is complete only when one lives or inhabits the auditory silence in the manner of an embrace, a source of complete auditory relief from the production of speech. When one feels inarticulate, silence is an alternative to the frustration of not being able to speak clearly. Silence may facilitate momentary escape from sights and sounds of the realities that surround.

Protective silence implies the presence of well defined but intangible boundary conditions that feel almost tangible. Respondents describe problematic silences in terms of what it is like to confront a solid object or impenetrable obstacle. Here the way one speaks seems to create, in a metaphoric sense, a linguistic wall or barrier. Here as well words and gestures are used to deny, delay, postpone, undermine, subvert, or prevent certain themes, textures, moods, or modes of sensibility from entering into the picture. It is talk that is in the service of ruling out talk. Most frequent are the sorts of references that allude to communicative conditions or symbolic enactments that feel like a wall made of wood, brick, or stone, closed doors, plastic bubbles, and an assortment of invisible barriers and imaginary impasses. In each instance someone takes refuge in the silence that accompanies the rhythm of words and gestures woven into a solid linguistic tapestry, choreographed, orchestrated, ritualized, stylized, with all sorts of presumptive sources of punctuation points and slanted interpersonal accents, both visible and invisible.

Such modes of sound and silence are often cast into the imagery of solid walls that remain stable and unbroken by even the most skillful use of the conventional tools of good communication. On one side is the observer who watches the coordinated movements—the interplay of word and gesture—of those who are located within confines of the immediate vicinity. On the other side are all the friends, family, lovers, and acquaintances who express a willingness to help one another open up and make use of the full range of each one's expressive capacities or resources. At the same time the full magnitude of expressed complexity, complication, difference, and diversity appears to stand in the way in the manner of just another fact of life to be accepted and confronted by each individual in his or her own way.

Not everyone needs so much protective silence. Some interactants find themselves located in social situations where they want to break through the protective silence of someone else. Individual A is a case in point. This person views himself as a very sensitive individual who has had a long-standing but inexplainable urge to become a priest. At the same time the young man is afraid to tell parents and friends of such a crucial decision for fear of getting a bruised ego. His loneliness soon becomes commonplace because there seems to be no one for him to turn to for guidance, direction, or inspiration. Finally, individual A decides to tell B, his own father, who is the coldest figure that A has ever spoken to. There appears to be an unspoken barrier between them that prevents B from understanding the lived circumstances of A. It is as though, from A's view, there is a solid stone wall between them. The condition has become so routinized that it seems to be a built-in or intrinsic constraint on mutual potentialities for engagement in a wide range of interdependent forms of interchange.

Protective silence implies a stance of distance, akin to the distance between strangers who have known one another their whole lives. Consider the many instances in which individual family members drift apart. Each member dwells on how different every member really is until a disturbing space separates each one. No one talks about anything that really matters. Despite an occasional guarded display of warmth and affection, everyone just goes through the motions. No one can relax and let personal urges flow. There seems to be an invisible wall between them. Some protective aspects of the encompassing silence arise from verbal gestures that make it seem as though each one is talking to a brick wall—it is virtually impossible to get through. At the same time no one in the family is willing to admit to being a source of stonewalling, for each one secretly thinks only the other members qualify. Hence, may sights and sounds are rendered null and void. One individual describes what it is like to try to break through the protective silence of other family members: one may plan to give a hundred percent, but nothing ever seems to change—the others seem encased in silence about the very things one wants to talk about in the most urgent way. In such a situation one could talk until blue in the face, trying five or six different ways, only to discover that nothing works. During each encounter an invisible barrier is assembled steadfastly by those who refuse to say a word. At times, at the outside limits, language may be employed to create a convincing illusion that each interactant resides in a clear, plastic bubble.

Finally, in the imagery of opening and closing doors, the movement into silence is defined in terms of one closing down or closing off the source of sight and sound, deflecting what the immediate presence of others makes manifest, deflecting attention elsewhere and reorienting one's frame of reference away from rather than toward those who wish to speak. One may even seek protection or relief from the levity of human sound, even the gaiety and revelry that fills a huge living room at graduation time. Everyone is gathered to celebrate the successful completion of one member's course of higher education. In the midst of all the laugher and applause, the one so honored senses privately in a powerful but unspoken way that a door has just been closed to an important chapter in his life. In the agonizing loneliness of a house filled with loved ones, it is as though someone else was participating in the festivities while the one who is the center of attention was really watching from afar.

WAITING IN SILENCE

Silence creates presumption. First there is the all-important matter of what registers *only* when one is silent in order to afford someone else the opportunity to speak. The decision not to talk alters the mix of active sensory modalities: one now sees, hears, touches, and moves in relation to what one does not say. This in turn implies a certain type of assumptive ground, namely the presumption that others cannot rely on the sound of the voice of the person in question as a source of either conveyed or elicited meaning. What registers in A's silence introduces, therefore, unknown, indeterminate, and uncertain elements in what others may attend to and recognize or not.

The very decision to remain silent is a fully observable condition. Individuals (A↔B) look directly at one another and both can plainly see that A talks mostly when B is silent. The silence of A may be problematic for B insofar as B lacks direct access to what A's silence brings to light within the lived circumstance of A but not in a form that is shared directly with B. It obviously matters whether one expresses oneself through verbal and non-verbal sense modalities simultaneously and concurrently or exclusively, one or the other. The distinct communicative significance of silence registers in the patterning and sequencing of speech acts. At issue is the appropriation and distribution of scarce communicative resources.

The way one chooses or is constrained to remain silent acquires additional stylized meaning as a complement to the way someone else presumes the right to talk or defer the opportunity. Individuals A and B *share* B's silence to be sure, but not from the exact same angle, vantage point, slant, stance, or skew. The inward-outward orientation of A's talk registers in the outward-inward orientation of B's unspoken replies. Such silence defers talk as a source of immediate gratification, pleasure, or delight. Whatever one gains or loses by talking shifts to whatever one gains or loses by leaving certain things unsaid. Moreover, what one talks about is an unfolding reflection of implicature—what one does not discuss in any explicit form. Hence, there is the *form* of silence infiltrated with the content or substance of what one does not say. In this important sense silence may be problematic for the one who produces or observes what the production of a given episode of talk accomplishes as well as what it does not.

One who waits in silence may use the silence as a means to recite privately what the individual in question really wants or needs to say to someone else in a given public setting. The other party, the one who speaks, may or may not be aware or have a clue whether any other observer or participant is currently engaged in silent acts of introspection assembled in the manner of a dress rehearsal of the shape of things to come. The anticipatory or expectational implications of silence (before talk) are potentially problematic insofar as the silence of one conceals in direct measure what someone else's speech reveals or fails to bring to the surface.

The one who waits in silence may produce private discourse that moves the other way, that is, backward, reflexively to imaginary or foregone possibilities: what one could have said but didn't think to say quickly enough. This urge unfolds in the manner of a personal lament, as in "if only I had my wits about me, I would have said." In waiting for the opportunity to speak, there may also register a secondary source of linguistic regret, what one was capable of but unwilling to say, what one really wanted to say or should or ought to have said. Here what actually transpires within a given succession of speech acts, whether framed in the context of present, past, or future tense, is richly multilayered and textured with silent modes of personal reflection and private discourse about the opportunities and limitations that unfold before one's very eyes.

Silence is a valuable personal resource. It allows any language user to conceal or hide given facets or segments of private discourse within the wider context of what transpires. What one hides in the silence is as open as the nature of the type of world one inhabits. Anything that registers within the totality of one's lived circumstances is fair game. Private discourse in response to language use in public settings may defer or deflect the expression of virtually any affectionate or controlling urge. It may be used to express one's implicit love or contempt, indifference or eagerness, for greater personal involvement. In the case of shyness one lives mostly wishing to be in a better position to be more verbal more of the time. Conversely, the one who fills the air with words may give off clues that signal an inability to tolerate one's own silence for any appreciable amount of time. Those who insist on the right to talk all the time presuppose or require the presence of those who will sit still and consistently say nothing at all. Here the sound and the silence fills the room in equal measure.

Silent mental dress rehearsals may indicate effort to wait for the right time and the right place to bear witness to some as yet unspoken aspects of one's lived circumstances. One individual equates waiting in silence with impatience over situations in which one does not truly grasp what is taking place in the immediate situation and lacks intent to reveal what one is really feeling or sensing at the moment in question.

One may wait in silence for something to happen that never does. In this sense the silence is without end. This is the case where two individuals engage in sexual intercourse and then act as if what happened between them really did not happen at all. Soon thereafter, the lovers go their own separate ways. In the subsequent protracted silence the two realize that they were never able to reconcile personal differences and at any moment either one could leave this world without ever having had the chance to *really* talk with one another. Here one waits in silence for the fulfillment of an array of communicative potentials never realized in any manifest form.

THE CODE OF SILENCE

At some point the urge, desire, need, or presumed right to be silent comingles with the obligation to be silent about x, y, or z. In this sense the margin of room to remain silent is a strategic indication of exactly where the expressive aspirations of self run up against the magnitude of felt obligations to others. Issues of willingness and necessity enter into the equation, particularly when the demand characteristics of interaction require careful modulation of the urge to speak up against the complementary need to shut down and say nothing more about a given matter of concern. The words and gestures one employs acquire meaning in relation to the stockpile of words and gestures that could be activated but are not out of some greater sense of obligation or loyalty. In contrast, rumor mills encourage gossip behind someone else's back. Likewise, ingratiation strategies generate discrepancies between what others will tell you to your face and what they will only say about you to others when you are not around. Here, tolerance of silence is relative to one's intolerance of certain modalities of talk and implicates, therefore, both the urge to save face and the possibility to impugn it.

Silent loyalty may be assumed or imposed. The situation occurs when respondents assume the need to remain silent as a matter of personal loyalty or conviction, even at considerable risk or cost, are numerous and varied. What distresses individual A about B is something A can't say directly to B but can share with C, D, or E (who also all know B). Here the governing personal logic is that it would hurt B to hear A's discomfort over B's actions. It may take repeated mental dress rehearsals for A to know how to bring up such sensitive and delicate matters.

Individuals A and B are members of the same sex who become intimate and have an affair. During the first year everything is wonderful, and each partner wants to share the joy and happiness with others, but each one also knows they just cannot afford to say a word. Thereafter A and B have to be extremely careful of everything they say or do together. At night they write love letters to one another in a semisecret code that requires heavy editing when read aloud to others. Individuals A and B find themselves constantly on guard, always overexplaining various courses of action, sneaking around, and getting jumpy at every little noise. Their code of strategic silence soon gives rise to much anxiety, which does not subside until A and B slowly let others in on such an intimate secret.

Collective silence is often an unwelcome burden over troublesome issues ranging from the decision to get an abortion, effort to avoid detection of a civil infraction, violation, or crime, and unmentionable forms of betrayal and disloyalty between what not even the closest friends may dare to say. Also numerous are family secrets designed to spare the outside world of any disquieting sign of deviation from the behavior of perfectly normal and well-adjusted families among whom the mere mention of anything that might be wrong is taken as a sign of disloyalty on fundamental matters that call into question the illusion of perfect domestic harmony and integration. Silence here covers a multitude of petty sins and minor infractions along with corresponding feelings of shame, guilt, or remorse over the inability of various members to live with the way things are rather than insist on the way they should be—in the manner of an unspoken communal fraud. Here the code of silence must do double duty.

Silence oaths of loyalty may also be extracted or imposed by implication, injunction, mandate, or command. The imposition of silence is taken as strained or coerced silence under pressure, tension, duress, or threat of further sanction or withdrawal of support of some vital resource. The children of alcoholic parents, in particular, are acutely sensitive to the full magnitude of the family secrets that must be protected at all cost. Such children quickly learn that even a hint of reference to the nameless problem is strictly taboo. In the extreme such coercive silence may lead to a deeper form of silence that is a source of much psychological entrapment to the controlling authority or voice of someone else.

#78 A's view: When I was in elementary school my father had a very bad drinking problem. I would wait up every night for him to stumble through the door so I could put him to bed before mom and dad would get into a fight. I spent many days in school wondering what would happen when I got home and where I should hide the knives tonight. I felt I couldn't express my fear, anger, hate, and confusion to anyone. This was mainly because my sister and I were told we couldn't say a word. My family of four became very good actors and should have won an Emmy. Instead we won ulcers and nightmares. In fourth grade I started attending Alateen where I finally realized I wasn't alone. There were millions of people out there living with the exact same illness. I learned that I didn't cause it and I sure as hell couldn't cure it. Since then, I have always had this support group, and today Alanon, that have given me a place to express anything. And there I am completely free.

FEELING TRAPPED INSIDE THE SILENCE

Sometimes silence can be oppressive. One respondent likens silent entrapment to problems that, once mentioned, open up a Pandora's box effect that can't be easily stopped. One's obligation to oneself is to stop whatever one is feeling from actually escaping. Yet somehow the unsettled silence always lingers while the problem is usually kept at bay. The greater the magnitude of the problem, the more it must not become an explicit point of reference, lest one's lived circumstance hurt or injure another person. Here one's troubled silences must effectively encapsulate what is at issue so that it is sure not to rub off on anyone else. Another respondent feels trapped by understanding two sides of a dilemma while not being in a position to express the issue directly to two other equally valued individuals who happen to be on opposite sides of it. Implicit here is a private sense of what happens when one begins to see other people in a different light than what they could ever envision or imagine. This condition may unfold even when one's affection and love for the others must be lived out mostly in total silence.

Also relevant are a long series of silent dislocations in human relations. There are times when the only person in a shared situation is asked "What is wrong with you?" One may see the others interact effortlessly and wonder why one never seems to be in a position to join in. It may also happen when all one really wants to say is how upsetting, nervous, and depressed one is while suffering through the disaster of a lifetime when everyone else just keeps on insisting or saying "It will be OK" and "Everything is going to work out just fine." Something similar occurs when one individual keeps thinking that it will never be possible to see one's best friend or ever even talk again. The silent pressure can be intense.

Silent entrapment may occur in the lived circumstance of the one who can least afford to be encased within the domain of the inarticulate, nondiscriminate, and unspoken. One respondent refers to a state of "feeling so broken" and in need of support from the one person who insists on launching into a condemning speech that leaves the needy person with nothing to say in return. Another source refers to shared situations in which one cannot say anything about what is going on and also cannot get out—a paradoxical injunction of the first magnitude. Still another is gripped in a state of anxiety and apprehension from initially feeling sure of how the person in question feels but when it comes time to speak discovers no clue as to how to say it before dissolving back into a state of not being so sure after all. Such circumstances are reinforced when given interactants stop talking because no one listens anyway. Silence at least provides some protection from shared situations in which everything comes out wrong and creates an even bigger problem.

For some interactants silent entrapment becomes a self-fulfilling prophecy. One respondent offers the following scenario: (1) one says nothing about a serious personal problem because of not knowing how to begin; (2) emotions get mixed up until one is not able to make sense of what is going on oneself amidst so much nonsense; (3) therefore one becomes gripped by fear that one will have problems interacting with others out of fear of being unable to express troubles in the right way; (4) because one now is transfixed by this deep personal fear, the majority of time it happens; (5) it is as if the fear becomes reality in the manner of a self-fulfilling prophecy and (6) ergo: the only alternative is to remain quiet and say nothing at all.

Some are tempted to give up and give in to the pressure of the encompassing silence that one seems unable or unwilling to break through. In the protracted sound, sight, and silence of a lover's quarrel, each one feels confused and hurt and cannot explain why. If one tries to convey all the nonsense, all that gets conveyed is confusion and misinterpretation over a heavy burden that must be born alone in sadness and private reflection over the fact that the other does not understand and can do nothing to improve the situation. Each party is left to lament in silence and feel the pain of looking into other's eyes and sense it seems easier not to talk rather than let things drag out.

Entrapment implies for some a refrain from saying anything because of the implicit sense that (1) there is nothing to say and (2) it has all been said before. Who can guide where one does not want to be guided? The end seems as unclear as the means. All that is left is to take what one has and go run wildly into the night. Sometimes the time to keep one's mouth shut is when there is nothing more anyone can say or do. One source attests to the fact of being subjected on many occasions to hard feelings and curt, hurtful statements and (1) not feeling free to respond or retort as one would like or (2) responding but being so misunderstood and thereby ending up causing the entire situation to be at risk. In one instance silent lament turns into profound guilt over losing the opportunity of a lifetime by not expressing something that might have saved a life, something that prompts the urge to turn the clock backward to the point where what was left unsaid could well make the difference between life and death to someone else.

ENFORCED SILENCE

#79 A's view: A and B interact in an educational setting where A has most of the (institutional) power and B has little of it. In a timed testing situation, B suddenly feels a strong need to go to the bathroom and asks A (teacher) for permission to leave. B does not allow A to leave the room, and A wets her pants in front of everyone. Individual A feels humiliation, embarrassment, and anger as everyone watches in silence. The child never mentions what happened to anyone and to this day, more than a decade later, she still has not fully recovered psychologically from what transpired on that terrible day.

#80 A's view: In many instances I feel I cannot say anything to my sister that I know she will disagree with. She is genetically depressed, sometimes mentally also. This means that anything said that is even slightly offensive to her will cause much anger, which sets off negative feelings that can set off a depressive reaction that in turn may set off a suicide attempt. I know I can't say things to upset her because I'm afraid she will become suicidal. Conflict arises many times because she drinks or takes drugs to "alleviate" her own depression. I don't like the way she depends on drugs but feel I can't talk to her or anyone else about this for fear of upsetting anything, any neutral balance, or any person who is involved.

Enforced silence may neutralize, deny, devalue, subvert, repress, undermine, thwart, or destroy the latitude of expressive freedom of someone else. Expressed sources of enablement are translated into unspoken injunctions and implicit constraints. The term "enforced" conveys a generalized spirit of impatience, calculation, and manipulation, an imbalance and oppression of someone else's urge to make manifest, speak out, or put things into words. At one end of the spectrum is the possibility of maintaining a state of silent terror or overwhelming fear of sanction, vengeance, disownership, or reprisal. In the middle domain resides a spirit of duplicity and mean-spiritedness, coercion and repression, by any ordinary means. At the ordinary end of the spectrum is unwelcomed exposure to a nagging spirit of criticism and negative evalution. Those who dominate soon discover that expressive freedom does not have to be actively destroyed, for virtually any means of personal abuse or neglect will do.

APPEASEMENT: SHARING THE SILENCE

In the production of discourse and dialogue silence emerges as possibility and necessity. The magnitude of opportunity to remain silent cannot be isolated from the margin of necessity. As such, discursive silence may serve as communicative resource or as liability. Insofar as the boundaries of silence of one source facilitate or promote a greater range of expressive and interpretive freedom on the part of any other, the tension between the unspoken and the spoken is apt to dissolve. Conversely, as the discursive silence (of one) makes it incrementally more difficult for others to express themselves in a free and spontaneous manner, the strain between the unspoken and the spoken is reintroduced. So unlike the psychoanalytic vision of constant tension and strife between conscious and unconscious urges in the reproduction of human texts, the terms of human interchange are envisioned here as open and fluid rather than fixed or static. After all, silence can become a problem in face-to-face interaction at any moment, then shift into a domain of problematic concerns for an unspecified span, before returning, in the manner of a restoration, to mainly nonproblematic conditions and terms.

In acts of appeasement, the sequences of silence are tolerated and sustained within the larger terms of unfolding dialogue. Individuals adapt styles of personal presentation that make it more or less difficult to facilitate the transition from spoken acts to unspoken urges. Consequently, appeasement requires a somewhat fluid and flexible stance of interaction, a process analogous to breathing deeply in and out but more akin to the mutually sustained urge to go *with* rather than *against* the flow of what emerges in expressed form. Maximum expressive freedom is accompanied by minimum interpretive resistance.

The significance of appeasement is largely compensatory. It registers in the magnitude of room to move in or out of the encompassing silence. Elements of deference enter into the construction of virtually any ritual, ceremony, or exchange relation. Demeanor fosters a sense of propriety through tone of voice, manner of dress, facial expression, plus patterns of eye contact, touch, and physical movement. What emerges is a distinctive sense of unspoken obligations and reciprocated contingencies in the overlap between deference and demeanor. Here each one is limited in the deference to be claimed by the demeanor each one is capable of and willing to display (Collins, 1975, pp. 162–163). Participant and observer must work together to uphold an idealized conception of what is possible. Matters of personal efficacy, status, prestige, credibility, legitimacy, and power are not an a priori given, but rather something to be reconstructed and renegotiated each time various individuals come into the immediate presence of one another. Thus, the very exchange of words and gestures presupposes an incremental buildup of an archriding worldview that is individually constituted but collaboratively constructed and therefore open to further question.

SILENCE AS SANCTUARY

This condition is rare and precious. Specific mention by respondents are few and far between. Nonetheless, there is a transcendent sphere of silence in which the ideal culminates in the real and whatever is subsequently brought to light. For once there is no tension between individual intent and unforeseen consequence. Through shared struggle to integrate transparent forms of discourse with penetrating modes of dialogue, the ordinary is transformed in and by the extraordinary. In any particular instance in which the respective sources are revealed as living subject matter, both individual aspirations and communal obligations come together, fuse, congeal, and coalesce in a spirit of restoration and renewal. Thereby the participants may rediscover themselves to be situated at the very center, the primordial ground, of whatever is revealed or concealed from distinct human view.

In the fusion of personal horizons whatever gets expressed is manifest as fully present. Here nothing is left out or undone. Life is shown once again to be surrounded by grace because affordable communicative resources are shown to be necessary and sufficient rather than unevenly distributed, stratified, or otherwise in scarce supply. Under optimum conditions the participants are in a position to maintain a level of interchange that permits each one to feel safe and secure. This significant communicative achievement reaches a point of culmination where individual light can become a source of common enlightenment. What is felt, thought, said, and done reinforces the presumption that this *is* the best of all possible worlds. Nothing that is expressed is found wanting—no sense of unfulfillment, deprivation, or deficit. For once again all is right with a world revealed in utterly transparent and translucent terms. Here the respective participants are free from the usual clatter, noise, and din, the friction, and strain, just long enough to make each one yearn for things to be exactly as they are. The human world is once again discoverd to be a sanctuary, our eternal home, the source of wonder and awe. Consider the following as a case in point.

#81 A's view: It happens when an individual works and lives in the Wisconsin Dells during the summer. It is hard to explain the freedom and joy and the delight of working in such a beautiful place. But it wasn't actually the job I loved it was all the people. We all found a human community for each one of us. There's no other place that can create such a strong sense of living in a human community. None of my friends, except the ones I made there, have ever had the privilege of living in such a loving and joyful community twenty-four hours a day, seven days a week, and three months at a time—wow! This is what has made it hard to define, describe, or explain to others. No one understands what an incredible experience I've had by spending three straight summers in the Dells. The kind of friends I have and the grand memories are simply wonderful. It's like a three month wild Spring break where you work your ass off, have a great time, and make a lot of money.

WONDER AND AWE

#82 A's view: A few years ago, my family and I were at our cottage for the weekend, one late afternoon we decided to go for a boat ride. I took my favorite spot on the seat at the very front of the boat. We were going really fast and the wind was cold and forceful against my face and body. The sky ahead of me was gray with large billowy clouds, the water was light green and a little choppy with little white caps. But when I turned around, there was a distinct, definite change; The clouds suddenly ended and the sky was bright blue and cloudless. The water behind me was blue-green and calm. The scenery is easy to describe—but the feelings I experienced were incredible. I was silent for the entire ride. I was so affected when I looked straight ahead; the wind was blowing my hair wildly, the feeling was one of power, danger, evil, an almost sexual urging. But, when I looked behind me, all danger was gone and I was reminded of childhood, games, summer, and lazy days and barbecues. It was like light against dark, evil against good. It was hard to express because the rest of my family was just enjoying our usual boat ride and I was feeling something—I don't know what—something profound; strong feelings were affecting me. I really can't express it, because I am not even sure what I was feeling at the time; it was like a wave of emotion—mixed emotions—fear and happiness, death and life. It was exhilarating to have my own private experience and yet it was lonely to know that no one else was aware or could know.

#83 A's view: It happens when one thinks of all the reasoning behind one's existence here on earth and becomes suddenly speechless. It is as if the way one grasps things is inexpressible to any other. Sometimes the world may be just a figment of one's imagination. Suppose that one is the only person really living and everyone one comes into contact with and everything one sees or thinks about is all really there because it's all there to affect oneself. Perhaps others don't think they experience the same awe as one does and one doesn't think that one experiences what they feel either.

#84 A's view: A is a member of a football team about to play a game with Marshfield. A becomes so pumped up for this game but is not sure why. During the game he makes two interceptions and runs one back for a touchdown. After the game A has this feeling of euphoria and excitement that could not be explained to anyone unless they were there. And who knows if they would have felt the same way? A feels that there are many experiences that people encounter that give them feelings that can only be understood by someone who goes through the same set of circumstances. You can express your feelings in words, but they never seem to describe the complete feelings.

#85 A's view: It happens at a time of complete euphoria. The euphoria was one of contentment and achievement of which A knew A would not witness again. A was not alone in this excitement as the event affected hundreds of others. At the time, it affected A each day for the following week. It wasn't the happiest day of A's life but possibly the one with the most joy, as it was somewhat sudden. Also a feeling of togetherness seemed to envelop the witnesses. Looking back, it is still tough to put exactly into the words what the feelings were. Even with the passing of time the images remain clear, as does the inner feeling of euphoria.

#86 A's view: There have been times when I have just been resting in the yard under the stars pondering the meaning of "Life." It is very special to ponder the world and its awesomeness and to thank God for all He has done for me but to adequately have explained "special" would be hard. The sheer magnitude of the sky looking down on me and the freshness of the air and how these made me feel would be hard to put into words. I have *really* enjoyed these "times" in my life. They have helped me to be slightly more humble in my life as well as helped me put things into proper perspective. I feel these "times" have helped me grow more than anyone will ever know. You just have to have been there or experienced it for yourself. Words just can't explain. Many times and through many circumstances in my life I have stirred deep emotions within myself. I feel I could explain very superficially these times to someone but to capture fully the depth of the experience would be completely beyond the capabilities of the mere spoken word.

#87 A's view: In the summer of 1986, I went to Oshkosh for the EAA Fly In. This particular year the Concorde was scheduled to fly over a couple of times and then land for a few days. We waited for a long time squinting in the bright sunlight to catch a glimpse of this amazing jet. Upon the approach it seemed to be like a very large bird, even the shape suggested this. I was not at all prepared for the "fly by." This aircraft came slowly closer to the grandstand area, seemed rather quiet, but as it approached it became a monster. It flew by, taking the breath out of me and it brought tears to my eyes. It was so amazing, even talking about it can't give an accurate impression. It was completely engrossing and somehow very emotional. The power and speed seemed to sap my energy and power. People around me reacted in a similar way, awestruck and speechless.

#88 A's view: It happens as a feeling that A has of emotions that can't be explained to anyone else. It's a feeling of happiness just to be alive. A will get this feeling sometimes when just sitting outside alone. A looks around at all the things that God has made and it just gives A this happy feeling inside. On a normal busy day A doesn't even notice the beautiful things all around. So when A does sit down and enjoy it, A gets a happy feeling within. It's just a warm feeling that A can't explain to anyone.

#89 A's view: I felt so deliciously unique. No one on earth I swore was feeling the euphoria I was. I had even convinced myself that never again would I ever have such a physical and mental intensity that brought such a strong emotion to my being. That memory would last for a long time to come. What was so special for these five short minutes was that the person closest to me, physically and emotionally, wanted so badly for me to disclose my feelings. But the physical feeling could not be explained as it was so fresh and new.

Entries 82 to 89 are assertive, optimistic, expansive, elaborative, miraculous, transcendent, timeless, and universal in scale and scope. At the center is the question of one's position and place among others in the larger scheme of things—a cosmology in which the force of words and gestures penetrate but do not exhaust the limits of what transpires in the human world. The opportunity for exchange and communication renews open-ended possibilities to set each member free as an alternative source of living subject matter.

An inclusive theme of spiritual silence invokes renewed faith in human possibilities to overcome whatever would resist or hold one source or another back. Particulars and specifics are placed in proper perspective. The one-among-many problem is recast, no longer merely assumed or taken for granted, but rather reframed or recast in the manner of an unfolding discovery and evolutionary quest. The human world, once again, is transformed, spontaneous, fresh and new. The risk of slippage and miscommunication is taken in stride, and free speech and interpretive response flourish and abound.

REFERENCES

Bateson, G. (1972). *Steps to an ecology of mind*. New York: Ballantine Books.

Brummett, B. (1980). Towards a theory of silence as a political strategy. *Quarterly Journal of Speech, 66*, 289–303.

Collins, R. (1975). *Conflict sociology*. New York: Academic Press.

Ehrenhaus, P. (1988). Silence and symbolic expression. *Communication Monographs, 55*, 42–57.

Ihde, D. (1976). *Listening and voice: A phenomenology of sound.* Athens: Ohio University Press.

Jawarski, A. (1993). *The power of silence.* Newbury Park: Sage.

Merleau-Ponty, M. (1973). *The prose of the world.* Evanston: Northwestern University Press.

Scott, R. L. (1972). Rhetoric and silence. *Western Speech, 36,* 146–158.

6

Miscommunication

C. David Mortensen with Morton S. Perlmutter

The study of face-to-face interaction remains elusive and fascinating precisely because so many things occur all at once virtually all the time. Each
source participates in the definition and direction of the shared situation,
and yet the totality of what is shared goes well beyond the grasp of any
given member. In symbolized interaction, no one is in an ideal, optimum,
or ultimately privileged position to know what takes place for the very
same reasons that there are no independent or infallible standards for
determining who is the most attractive, mature, sexy, sane, or wise member
of any given speech community. In matters of what separates this from that,
more from less, or better from worse, every participant has an unspecified
margin of opportunity to make a difference in what transpires and yet at
all points along the way each source also maintains a distinctive slant,
angle, and view of the larger scheme of things. In other words, every
participant expresses more than what any other can grasp or comprehend
about a succession of expressive acts construed from multiple vantage
points. In effect, each individual provides an alternative method of account-
ing for what takes place collectively. Hence, no one individual grasps all
there is to grasp because the very definition and direction of what transpires
is simply the individual definitions added up in a constructive and accumulative rather than a strictly reductive manner. Complex activities, as a
rule, do not lend themselves to simplistic modes of definition, classification,
or explanation.

During episodes of mundane conversation, virtually anything and
everything that happens counts one way or another, but that does not mean
everything counts equally. For what source A, B, and C take to be the case
about their respective encounters and involvements is the *real* definition of

what unfolds between them. Consequently, each one can be expected to take shared matters into account without ever being able to grasp or understand the multiple calculations and shifting equations produced by everyone else. It is a matter of simple intellectual honesty, then, to recognize that A, B, and C, as separate and autonomous entities, maintain full access to their own lived circumstance but only incomplete, partial, segmented, and often interrupted, distorted, or severely distanced access to the lived circumstances of one another. This logic seems to apply no matter what any one source does or does not feel, think, say, or do.

For these reasons, participation in the process gives rise to a sense of what remains tentative, provisional, uncertain, indeterminate, or otherwise unknown about the subsequent turn of human events. What each individual strives to accomplish is actualized through anticipatory and responsive phases of coordinated action. This in turn suggests that what a particular individual achieves is an open-ended expression of what the source in question is capable and willing to be and do in the eyes of others. It follows that whenever individuals interact directly with one another, afforded communicative resources register in a succession of activities permeated with implicit urges, desires, needs, wants, intentions, and alternative modes of interpretation for multiple goal-directed yearnings and strivings.

Communication, after all, is what two or more individuals feel, think, say, and do (together and alone) without any one member being in a privileged position to figure out what makes it possible and necessary for collective things to work out just the way they do. At the center of human action is an unfolding, incomplete, and unfinished communal struggle over selective and strategic aspects of discourse and dialogue. Participation in the process may or may not reveal the source of two major ecological secrets, namely, what makes individual discourse possible in the first place (potentialities) and what mutual dialogue makes possible subsequently (unforeseen consequences). It turns out that the what may reveal little or much about the why, when, or how of what transpires but, of necessity, only in partially illuminated light.

So what counts as the communicative value of face-to-face interaction turns out to be at least as complex as the magnitude of changes set into motion. The participants may know full well in point of fact that they *do* make a real and decisive difference in the personal conduct of one another without any one source ever being able to pinpoint exactly what the consequences may happen to be. Any direct personal encounter is apt to produce a rich mix of implicit urges, desires, intentions, expressions, coordinated lines of action, structures, functions, effects, and consequences. Distinctive features add up in a holistic and synthetic manner that does not reduce itself to simple verdicts over whether message sent equals message received. In effect, B's response is amplified in response to A's response.

What matters most is how vital and fully animated systems of human communication simultaneously and sequentially conceal what transpires. In an ever-changing litany of sign-making activities that differ in degree of clarity ranging anywhere from the transparent to the opaque, signs of disclosure and concealment are located on all sides. Such a condition rules out the possibility of self-evident modes of translation and interpretation. In any reference to the linguistic construction of reality, it is necessary to incorporate elements of the misconstruction. So the main task here is to locate a range of sensibilities in which an acute sense of miscommunication or problematic conversation occurs within some larger sphere, scope, or domain of what is presumed to qualify as communicative.

WHAT DEFIES DESCRIPTION

The first exemplar or prototype is a set of instances in shared situations (A↔B) where A's view of (A↔B) remains somewhat inexplicable to A, based on A's own frame of reference. In effect, individual A manufactures, produces, or responds to the very conditions that elude A's effort to make sense of some vital matter to someone else. What arises is some critical threshold of linguistic complexity where the central consideration is the *plurality* of what one feels, thinks, and attempts to say. Such conditions are most acute when dealing with unusual, confusing, or new feelings and sensations that prove difficult to convey to anyone else on the strength of words and gestures alone.

What defies description are complex, multifaceted, and innovative aspects of sensory activation a given source has never dealt with before. At the moment the source in question may not comprehend or understand fully his or her immediate circumstances and thus find it extremely difficult to describe what is being felt in a concise or clear manner. At such moments words leave one feeling incomplete. Someone claims to be "happy." What does it mean to be "happy" anyway? What is "sorrow"? What is "pain"? Each word can be broken down in varying degrees of salience, amplitude, or intensity. But who is to know just *how* happy, scared, or sad someone else happens to be at any given moment? It can be quite trying just to make the effort required to articulate what one is experiencing (at the moment) to someone else. Others *claim* to be able to understand. Hence, you may feel better after getting complex feelings off your chest and still wonder whether the others really understand what you are trying to say and never be able to decide one way or another.

There may be times when there seem to be no words in one's vocabulary to express *exactly* what is being felt at the time. Sensations jumble into a knot. One can't convey the jumble until complex elements are worked through and straightened out in one's own mind; and only then might it be possible to identify, dissect, pull apart, put together, and finally identify distinct features of uncertain conditions and circumstances one shares with others. Such moments resemble what it would be like to look into a dark room and see only the outline of an unknown object and later tell a friend what it was you saw. The friend will not go away with a clear idea of what you saw because you do not know yourself what you saw.

Individual A sees herself as a very sensitive person. Across many different types of social situations, individual A tends to internalize everything that happens, and this means that everything happens *to* A. This means that whatever goes right goes right for A and whatever goes wrong goes wrong for A. Individual A's style is to project what A feels is safe. This means that A will not expand on any personal feelings but rather holds back because A questions the validity of those feelings, whether or not others think they are right or wrong, good or bad. Other respondents describe the struggle required to face up to the task of opening up and sharing inner feelings. Having to face complex emotions is sometimes too difficult for some individuals to do. The most compelling cases in point occur at the far ends of the sensory spectrum: the ineffable textures of pain and the exhilaration associated with hearing fine music.

At age thirteen individual A is diagnosed as epileptic. It is difficult to explain the intensity of the pain of a seizure to those who have never experienced the condition themselves. Whenever A has a seizure—in the past seven years there have been plenty—she has to tell doctors what has happened physically and mentally so that they can figure out what type of seizure it was. General symptoms include tingling sensations, different types of headaches, and a variety of dizzy spells. When A must describe the symptoms in minute detail for the doctors, she must choose her words very carefully. The most painful descriptions are saved for the doctors because at least they know something about the subject. A's parents, who have always taken care of her and made her feel understood when no one else would understand, are helpless and clueless. They see what they see when A has a seizure, but she finds it hard to even try to explain what her *brain* feels like. This goes for friends as well. They feel helpless, and she feels frustrated. One day A was sitting in a high school biology class and suddenly lost control of the ability to speak or understand speech. She struggled to maintain visual focus, but everything was blurry. It was so embarrassing. The small seizure would have been over within a minute, and no attention needed to be drawn to her. Yet A couldn't form words and had absolutely no vocabulary bank. Another instance involved a walk around the hallways. She was walking back to class and once again lost control of language. This time she lost control of depth perception as well. As individual A passed people in the hallway, she tried to call out for help, but it did no good. Her tongue could not form the words. Soon A got lost in her own school. She had no sense of direction. The episode ended two or three minutes later. It has lead to a very insecure feeling that takes over every so often. Trying to deal with it (if A is conscious) is as difficult as trying to explain the feelings to others. Sense is at times more easily felt than described.

Part of the pain associated with having one's tonsils taken out is the sheer inability to talk. Even painkillers may not compensate for the sudden inability to describe what is wrong to others. During acute periods of personal suffering one may just need someone else to understand the nature of the discomfort, but even that can become virtually impossible. Because of lupus, person A often finds herself confronting many problems that are very difficult, if not impossible, to share with other people. When she falls out of remission, she knows exactly what is happening. She can tell because of slight bodily changes, but they are often not measurable changes, so doctors will not catch them right away. Since the doctors don't catch them, it is very easy for her to deny them. Moreover, A doesn't talk about them to anyone because she is scared and doesn't know what to say. Lupus also makes A feel very different when it restricts her from doing ordinary things. The summer is the worst. Staying out in the sun is a major pain (skin growing with whiteness), and she must miss out on a lot of fun things—going to the beach, swimming, softball, and so on. Although this can all be worked out, it is still a real psychological downer. Person A is not in a position to do these things so it is easier to act tough rather than to open up about something like this. Basically, A does not know how to explain such a baffling condition.

Less intense maladies apply as well. Since the age of six A has gotten these "aches" in the legs occasionally. A doesn't know what it is. She calls it a "legache," but God knows A's never been able to explain to anyone else what it is like and why she still gets them. Her mom has always pretended to understand so that she wouldn't have to hear A try to explain it. "Oh, poor Sue has a legache—the Ben-Gay is in the closet." But what is worse is to be on the receiving end and not be able to understand what someone else is feeling.

In the following two entries, expressive urges remain elusive, diffuse, and somewhat inaccessible in the interplay of discourse and dialogue between one interactant and another.

#90 A's view: The circumstances could be described as a transitory period in my life. Neither words nor gestures could effectively and precisely convey such ambivalent and ambiguous emotional conditions. Moreover, I was unable to understand what I sought to express which in turn helped to create even more of a sense of helplessness. I chose to look for the answers to my confusion inwardly, and by myself. At the same time I became set on the fact that nobody could understand me so obviously nobody else could provide me with the particular answers I sought. Second, it was the sense that nobody could understand my emotions unless they had experienced the exact set of circumstances and this intensified my belief that I could not express the abrupt and dramatic changes in my emotional well-being before others. More importantly, even if others did experience similar circumstances, their understanding was impossible, in relation to my frame of reference, because they didn't understand the internal complexities which affected the make-up of these emotions. Ultimately, my fear of being at the mercy of such circumstances rather than in control of my own fate rendered me at a loss for words. This feeling of being 'out of control' was foreign to my previous experiences in life. I am sure this made it all the more difficult to express what I was feeling at the time. Although I did understand one thing—my crazy emotions were a direct result of new and unexpected events.

#91 A's view: Several factors contribute to my inability to express myself. Most often I simply feel that I am *unable* because something is missing. It's not as simple as saying "I'm excited" or "I'm bored." Many times something will happen and I'll feel something but I don't know what. I can't identify what I'm feeling. I can't put a label on it. My stomach may feel knotted up or I may feel heady, but am I nervous, scared, excited, or in anticipation of something? Maybe a little bit of each one? I don't know. I could describe the symptoms perhaps of the actual physical feeling I'm experiencing. But even that can be hard. And the question still remains, "What does it mean?" No word feels right or satisfying in trying to express what I am feeling. Maybe part of the problem is a lack of solid, concrete, and unambiguous terms. That is, where the search for sensible labeling and naming procedures gets more difficult and I resort to my "I don't know *what* I'm feeling. But I do know I'm feeling *something!*"

The description of pain is problematic in a multiple sense. First is the singularity of a burden that remains inexplicable. The ultimate source of personal suffering may not be subject to strict standards of identification. Acute distress often seems to come out of nowhere and disappear into nothingness. Second is the effort to locate the cause, rhyme, or reason as a means to discover the cure. Respondents frequently report the inability to know how to classify or label the nameless entity that then becomes an additional, second-order source of distress. Conversely, just knowing what it is or what to call it may provide some measure of existential relief. Third is the aftermath of the mediation of self-reflection: "What did I do to deserve this?" or "Why me and not someone else?" Fourth is the discovery of the magnitude of distance, distinction, or difference between the direct experience of pain and the degree to which others are in a position to grasp indirectly what one is experiencing firsthand. In the final analysis, it may be virtually impossible to separate the impact of the pain per se from the manner in which it is conceptualized and expressed, through diverse processes of mediation, to observers or from bystanders.

At the opposite end of the sensory spectrum are varied appeals to the splendor of hearing fine music in one's own ears. What registers mainly here is an overpowering sense of how good it feels, particularly if you have a deep love for fine music. Consider this description of a spectacular local custom.

#92 A's view: It is practically impossible to explain the feeling I get at a drum and bugle corps show. The feeling is even more intense when the corp I am 'rooting' for wins the championship. Drum corps do not have any woodwind instruments. They only have brass horns, percussion, and color guards (flags and rifles). The sound is very different from that of a marching band. It is so much more intense, solid, and sharp. You can literally feel the music pounding inside of you. The sound is electrifying and emotions run so high that there is no way to describe what transpired unless you experience it yourself. Moreover, you can't really experience it for yourself unless you have a deep love for music—all kinds of music including blues, jazz, opera, soul, and rock. In 1988 the Madison Scout Drum and Bugle Corps won the Drum Corps International Championship. It was one of the most exciting times of my life and so indescribable. When the Scouts marched onto the field, you could see and feel all of their pride. The way they marched and carried themselves was enough to touch any person. To hear the music moved everyone. When they play you can feel the music inside and outside of you. It brings "goosebumps to your skin." On that hot August evening in Kansas City, the Scouts won. It was one of the most emotional moments of my life. It brought tears, happiness, excitement, and pride. It is a feeling no one could ever put into words, not even with other people who were there. They just say, "Yeah, I know how you feel." I've gotten to the point where I don't try to explain anymore because people just cannot understand why I get so excited about going to a drum corps show.

#93 A's view: First of all, an experience might seem magical, extraordinary, joyous, or awe evoking. Trying to tell someone could "break the magic" and dim the experience. One real problem is the lack of appropriate words especially when describing complex emotions. I've experienced "magic moments" in my life. Some weren't necessarily major events, just minor special happenings. For instance, music: there have been songs, voices, instruments, even certain musical notes hit just right that for some unexplainable reason caused goose bumps. One specific instance occurred in a concert hall where I was working. One of the performers played an electric (or amplified) violin (solo). It was a gospel music show, something to which I've had very little exposure. The violin had an extraordinary sound that *filled* every nook and cranny of an odd-shaped building with a sound that was magical—very dramatic, very moving. But you can't really share that sort of feeling just by attending to my description. The feeling cannot be re-created with words. I could express my experience to you but my words would not really capture the magic of the moment.

The juxtaposition of such extreme forms of pain and pleasure illustrate an important principle. As a rule, the singular burden of pain intensifies in direct proportion to the inability to express what transpires before others. However, the euphoria associated with hearing fine music intensifies the magic of the moment precisely because of the full depth of what does not transcend the bodily boundaries or auditory thresholds of each listener.

QUESTIONS WITHOUT ANSWERS

If life is the brute fact, it is also the ultimate source of all unanswered questions. From the beginning to the end of the journey, the quest for definition and direction in each one's uniquely inhabited lived circumstance is at stake. Hence, the definition of life is discovered as a distinctive way of life. As a consequence, questions arise over how to live in or out of the immediate presence or absence of others. Unresolved questions over the parameters of communal activity require a margin of opportunity for additional inquiry and exploration. At issue is how each source serves or functions as a model (type) and example (instance) of modes of personal conduct that remain in question, at issue, or otherwise under scrutiny.

From a communicative standpoint, it takes two or more sources of expressed activity to produce the working definitions and directions afforded to each one. From the same perspective, each life acquires personal identity through a succession of concrete acts and practices. The process implicates networks of specific acts of presentation (by one) in relation to multiple modes of *re*presentation (by every other one). At issue are questions without answers that have the greatest implications. Most concerns are grounded in unresolved tensions over the particular position and place of certain individuals within the surrounding community at large.

Individual A questions who A wants to be and what A wants to do in the remainder of A's life. Individual A feels pressure to answer these two types of personal questions for friends and family, but the questions are much too complex to answer during the most complicated period in one's life. Another individual assumes everyone, at one time or another, goes through times or periods when life seems to make little or no sense at all. Some admit and others deny such moments occur, but those who deny do so only to protect themselves from any further harm. It is a matter of self-preservation after all. Still another source feels unresolved tensions gradually building over time. Eventually this individual (A) finds it is nearly impossible to work, think, or sleep. Individual A feels like someone who wanders around in a cloud—almost half-drunk—where one just can hardly register any information before others. People ask A questions, and A does not respond. Individual A just isn't there. He is merely present, just going through the motions. The trauma of a recently dissolved intimate relationship leaves A feeling a part of A was dying, and A wanted to mourn. Everything else was secondary.

In another context respondent B asks A about another person (C), and A is very reluctant to answer. Individual A thinks most questions about other people are intended to find out something either very personal or source dependent. Individual A doesn't believe in making self-disclosures about other people when they aren't around. It is hard enough to make your own choices about others and to do it for someone else is potentially damaging, ludicrous, and often based on pure conjecture or a breach of trust in many cases. If someone asks a personal question about someone who is not present at the time, individual A will play dumb, say something positive, or reprimand the one in question for spreading or generating hearsay.

INTERPRETIVE CONSTRAINTS ON EXPRESSIVE FREEDOM

At some level participant and observer struggle to reconcile what transpires, takes place, or makes sense in the past, present, and future tense. In some ways what one experiences in the present is cast into linguistic form before and after the fact. Here there is tension between the immediacy of the existing moment and what unfolds before and after from one vantage point or another. One strives to express the condition one is in by what one does, but the two (being and doing) may or may not be effortlessly aligned. Here is potential tension and strain between one's state at one moment (T1) as it dissolves into something else (T2).

It seems possible that what one does to reveal or conceal the condition one is in (at the time) is transposed or recast in the very act of translation (over time). To define a little bit one may have to describe a lot and by then it can be too late. Any element of definition may call for additional aspects of description and explanation. To describe, in effect, is to both expect and anticipate and still recount, recast, and reconcile. Hence, the expressive freedom of the moment is framed through a succession of interpretive constraints on conjoint activities that unfold over extended time frames. As a case in point, individual B tells individual A something shocking. Individual A reacts, more or less articulately, but afterward, when A tells someone else about the shock, A fixes and defines the exact moment of shock. A writes the story of A's reaction in a spatiotemporal process that becomes at least as real as A's feelings during the original moment in question. What enables expressive activity is exactly what constrains it, namely a state of interdependence between one source and another with an alternative frame of (expansive or restrictive) reference.

Such a realization need not be the cause for alarm or despair. In fact, it comes to some as a great relief to ponder the possibility one can never truly know if he or she is conveying something correctly to someone else. The point is that a state of communicative correctness, in the sense of simple correspondence between the position and place of two or more sources, is strictly ruled out. Others may view one's expressive acts in a quite different light than one intends. In this sense no one can ever *fully* express what transpires at a given moment or over time. One respondent concludes the only way two beings would ever be in a position to express fully what they experience at a given point in time would be if each one had lived exactly the same lives and viewed things in exactly the same light. This astonishing diversity in the communicative capacities and practices of human beings makes such reasoning plausible and beautiful. It would be, after all, a colorless world if all human beings experienced each event in such an identical manner as to be able to express fully rather than approximately to what is given to each one. The following entries convey several essential themes.

#94 A's view: There are many times when what I've experienced cannot be explained accurately to someone else. Sure I can tell them what was said or what actions took place but what was *really* going on, and what it really meant to me, escapes the grasp of words. I am acutely aware that meaning, full meaning, never gets conveyed or understood fully. Often times like these happen with my closest friends. There are people who know me well and we are very close. It is with topics of such gravity or intimacy that this "non-understanding" takes place. Although we often try for hours to be descriptive the understanding of meaning does not come across. For lack of a better word—intuition—tells me that this "nonconveyable" element of "non-understanding" seems to have something to do with "being." When I want to share this with someone, I can't tell them. Oh, sure, I can verbalize. If understanding is going to take place—it does—and that is a wonderful feeling. But if it doesn't happen, it can be one of the most isolating and fearful times in one's life.

#95 A's view: This situation is very common. I find I will be interacting with a person, perhaps dealing with feelings and sensations seemingly caught inside my brain, and yet I am unable to illustrate fully what those feelings are. I begin to express my ideas only to find myself ending in confusion and signing off with "Never mind" or "I don't know." This could be because I'm not exactly clear what I am feeling or it could be because there aren't words in our written language to capture the full range of one's own feelings. Another idea is that I am unable to integrate my ideas into the proper phrases—there are words I can use to express my feelings, experiences, or ideas but I just can't find them. Sometimes when I am looking at poems or cards out at the Hallmark shop, I'll come across a phrase that lays out so clearly ideas or feelings of my own past experiences. Then I wonder why I couldn't have thought of saying it in that particular way. Usually I'll end up buying the card. Today a close friend and I were talking about in-depth feelings. He said he had these images inside his head he wanted to share. I would have liked him to explore these images but he would not continue. He said his words would not do his thoughts justice. He was unable to translate his images into a form so that I could recognize them in the same light as he did. The transfer of thought to word and to subsequent interpretation is not always straightforward or uninterrupted.

WHAT IS REVEALED ON THE INSIDE BUT CONCEALED ON THE OUTSIDE

Some distinctions are more troublesome than others. When interactants search for a collective explanation of what they strive to define or describe individually, there is a tendency to try to locate an array of particulars within the larger scheme of things. This involves a mutual search for a sense of place, position, and location: where this belongs, when something will begin, what happens to this or that, how things start out, change over time, or how they end up. Since each source within the systemic domain of expressed activity is an absolute source of origin of what is in question, each one also qualifies as medium and point of termination for other sources. Considerations of who functions as source or object are bifacial. When 'A & B' are in the immediate presence of one another, what A expresses to B is alternatively oriented: (inside-outside) from A's unique vantage point but (outside-inside) from B's equally unique vantage point. This condition gives rise to a litany of issues over the degree of connection or disconnection, alignment or misalignment, in various frames of reference and lines of coordinated action.

From a strictly analytical point of view, efforts to distinguish the inside-outside participatory orientation of what A expresses in relation with the outside-inside observational stance of B are bound to be fraught with convenient fictions, dislocations, and misattributions on all matters of cause, logic, reason, or consequence. From the first-person perspective of A talking to B and trying to take B's second person response into account, miscommunication may occur insofar as A assumes that A is engaged in an expressive act that reveals within what is concealed without. Furthermore, if A assumes what A takes for granted is consistent with A's response to B's immediate response to what A has to say, then a double fiction is introduced: A can see B can't see that A conceals (from B) what A reveals only within A's body boundaries. Such a presumption may or may not be subject to visible or observable challenge. What is of interest are the sorts of communicative milieu where these conditions are presumed to operate from the stance of participant and observer alike. What follows are eight relevant entries.

#96 A's view: It occurs when A is in a situation in which someone A cares for deeply wants someone else (freedom, another companion). The hate, pain, sorrow, aggression, confusion, etc., involve an extreme range of sensibilities. People tend to claim that they know how A is feeling. To A, that seems impossible. Someone can understand the ideology of a feeling (hate) but that does not mean they understand the particular interpersonal factors that motivate such a feeling as intense hatred.

#97 A's view: The experience I found most difficult to express was when I was feeling attracted to my female roommate. She and I had been living together, along with two other people, and I thought maybe we could make our relationship more intimate. However, I have never been in a lesbian relationship before. Neither has she. I didn't know if she would freak out if I told her how I felt. I was afraid of messing up our friendship. So I put off telling her for two months until I felt I just had to let her know. It was very difficult. I didn't know when to tell her, or what words to say, given the delicateness of the situation. I have never felt that way about another woman before and didn't know if I could even act upon such feelings. Unsure about my feelings, I had an even harder time trying to express them to my roommate. The circumstances were further complicated by the fact that such feelings are considered "taboo." In our society, it's not normal to feel sexually attracted to a member of the same sex. Although I knew my roommate was open-minded, it was still very difficult to confront her with my so-called "taboo" feelings.

#98 A's view: A and B are sisters. A becomes very close to a young man, C, and they develop an exclusive relationship. One Friday night A comes home to find B and C together. She is furious and storms out of the house. Later, A can talk to C about it but for some reason cannot discuss the matter with B. How do you tell a family member they have made you feel so awful? It seems as though no one could possibly understand. Person A just can't figure out a way to explain and justify her feelings. She thinks that everyone would think she is just blowing the whole incident out of proportion. It seemed that it would be OK to feel anger but to stay quiet rather than bring the whole family into it. A cannot figure out a way to discuss the matter so that it would make sense. Even though A had a lot stored up inside, she could not find an appropriate way to express herself. By discussing things A thinks she would worsen the tension and spread it to other people. Therefore, A stays quiet and never really mentions what she is truly feeling. A knows her sister sensed what she felt because of her actions, but she never explicitly shared her feelings with her sister.

#99 A's view: I have a tendency to keep personal problems hidden from those closest to me, including members of my family. For this reason, I prefer to keep this type of situation to myself, whether it is because I don't want people to know of the situation or I don't want to admit to myself the possibility I might be the cause of the problem. I detest it when people disagree with me and think that I am wrong. It makes me feel like a bad person. Recently my mother and I had a major disagreement and I left home without saying good-bye. We went for a month without talking. It was really difficult for me to handle but I didn't feel I could talk to anyone about it, thinking no one would understand my reasoning. I was lucky we talked things out, but the last month was most strenuous.

#100 A's view: When I was seventeen I began to have sexual intercourse with my boyfriend. I knew we had to protect ourselves so I decided to go on the pill and my boyfriend started to use condoms. I was afraid of getting pregnant and getting AIDS. I knew what I was doing was right but I could not tell anyone in my family. I come from a very Catholic family or should I say we were practicing Catholics. My father and mother explicitly stated their views against premarital sex, abortion, and birth control. I knew my mother was once on the pill but went off of it because of the side effects. She believed it would do damage later on, plus I found out that she was on birth control when she was pregnant with me. My father would permit no talk about it. So here I was taking two major steps in my life and feeling quite guilty about it. My boyfriend sensed my anxiety over not wanting to engage in sexual intercourse as often and I became more distant from him. I began to blame him for all of my guilt. In the end my own guilt became so great I immediately went off the pill and wished I had approached others on the subject sooner.

#101 A's view: A and B undertake a video project. At first A likes B but later begins to dislike B. A sees B as having a way of twisting situations to get what he wants. B uses people without their knowing it most of the time. B persuades people to say things on videotape or tape recorder that benefit his purpose but have the potential to embarrass the speaker, his or her image, or reputation. A has very strong values and does not like it when someone is taken advantage of, so he feels guilty and frustrated with everything that is happening. The situation gets to the point where he can't take it anymore. This is when he had terrible problems trying to express what he is going through, how he feels, what he thinks, and how frustrated he is. A has never felt anything like this before and hasn't since. It is scary because he feels so scared, helpless, and alone. The more he struggles to get back on track, it seems the more he becomes stuck in the situation. Soon A begins to feel like a caged animal—trapped and blocked out from the rest of the world. Wherever A goes, he feels as if everyone can see right through him and knows what he is thinking. All of these strange, different feelings are going through him, but the worst part is the feeling he couldn't explain what was going on because it seems that when he talks about the situation, it only makes others dislike him even more. A then goes from being a confident, optimistic person to being very insecure and pessimistic. A is the kind of person who hates to keep things inside, but that's what is happening, and it is contrary to his nature. The more he thinks about it, the more he begins to panic. It is a perpetual cycle. A soon becomes so overwhelmed with thoughts and emotions and so "keyed up" that he has trouble falling asleep. He worries about what people think of him. The less able he is to express himself, the more he wants to hold back. Soon he wants to seal himself in a place away from the rest of the world. He is afraid of saying what he feels for fear of looking like a fool. Later, looking back, A now realizes how he himself perpetuated his internal fears, real or imagined, by not telling anyone. A then talked to his pastor, who told him he hadn't done anything wrong but because he was so sensitive about other people's feelings, he picked up on other people's troubles that weren't necessarily due to his own actions and, as a result, felt guilty for no real reason.

#102 A's view: A and B create a romantic relationship for a year and then break up as a couple. A doesn't think he could talk to anyone. He is experiencing a sense of loss. He also feels as though he can't open up to others or ever become close to someone else again. A doesn't want people to realize how he is feeling, so he has to put on a "mask" just to keep his so-called image. Looking back, A now realizes that if your friends think less of you as a person because you reveal your true feelings, they aren't much as friends. A now realizes that it is important to express your feelings to others, no matter what those feelings are.

#103 A's view: A has recently experienced seven months of living hell with his girlfriend. Many of the people around A question A's intelligence, asking why A continues to put up with such a shitty situation. A also questions himself thoroughly, as to what it was about this person that was so special that A would allow himself to get walked on. A is aware of the good qualities she possesses and the things she has brought into his life, but it is virtually impossible to explain to anyone what A felt, mainly because A doesn't want to waste his breath explaining the importance of her in his life. This is something A feels is understandable only within the framework of his own experience.

#104 A's view: I am very good at concealing my thoughts and feelings through various 'masks'. I've actually become so good that sometimes its even difficult for myself to distinguish which mask I may have on. I'm expected to be this "shiny, happy person" who has nothing wrong—a lie of course, so I pretend to an extent even with my friends.

Miscommunication is closely associated here with discourse and dialogue that operates in exceedingly complicated and unstable communicative situations. First there is an initially heightened and pronounced distinction between the interests and vested interests of first and second parties, the mix between those who witness with their very own eyes in relation to those who constitute all the rest. Closely related is the presence (within the lived horizons of one) of an all-pervasive longing for interdependence coupled with a deep sense of identification with multiple manifestations of the same thing (from one source) in relation to singular manifestations of many different things (from any other). Moreover, there is also the pervasive sense of constraint, prohibition, and restraint on matters of self-expression or the degree of absorption on the part of another. What some source ends up expressing is a highly condensed epigram, a prolonged act of severe understatement of the true magnitude of one's implicit desire for what is revealed on the outside to be revealed in full measure on the inside (of each participant). Existing interpersonal boundaries appear insufficiently permeable or rigid when much too much is presumed to be stored inside to be of much personal use outside.

There is considerable private discourse and self-reflexive concern over what does not happen in a given system of communication but can be envisioned as a possibility. Below the surface implicature abounds—what is hidden, covered up, false, misleading, masked, or elusive. The inward-directed search is for cause, logic, reason, warrant, or justification for not expressing something, usually based on the presumption of a fleeting inability to grasp some underlying urge, motive, or intention associated with the display of unspoken feelings or sensations. The emerging salience of unactualized urges (sexual) coincides with implicit tension over the decision to delay or put off the moment of explicit disclosure until external circumstances become more manageable or subject to tolerable levels of personal control. Finally, there is guilt, regret, and remorse over imagined interaction that did not take place. The risks of future interaction are weighed against the risk of indecision, avoidance, and inaction (toward a given means or end).

Also relevant is the larger consideration of who is on the inside or the outside of an existing interpersonal boundary characterized by much sedimented tension and accumulative strain over who else may be deemed worthy of being brought close together or held far away. Hence, 'inside\outside' distinctions coalesce with a mixed sense of source and subject matter somehow located near (accessible) or far (inaccessible) away from view. Closely related is the implicit presumption that one or more of the respective parties cannot figure out a way to discuss the matter in a way that would make sense. The tension would surely spread to others. Sometimes words speak louder than actions. Here personal problems remain hidden just below the surface of public appearances from those who are closest. Disagreement over minor matters can indeed make a participant feel like a bad person. Eventually some may be tempted to place exclusive implicit blame on someone else. The risks are multiplied if the respective parties have a way of twisting situations to get what they want even if it means others get to the point where they can't take it anymore.

Still others fear everyone else will see right through them and eventually know everything they may be feeling, thinking, or about to say. Sometimes strange, different sensations and implicit speech prevail. It can become a perpetual cycle. One may start to feel guilty or responsible for no good reason. It gets easier to become trapped between the urge to open up to others and the constraining need to close down. One may be tempted to wear the most convincing mask possible. The trick, of course, is fooling others without running an undue risk of fooling oneself, as in the discovery of fool's gold. It is even possible to become so good at wearing masks in the manner of a convincing illusion (Becker, 1973) one can no longer distinguish which mask one is wearing at the time.

INDECISIVENESS: NOT KNOWING EXACTLY WHAT TO FEEL, THINK, SAY, OR DO

Face-to-face interaction may not necessarily reduce initial levels of uncertainty or apprehension; in fact, it may well increase one's sensitivity to what one does not know or what others are not in a position to define or determine. In the following set of entries, a sense of uncertainty is coupled with a state of indecisiveness over what to feel, think, say, or do in anticipation or response to what the expressed activities of others reveal or conceal from human view. When one participant becomes uncertain and indecisive simultaneously, a vicious cycle may begin. The more difficult it becomes to make sense to self and others, the less one can expect subsequent sequences of interaction to make much sense to anyone. Often there is no one who wants to hear what is wrong with the lived circumstances of one particular individual. Hence, the one in question is resigned to keep personal problems to him or herself. Matters of uncertainty, indecisiveness, and misinterpretation and misunderstanding go hand in hand. The very thought of talking to someone else about matters that one can't figure out oneself becomes utterly preposterous. One who does not know where to begin risks making everything else come out wrong. Not knowing the answers for oneself may lead to the deeper implication that one would ever find them anyway. In such a situation, where no one seems to know what is right, the source in question is left to struggle with the renewed discovery no one can know your exact feelings or replace your thoughts.

#105 A's view: My experience stems from my job. Although I tried to express my feelings to others, nobody seemed to understand my problems with my job. At my job, I was hired to sell men's high fashion clothes but as it turned out I was nothing more than a gofer and delivery boy. Every day I was sent out to get various things for the owner of the store. None of these things were associated with selling clothes. At first I did not want to discuss my situation at work with anyone, because I thought people would put me down for not wanting to do my job. But as the deliveries and errands continued, so did my dissatisfaction with my job. I decided to express my anger with people who were closest to me. As I tried to explain my problems to them, their responses were just what I expected. Nobody wanted to hear what was wrong with my job but what I liked about it. Over time the problems got worse. I decided I would be better off to keep my problems to myself. Finally, I decided that I had enough and I quit my job. Even though I tried to express my feelings to my family and friends, they never understood what I was going through.

#106 A's view: Sometimes I know how I am feeling but I have trouble explaining it to others and other times I myself can't even figure out how I am feeling. When I don't know how I am feeling, and can't begin to talk to others about it, I feel it is because if I'm not really sure how I am feeling, where will it get me to talk to someone else. I try my hardest to sort it out within my own head. On the other hand, if I know how I am feeling and still can't express it, it is probably because it doesn't fit into words. I fear others won't understand me or that I would rather keep things to myself. Instances like this could involve how I look at life or things I think should be happening to me but aren't for various reasons. This feeling frustrates me, usually to the point where I feel very alone. I could have lots of relatives who care and all the friends in the world but a feeling like this causes me to feel all alone.

#107 A's view: A could not give a complete answer because A could not collect his thoughts enough to explain the problem. A does not confront B with the problem because he doesn't know where to begin. His emotions are so mixed up that he can't even express the problem to himself. The one time he does try to express himself, everything comes out wrong and it creates a bigger problem. Whenever there is a problem concerning himself, A has problems interacting with others because he fears he will not express his feelings properly. Because of this fear, the majority of the time it occurs. It is as if his fear becomes reality. When he has something important to say, he practices it many times. When it comes time to confront people, A's thoughts become mixed up, and he doesn't end up expressing his true feelings. Quite often A feels that he cannot tell people how he feels and therefore must keep it to himself.

#108 A's view: The time was when I was going through my identity crisis. I did not know who I was, what I wanted, or who to turn to. Because I could not answer any of these questions, I knew no one else would be able to either. I gave indirect cues of confusion and became irritable at unusual times. No one understood me and I knew that because of replies such as, "What's the matter with you?" or "Why are you acting that way?" The scariest thing was that I didn't not even know the answers myself and I thought I would never find them. It was a very lonely time in which I felt different and isolated. I wanted to reach out to others but I did not know how. Sometimes I felt as though the way I was feeling was "wrong" and that I should not burden others with my problems, as if they were very minor and could be easily resolved. I felt as if no one knew what it was like to be me and that everything that happened to me was unique. There was no way to prevent bad things from happening and if they were to happen, they were to happen to me. During this time, I was witnessing a lot of peer pressure. My friends would tell me one thing, my parents another, and my boyfriend still another. I did not know who to listen to, who was right, or who was wrong. This contributed to me not wanting to talk to others because I always received conflicting views. No one seemed to know what was right. I was convinced that I was the only one I could turn to and this was scary because I certainly did not have any answers. In short, I did not know who I was, where I was going, or how I was going to get there. And deep down I knew that I was the only person who could answer these questions; other people were there only to help guide me. My issues and problems were so personal that no one could see what I was really going through. Actually, my parents probably knew what I was going through but I knew that there was no way that they could give me the answers to my problems. I went to my friends also but most of the time that only made things worse. They were much more judgmental and critical and did not really seem to understand. I felt like I should have done what they did and acted like they did. They seemed to be handling things well, so I thought that I should be more like them. I did not know where to go or who to turn to. I wanted this stage to end quickly but I thought it never would. Years later I am seeing things more clearly. I am not sure if I am through with my crisis but I do know there are still many things I am unsure of about myself and there may be no one to turn to who can give me the perfect answer. But there are others out there who are willing to help and I have learned to give them a try. Even though they may not be able to give the exact answer I hoped, they can support and help me along the way. Because they have problems, like mine, that take time. No one can know your exact feelings or replace your thoughts and I realize that now. This makes me more sensitive toward others and I now look for cues of pain or hurt in others so that I may make their own issues a little easier to deal with.

States of indecisiveness are equated mainly with unwelcomed types of behavioral and environmental constraint. Interactive restructions diminish the scope of one's total latitude of expressive freedom or room to move about. Others are viewed as a liability rather than a resource. The search for certainty is undermined by the degree of uncertainty in the responses of others. Self-reflection fails to clarify the sense of being confused or mixed up. Personal identities are called into question. Episodes of harsh criticism and adverse judgment multiply. The risk of miscommunication is compared with the unforeseen consequences of denial and avoidance. The central issue is whether to engage in future interactions or to negate the opportunity.

WHEN ONE CAN'T EXPRESS ONESELF TO ANYONE IN THE IMMEDIATE SITUATION

Here miscommunication unfolds in an extraordinary manner, even in quite ordinary social situations. When a set of entities (A↔B) interact with one another, dialectical tensions may give rise to a indirect sense of connection with other sources who are not immediately present at the time. At this point what can/cannot or does/does not transpire between the respective parties is measured against what could, should, would, or might take place between either A or B and someone else—an alternative source, a hidden presence. Furthermore, A or B may not even be in a position to know whether a given sequence of speech acts are being interpreted or understood in implicit and highly mediated relation to the communicative capacities of some other indirect source of reference.

The most common central theme unfolds in a shared situation where source A is unable to express what A is feeling at a particular time but thinks he or she could explain it to some other person who is not located within the immediate vicinity. Such a condition can be experienced by the most verbal, open, and outgoing persons. It is puzzling to find one can express condition X to friends or relatives, but not to those who are most directly involved at the time.

#109 A's view: This usually happens when I'm experiencing something really intangible, something I myself don't conceive through words or even concrete 'thoughts' but rather vague feeling or intuition. Last week my boyfriend and I were at Ken Kopp's store. Behind the butcher's counter the wall is covered with mirrors, much like a bar. We were standing at the counter for awhile and I knew there were mirrors there but even so I felt as if I were in a large bustling grocery store. This feeling took over my perceptions and I began to feel more altered and excited, sensing there was some heavy action going down somewhere (like at a bar?!?!?!?!?!?) and I only had to explore and find it. Then my brain said, "Hey, it's a mirror! You are in Ken Kopp's, stupid!" This happened a couple of times and I finally asked my boyfriend, "Doesn't that mirror weird you out? It makes this place look so big." He responded, "It's a *mirror*." I said, "I know it's a mirror but it still makes me feel like I'm someplace else—not Ken Kopp's. Know what I mean?" He replied, "No." I dropped the subject because I knew even if I explained it fully and as completely as I could, he couldn't understand. That is, he might recognize that "Yes, she feels as if she's someplace else because of this, this, and this" but what he couldn't *understand* was because he wasn't feeling the same way—so what is the use of even trying to explain to someone when they're not experiencing the same type of thing? Obviously, if this poor communication was in different areas, a topic vital to our relationship, we would have thought about it. But instances like these I don't bother to tell anyone because they just can't understand—unless they have been there themselves. This brings me to a different example of the same type of thing—phobias. I'm afraid of heights, especially open air walking bridges, and stairs. Railroad tracks are the worst—I've only walked a couple in my life and it's scary as hell. Usually, the person I'm with will automatically take my hand or whatever and then I really freak cuz as soon as somebody touches me, I feel instinctively that they'll draw me to the edge and I'll fall off. I get this feeling on steep stairways or even when I walk by a steep stairway going down. Once again, people who don't get this feeling can't really understand it because they can't feel it themselves and so can't express what they don't feel at all. (I can barely put into words all the things I'm feeling when I am in that situation.) However, last summer I worked with a woman and one day we were gabbing and somehow the subject of heights came up. She had the exact same phobia I do. Even though she tried to explain it, she didn't say what I would have said and her explanation was not the same as mine would have been. Once she said it I realized it too was a small part of all the things I feel when walking over bridges. She is the only person I've ever talked about such a subject who really does experience the same things that I do. I know that our experiences aren't exactly the same but close enough that we *understand* what the other is saying.

#110 A's view: It began happening approximately a year ago when A noticed she was having problems in her marriage. Since they had not been married a very long time, it was hard to admit to anyone, much less herself, that she was having problems with the marriage. After all, she was supposed to be in the honeymoon stage—the problems were supposed to come later. At first A tries to rationalize the problem—things would get better. They only had to survive like this for another year until she would get out of school with a master's degree. It is the tip of the iceberg—she doesn't want to admit it to herself. Inside, however, A is hurting and feeling she has no one to turn to. So she hides all of her feelings and frustrations inside. She deals with the stress through food and ends up gaining thirty pounds within eight months. No one knows what she is going through, not family, people at school, or even best friends. Six months later one of her best friends starts putting the pieces together and confronts A about it. A finally gives in and tells her what is going on. All of the emotions that A has kept inside for months come out, and she feels so much better. This huge secret finally comes out. It is like a big rock being lifted off A's chest and she could breathe again.

#111 A's view: A often finds it hard to express himself in front of strangers. He is not that shy a person; in fact, his friends would say he is socially obnoxious. Moreover, when it comes to intellectual conversations, A is often frustrated by the lack of ability to express his ideas, opinions, and arguments clearly. With his closest friends he can talk and talk about the deepest subjects for hours, but in university classes and in small groups, he is usually termed quiet. This is very frustrating, since he has a lot to say about things. He feels trapped within himself and by the severe limits in his communicative abilities—this is probably the reason why he acts obnoxious at other times.

#112 A's view: After A and B date for a year, A feels the relationship begin to deteriorate. A can't figure out what is wrong, what the problems are, and bit by bit is starting to feel unhappy. Initially, A ignores the internal conflict. After all, B is very much in love and happy, and A doesn't know how to go about tell him something is wrong. Little by little things are bothering A. Rather than express her feelings, A keeps them inside. This causes added confusion, tension, and frustration. A becomes irrational and oversensitive as the stress increases. A finally reaches the point where she has to do something. She decides to confront B without first sorting things out in her own mind. A isn't able to back up her accusations nor clarify her feelings. She becomes frustrated at not being able to explain to B exactly how she is feeling. B feels the frustration along with his own anger. B is angry that A hasn't spoken to him sooner.

Entries 109 to 112 underscore a central theme. In calculating the consequences of episodes of miscommunication with any given sets of interactants (A, B, & C), it is critical to be in a position to envision alternative sources of reference (D, E, & F). The lines between the 'actual' and the 'imagined' lines of connection and disconnection merge, blur, cross over, penetrate, intersect. Much of the clamor, confusion, and panic associated with sequences of exchange (in the immediate situation) may be alleviated in compensatory acts of imagined interaction.

ANXIETY: NOT BEING ABLE TO FIND THE RIGHT WORDS TO SAY

Anxiety undermines the fulfillment of expressive urges. It also interferes with the desire to be explicit, articulate, and discriminating. The process of making sense is integrative and constructive in definitional and directional force while a state or condition of anxiety becomes disintegrative and deconstructive of those same efforts. When respondents strive to account for what makes them anxious, they may be susceptible to Wittgenstein's dictum—what one cannot say, one must consign to silence. Anxiety is free floating. It has no distinct point of beginning or specific location. It is roughly akin to numbness or vague aches and pains you feel all over, but the feelings left behind are not distinct enough to define or classify. Sometimes it takes little effort to assign names to things. The words fall off the tongue as automatically as the blinking of one's eyes. At others social conditions may not be favorable, or the requisite skills become inaccessible for no apparent reason. In each case what is missing is the capacity or willingness to find modes of representation and reference that can be subjected to public scrutiny.

The decision to give expression to one's own anxiety before others is risky. At one level resides the possibility of calling attention to what strikes others as either meaningless or nonsense. Those who admit to being nervous over what they cannot say invite mindless responses: "Relax—everything will be OK." "Just take it easy." "Try to keep things in perspective." Often there is concerted effort to stay in the race, and keep up the pace, while not knowing what to do or how to let go of unsettled burden, worry, or doubt. One respondent equates shared anxiety with the constant twisting of the words and gestures employed to account for it. Another retreats behind vague pictures. Still another invokes a private sense of being enclosed in a space about the size of an elevator without a door. Friends sit around and say "not to worry." She would agree with everyone but still not be able to explain the irrationality because she doesn't know its origin herself.

#113 A's view: Over a period of time person A develops a serious case of anxiety. Individual A becomes nervous, sleepless, and loses much weight. All of A's friends say, "Relax, just do the best you can." So A tells herself the same thing yet for some reason can't calm down. Moreover, A can't explain this nervousness because it is so ridiculous. Eventually A becomes so exhausted and worn down that she has to learn to teach herself how to relax. She feels she is relearning the entire process.

#114 A's view: When I write poetry I experience such intense emotions and thoughts which are (seem at the time) so high or so low I do not wish or try, at that time, to express them to anyone else. Further, the experience of actually sitting down and writing is a mystery-process. On the one hand, it just sort of happens, and on the other it involves very hard work—the juxtaposition of these two processes make for an odd mixture which is hard to define. I believe I do not, furthermore, desire to share some of the deep feelings and yet I do but in the form of the finished product of the poem (which I almost always share).

#115 A's view: I have felt at times that my emotions were too complex for me to explain or for anyone else to understand. One example is a feeling of panic that has struck me before the beginning of some new experience. I've tried to explain my anxiety to people but not only did they fail to understand my physical distress but they could not comprehend the intensity of panic I felt. I could not explain how terrified I was about something that no one else seemed to think was particularly traumatic. Eventually I have found the means to face whatever crisis has emerged.

BLANK SPOTS

Miscommunication may be equated with vital but missing information about the origins of someone's lived circumstances. Interaction in families with adopted children provides a particularly striking case in point. Sometimes the discovery comes much too late. The one who has not been told all too often becomes also the one who does not belong (genetically). Even small children notice stark but unexplained differences, for example, being the only fair-skinned, blue-eyed, blonde child in a very large family where everyone else is dark-skinned, brown-eyed, and has dark hair. Such stark contrasts go unnoticed in the manner of a code of silence.

When individual A was very small, she was the most loving, giving, extroverted child. At age eleven she found out that she was the adoptive daughter of parents well into their sixties. The way she found out was completely blanked out. She remembers making some small comment, and her mother said they had adopted her and didn't she remember? Individual A honestly did not. Thinking back, she thinks it was all handled very lightly, and not much care was taken on her behalf. Ever since then A has sort of felt she was tricked into living with them and pulled into herself. Consequently, she was never able to tell anyone she wasn't sure that she really loved them after that. People would have thought her nuts—"What—you don't love your parents?" For a long time individual A wasn't sure that the relationship with her mother was normal because of their different biological makeup and the unsettled feeling that love was not really present—it was more gratitude for rescuing her from anonymity than anything else. To this day she refuses to rock the boat or ask for anything. Person A does not want to need them. It has affected her love relationships with men. She gives and gives and hardly gives them a chance to love her back because A feels somehow unworthy of anyone's love—as if she is not real. Her blank spot has an impact on face-to-face interactions vastly extended through time and space—in effect, for the rest of her life. Another respondent in a similar situation presses the issue of not knowing his real father. In the back of one's mind resides a picture of a father that one has never seen. One feels fatherless, a hollow feeling that gives rise to a question: Does he look like the father he has never seen?

FRUSTRATION: OVER NOT KNOWING WHAT TO SAY OR DO

#116 A's view: It's as if A knows exactly how A feels but can't say what it is. During the moment of truth the exact words are contained within, but A keeps repeating them over and over. He is practically mouthing the words, but the sounds are never heard. All of a sudden, when it is A's turn to express affection for another person,

A gets extremely tense and tight feelings all over, palms practically dripping with sweat. Then A proceeds to change the subject and get out of a sticky situation.

#117 A's view: Sometimes the English language doesn't seem to have enough adjectives to express what A really feels. It seems certain words are used so often in so many contexts that if there is an extraordinary situation, the adjectives don't seem to convey A's real feelings. Different people have so many different meanings for the same words or gestures. One may feel so deeply about the meaning of one's own words, and the other person who hears those words may not feel those same words very deeply at all.

#118 A's view: A's problem is a conflict within, something that A does not know quite how to deal with. A struggles to try to solve this problem and in so doing becomes quite frustrated. Other people begin to recognize A's frustrations also. A starts to think about it all the time. A is not sure if it was that A just couldn't express the feelings or that A truly had no answers. Basically A is confused with what A feels and thinks is best. A really tries to discuss these feelings with others, as he thinks it would help. However, A just can't make sense out of it. It wasn't until one particular person (B) finally sets A down and makes A express these feelings. He accomplished this by first expressing all his feelings to A. This opened up a strong trust between them. Because of B's actions, A could eventually share A's feelings with another person.

#119 A's view: I do a lot of writing for my internship and classes. I find myself pumping out press releases, PSAs, papers, and letters left and right. As the sentences and paragraphs come together into the final draft, I am always stopped by the "lack of the correct or appropriate word." This is frustrating to the mind—to think of that one word that will bring the piece together. Sometimes I find refuge in a thesaurus. But there are times when no words can be found or accurately used to replace an awkward phrase or a word used too often. This limitation of our language to capture the expression you want is very frustrating. Sometimes you feel that one special urge but you can sit and stamp for about five minutes and yield nothing.

#120 A's view: Once, at work, I got a phone call from a woman with questions about a report I had completed. While on the phone with me, she was also talking to someone else in the room with her. This made me very uncomfortable. She then started laughing and basically hung up on me. At this point I was very frustrated because I didn't know what was going on. Then I got mad because I realized she was laughing about the matter with another employee. The next day I went to see her so I could express my feelings about the previous inappropriate and unprofessional behavior. This is the part that gets weird. She tried to make it seem like she hadn't done anything wrong, but I could tell that she was uncomfortable with me being there. It was as if she didn't care what I was thinking and just wanted to get clear of the situation. It was so creepy. I can't fully explain how I was feeling except for being cheated and really frustrated. Anyone else would have to experience it directly to know how I felt at the time.

#121 A's view: Whenever I feel upset for any reason at my close friends, I find it very difficult to express my anger or aggravation to them. I never know if I should tell them how I feel, or just let it slide. If I do, then they generally get mad at me and tell me "it's their life and none of my business." I then see them as doing something that is hurting them but I am trapped in a situation where I can not say anything about it, in fear they will be mad at me. If I do not say anything, I just get more aggravated to deal with circumstances such as these. I tend to write letters to express my anger and frustration. I keep these reflections to myself and try to deal with them at later points in my life—in some similar situation to deal with them better myself.

#122 A's view: I have a very hard time dealing with most emotions. I tend to avoid having to open up and express my inner feelings. Having to face these emotions is sometimes too hard for me to do. It drains a lot of personal energy and patience. I have had times when my mind gets blown away and torn apart. 'Frustrating' I think is a good word for it. I feel very frustrated and very angry, so angry and mad I just want to scream or break something, maybe both. I feel so helpless because there is something going on over which I have no control. I space out and begin to freak out. I feel my whole body tense up and no matter what I try to do, I do not seem to be able to relax. I feel myself going deeper and deeper down into a hole at times where I am not able to chill out and get a grip on myself. I end up bringing myself so far down that I feel as though I am stuck here, somewhere inside of me where I do not want to be. My mind stops functioning in a rational way and I become blinded to everything and to everyone. Nothing else matters. Nothing. I get so much energy, negative energy. My mind is working so fast and in so many directions. I feel as though I do not know where I am at or where I am going. It involves loss of control, fighting against limits. Something holds me down and will not let go, something I cannot change. My mind keeps searching desperately for some kind of answer, but for some reason I am too overcome with the sense that I am burning up. It hurts to think. I am too wired, too pissed off to think, let alone think straight. I want out and I fight to get out. Certain feelings, moods, temperaments that I do not know "erk" me the wrong way and when certain areas get touched, I lose it.

#123 A's view: A finds these types of situations really frustrating—especially because he considers himself to be fairly articulate and sensitive. Yet, a lot of times lately, A has been unable and maybe unwilling to explain to friends and family how he feels. A is at a point in life where his goals and values are no longer the same as close friends'. Every day something different appeals to him. Some days it is the appeal of a serious relationship. Other days he wants to move far away. Still others sitting in a bar and drinking with friends is all that matters. Finally, sometimes he doesn't want to get off the couch or bed. A claims that he doesn't know how the fuck to explain clearly what he wants or what it is like to be living his life when he has absolutely no consistent idea of who he is or what he considers important.

#124 A's view: Individual A is the sort of person who has always been taught never to cry or show any strong emotions besides anger, hate, and lust. It is frustrating not to be able to say what you believe without becoming the object of laughter. It's a frustrating way to live ones life, bullshitting half of the time just to satisfy other members of society.

#125 A's view: The experience is one which A could not and to this day cannot express. Although part of A has come to the conclusion this experience is inexpressible, for some reason another part strives to express what A felt. This leads to inevitable frustration. For no sooner than A begins to fantasize that for once A has expressed the "inexpressible" to another person, the other person says something that clearly indicates they do not understand. The frustration stems from the overwhelming desire to share a common experience. A thinks that every human being has this desire to construct a sense of mutual significance.

#126 A's view: Every minute that I am awake, and often when I am asleep, my head is full of personal thoughts and perceptions of what I am experiencing. When I process these thoughts I feel as if am having a conversation with someone inside of me. Who is this person? I believe it is my "inner self," the place where my "feelings" and everything that makes me a unique person are kept. Every time I wish to express a feeling I must consult with my "inner self." This leads to extreme difficulty in expressing myself to others and frustration within myself. My "inner self" and the real world speak two different languages when I experience something that I wish to share, or even when my "inner self" just wants to tell something to someone in the outside world. The words and thoughts I am thinking never come out of my mouth. I understand my thoughts because they are in English so why don't they come out right? I often feel like I am in some faraway land where nobody speaks the same language that I do. The only conversations that I allow myself to have are ones that I practice within first.

If anxiety promotes heightened uncertainty or apprehension and aware-ness of blank spots with what is missing or left out of given interactive sequences, then frustration registers as active interference with strategic aspects of sense-making practice per se. Oddly, it is a condition in which one source unwittingly brings into play the very forces that undermine or subvert the *continuity* of activity each one is seeking to maintain (or fulfill). At the moment of truth either the words will not come out right, or the accompanying gestures will fail to compensate for what's gone wrong. Some respondents speak of a gap or lapse in the flow of interdependent activities. Others construct retrospective notions of (1) undifferentiated feelings and sensations, (2) incomplete transforms or relations between feeling, thinking, and talking or (3) lapses in syntax, reasoning, logic, or theme. Most salient is a loss of comprehension or sense of coherence in the production of the discourse or the dialogue.

Frustration with what one expresses is highly correlated with what someone else fails to grasp or take into account. Sometimes there is only fleeting disablement and at others the decision to change the topic or get out of an unmanageable interchange and not look back. Here what occurs at an unintentional level accentuates a sense of futility while intentional types of interference work on the side of subversiveness in conversation. When the content of the discourse does not satisfy the intentions or objec-tives of the participants, some are prone to conclude it is futile to continue because talking seems to do no good.

Seldom is there recognition that one may be frustrated at the literal level, where words and gestures have no significant results, but at the meta-level of tacit implication—presumption, inference, ascription, and attribution— the decision to keep talking at least preserves a process in which both parties have cooperated to change. At the international level, for example, the Israelis and Palestinians have engaged in "peace negotiation" for the first time in over forty years. At the literal level, talks appear to have produced no significant results to date, but at the level of metacommunication, the exchanges invoke a process in which both parties have cooperated in making change. Such a process wards off the futility of interchange at the literal level. Moreover, the decision to agree to disagree across conference tables is a radical change (second order) from their previous violence. In so doing, the respective parties are, in fact, changing the game and decreasing the possibility of futility. While their use of words and gestures may appear futile, each one produces the medium for the unfolding negotiation of that futility.

Frustration invites a sense of futility when the intent of what we express to one another becomes consistently distorted—amplified, diminished, or unappreciated. It is heightened when we continue to explain what we alone construe to be the rhyme or reason for apparent miscomprehension, inattentiveness, or lack of appreciation. Such a state is akin to the experience of feeling unsettled, lost, and adrift in the litany of meaningless gestures. To be the object of subversive tactics often only makes matters worse.

The logic of subversive conversation emerges, for example, when two people who are engaged in discourse have an overlapping agenda that operates at both literal and tacit levels simultaneously. What implicitly subverts to the point of overt frustration is an overall strategy designed to maintain the integrity of A's own self-definition at the expense of B's. Thereafter, each strains to identify the other's problem, implying that A has been observing B's pathologic condition ("your problem") outside B's own awareness. If individual B responds in kind, a mutually escalating game ensues. Here the hidden agenda, as exemplified by the accusation of the other's "problem," introduces a new level of subversiveness and enables each participant to become more mindful of the other's intention to neutralize, thwart, or destroy their own unique identity.

To have a problem suggests the superiority of an observer at a point when neither party can admit to the reality of the other's claim. When subversive intent is the tactic of choice, no amount of talk will change it. There must be change in the process and a willing suspension of subversive logic in the personal conduct of everyone who is concerned.

THE UNIVERSAL RISK: DISAGREEMENT AND MISUNDERSTANDING

#127 A's view: The times A experiences something A can't express to anyone else begin in things A can't understand. Something may be bothering A and yet rather than logically trying to figure it out, or even accepting that A is being bothered by something specific, A will just be quiet or feel depressed. When A comes to an understanding of what is bothersome and cannot express it to anyone else, A feels so much inner tension that A is extremely irritable and will behave insultingly toward the people A comes into contact with—especially if they try to find out what is wrong. A either represses the feeling until a more pleasant state of mind overrides it or will struggle to make someone understand how A feels. Often, when trying to express something, A will say that other things are bothering A or are the source of a bad mood and make an issue out of some fairly insubstantial complaint, rather than trying to actually say what A is feeling or coming out with the source of irritation.

#128 A's view: A and B are lovers. Sometimes there is a lack of communication between them. A feels confused and often hurt and cannot explain why. If she tries to explain these feelings to her lover, all that is transmitted is misinterpretations and a bit of sadness (for the fact that she is upset but he can do nothing to help and doesn't understand). At these times she cannot relate to friends either. It is as if there are ideas with emotions attached to them, floating in her brain, but she can't seem to make a connection with them in order to deal with the emotional part of them. They stay within her, constantly reminding her of their presence. She still cannot explain them. No one else in this world, even those closest to her, can ever know what she is feeling.

#129 A's view: A and B have known one another for seven years and usually feel very comfortable with one another. About a month ago A and B had a conflict, and A began to feel frustrated whenever A tried to express A's point of view on the subject. A would let B know how A felt and B would talk about it for a little bit and then move on to the next topic very quickly. This would make A wonder if A's ideas were expressed clearly. Then A tried to state the problem differently, and each time the exact same thing happened. The feeling of not being clearly understood is very frustrating to A, but each time the topic is discussed, it is handled the same way, and no resolution is ever found.

#130 A's view: I often feel that I am not being understood. People hear my words but do not understand the true meanings. Often, I listen to my own words and think that what's coming out of my mouth is paraphrasing for my brain with all the subtleties left out. I feel misunderstood because people haven't shared the same experiences as I have—they don't look at the world the same way as me. It's very frustrating to talk to someone and know that they are walking away having missed the point. Sometimes I blame my failure to express my thoughts effectively to my *overall* ineffective communication. Other times I blame the person to whom I'm speaking for not really trying to understand. I think that the only way a person can truly understand another is if they have shared all the same experiences (alas, impossible). This pessimistic view is very frustrating to me. As I get to know myself better, however, I find comfort in believing in my own reality and not caring so much that I am misunderstood by others but caring instead about my own convictions.

#131 A's view: I am sometimes inhibited to express my feelings for fear of being misunderstood. For example, I have this friend who I care a great deal about, in fact I can say that I love her in a much deeper way than I have ever loved any of my female friends before in my life. Though we are close I feel that I can't share these feelings with her or anyone else because I think they would be misinterpreted. I am by all means a heterosexual person and I have no sexual feelings for this person. Her presence just makes me feel content and I enjoy being around her and talking with her. She nurtures me. However, I'm afraid telling her this would put a dent in our relationship.

Acts of disagreement and misunderstanding are powerful forces. A state of agreement may be construed as a point of convergence in the alignment of multiple viewpoints. Likewise, one of understanding involves the mutual realization of the basis for the agreement. At a personal level, acts of disagreement and misunderstanding become powerful insofar as they call into question the presumed or strategic aspects of personal identity. Part of the issue is the interplay between source and subject matter. Interpretive responses to what one expresses introduce punctuation points of affirmation and negation, support and threat, confirmation and disconfirmation of the one who speaks. Implicit in much personal disagreement and misunderstanding is the threat to disconfirm or disenfranchise valued aspects of personal identity, either by refuting or being unable to make sense of the constructed meanings of the other. As human animals, we are meaning makers. We require confirmation of the identity who produces the meanings, or we are faced with unvalidated or invalidated meaning, hence the disenfranchisement of self. This does not imply that all disagreements or misunderstandings are necessarily invalidating.

The need of individuals to have others validate matters of personal identity covaries with the fear of having others reject them. This need for affirmation, and fear of rejection, often leads to paralyzing interchange, subversive logic, and false pretenses. The urge to maintain a carefully guarded image, while trying to make others accept it at face value, makes it real. The twin themes of withdrawal and cover-up accompany acute efforts to avoid the disclosure of one's true feelings and emotions. Here miscommunication involves the removal of one party from a position to engage in any meaningful communication. Subversive tactics may be directed toward unresolved matters of personal identity likely to meet with rejection on the part of others. Symbolic enactments maintain a facade of civility or normalcy, but the price is considerable distress and interaction tainted by false or unauthentic realities. Layers and layers of symbolic cover may ease one's sense of weakness, vulnerability, or susceptibility to manipulation and exploitation. On the other hand, it may also promote a double life in which public appearances are quite out of sync with private reality, that is, identity. Presentational masks are weak sources of protection from the painful truth that things are not what they seem or what they appear to be.

All negotiated contexts are grounded in patterns of rules that contain meta-rules for the conduct of disagreement and misunderstanding. In legislative practice, for instance, the operant meta-rules involve debate and advocacy and the clarification of issues. In marriage, however, most people believe that disagreement is synonymous with conflict and that misunderstanding is synonymous with intimate connection. The differences between these discursive contexts are essentially expectations concerning the centrality of matters of personal identity and identification—the socially constructed sense of self as active agent. In legislative practice, one's sense of personal identity is assumed to be irrelevant and a nonfunctional part of systemic process. Marriage, however, is essentially about the elaborated definition of self and other and the ability of each partner to validate the self over the other. Disagreement and misunderstanding cut to the very heart of marriage as a system of mutual validation and qualification and threat to its stability. Legislative systems, on the other hand, employ disagreement and misunderstanding as central to the very processes by which they maintain homeostasis or balance between a changing lineup of constituents.

The dangers of disconfirmation of personal identity are great and often result in destructive sequences of events. One response is to defend one's sense of self from others in ways that others think invalidate them. If nothing intervenes, the process may escalate to the point of physical as well as psychological damage. A second scenario occurs when attempts to create agreement and understanding result in the nullification of meaning. As each party struggles to make and convey meaning, they often attempt to move beyond existing levels of ability. In effect, they simply run out of the capacity to make meaning. One or both may become insane and leave the field of mutual comprehensibility and enter into the creation of surreality through the creation of neologistic inventions.

A third potentially disruptive result of the disenfranchisement of self is leaving the field of transaction itself. Some people simply choose to vitiate the discourse and physically move out of play. This tactic is not necessarily disruptive to a system's ongoing process, since it can lead to continued information exchange in another time, another place, and in another mode.

A fourth result of the disenfranchisement of self is the change of self. Most of us hold the notion that it is possible to prevent change and engage in all manner of tactics in order to maintain unchanged personal identities. These tactics include disqualification of alternatives, the maintenance of rigid censorship over all new information, and the nonconscious refusal to acknowledge inevitable developmental change—in other words, refusal to know what one knows or that one even knows. The universal wish of changing self is believed to be the risk of loss of identity to most people. But in that way of thinking, there is a false assumption, namely, that a punctuation in a sequence of events is synonymous with the termination of all events and all processes in an open system.

Perhaps the risk to matters of personal identity that is inherent in much widespread disagreement and misunderstanding is minimized if we keep the "and, then" premise of life. That premise rests on the assumption that the definition of personal identity is a process that we and others peri-odically punctuate "and, then" continues. One's sense of personal identity will be changed, but within an evolving context of continuity and consis-tency in matters of personal conduct with others. The Western mind, in its devotion to a science of mastery, dominance, and control of words and things, assumes that the objectification of self allows us to control it as though it were a thing rather than a consequence of emergent transformation. From this perspective, if security exists at all, it is to be acquired in a discovery that self is invented through collaborative practice.

MISDIRECTION/EQUIVOCATION/VAGUENESS

Face-to-face interaction provides open-ended opportunity for participants and observers to create internalized streams of reflection and expectation about the personal relevance of the explicit sequences of interaction per se (Sperber & Wilson, 1986; Atkinson & Heritage, 1984). Presumably, then, the very use of words and gestures exerts some influence over the idiomatic formulation of assumption, inference, implication, and attribution of intent and meaning that register from within but without exterior trace or imprint. Moreover, these invisible consequences of visible interchange are not apt to be evenly distributed among the respective participants. It is within the elaborated stream of linguistic form that matters of direct expression, misdirection, and indirection coalesce.

Stylistic forms of misdirection introduce variation in the strain of linear, sequential, and symmetrical modes of exchange. Heightened spontaneity provides relief and resistance to straightforward modes of expression and reciprocal influence. There is also a willingness to blur distinctions and the urge to divert, disable, exclude, and subvert linear movement from A to B and back again. Misdirection and deflection operate at the fringes of rule, role, norm, and custom. Misdirection exploits ambiguity instead of minimizing it. Hence, it is very responsive to complexity, diversity, ambivalence, furtive misunderstandings, and subtrafuge. The infusion of metaphoric considerations gives participants permission to fill in the gaps, explore implicit meanings and exchange of subtle, semisecret feelings that trace hidden analogies and, above all else, condense, compress, and displace the conventional with what may be taken as strange, uncertain, irregular, or unfamiliar deviation and mistake. In short, elements of misdirection are embedded within the direction and definition of interaction. Stylistic modes of indirection (1) suspend the application of the ordinary in favor of the extraordinary; (2) promote lapses of disorientation; (3) replace the transparent with the opaque; (4) promote a temporary, transient sense of disorder, imbalance, or thematic opposition; (5) celebrate exclusionary, detached, amoral, nonlinear aspects of expressive activity and interpretive response; (6) insist on this and that operating at the same time; (7) move toward the diffuse; (8) exploit inequality of opposing forces and radical disproportion; and (9) sustain the open-ended, maniform, protean features of discourse and dialogue.

In this study conditions of misdirection, equivocation, and vagueness are highly correlated with states of disagreement and misunderstanding while direct, clear, and straightforward interchange is mostly associated with conditions of agreement and understanding. Mutual sense-making practice produces a solid and in-depth level of common ground, coorientation, and consensus while the inability or unwillingness to reason together leads to systemic disorganization and chaos. The more problematic the level of exchange, the more evidence we have of protracted intolerance of the slippage, gaps, and lapses in sustained effort at meaning-endowed activity.

DILEMMAS/CONTRADICTIONS/PARADOX

Communication is never effortless nor automatically assured. The condition is manifest as an overcoming of resistance against whatever would hold it back. In effect, communication entails struggle over inertia and status. As such, it is an achievement that either occurs or does not. Linguistic success is never infallible nor inevitable but is rather established as a matter of kind and degree. There is, after all, only so much room to move in or out of relation with this or that particular source(s) of opportunity and constraint. We enable and constrain one another simultaneously. It turns out that the myth of perfect fidelity or union between two or more living beings is just as unobtainable an ideal as the presumption of singular escape into splendid isolation. Conclusion: miscommunication is inherent in communication within open systems.

Perhaps the quintessential dilemma of human communication lies in an inherent paradox. We are genetically programmed to transform matter and energy into information for survival purposes. At the same time we have an acquired capacity to engage in highly symbolic interactions that may be used to support the most profoundly bizarre belief and expectation, that is, the supposition that our limited physiological constitutions routinely convey complete and accurate information that need not be called into further question. Moreover, it is possible to expect informational exchanges to transliterate nonconscious signals, hints, innuendo, and necessarily, fleeting and transitory definition and description of shared action with such precision that no one in the exchange is beyond the pole of meaning.

Fights between spouses, for instance, often emerge out of their separate needs to be understood, but also out of their inability or unwillingness to comprehend that they simply cannot be understood as clearly or completely as they might wish. This is most often expressed as disbelief that their demand for their own personal conduct to be interpreted with total omprehension of understanding. Conversely, their spouse has the equally impossible task of conveying their reality as reality which includes their inability to grasp the significance of what the other attempts to convey.

Contradiction, as well as paradox, exists in this tangle. We really do appreciate the intent in one another's messages but refuse to believe that we do. We have adapted a mechanistic view of communication and believe we convey the intent of our shared actions, much as a truck transports goods. We assume that communication is merely a medium or carrier of a set load of information that arrives intact, and we have carefully taught ourselves to ignore the basic characteristics of the entire system of exchange.

Messages do not activate empty or neutral mechanical receptors but rather highly reflexive and sensitive modes of transformation—a rediscovery of what someone else discovers in our midst. In order to grasp and comprehend, one must take into account alternative pathways and means of taking into account. This requires a completely different way of knowing. The two spouses in question, for example, would have to discover means of sense-making that entails a process of sharing and joining for purposes of creating a wider range of more fully elaborated systemic processes. Such a way out of the dilemma would require considerable refocusing, less on causes when one party wants to obfuscate their own intentions in order to find cause with the flawed actions of the other and more mutual effort to know their connections in terms of the processes they are using in the context of not understanding or appreciating the meaning of the other.

#132 A's view: At a time when A has just decided to take some time off, a strange, strange set of feelings overtook her. It was almost as though A was feeling contradictory things at the very same time. For a while A feels excited yet scared about her "new freedom." She finds it strange to be completely on her own. A is also happy and sad at the same time. It is very hard to describe because A has never felt quite like it before. She actually feels both things—like laughing and crying in the same second. She can't control the way she feels—walking along and maybe a tear would drop or maybe she would just break out into a big grin that she could not wipe off her face. A wants to talk about it with people to make sure she stays rational about the whole thing and does not go overboard one way or the other. The difficulty is mainly that A is not sure exactly what she was feeling and so she couldn't describe it to anyone else.

#133 A's view: I felt that as well as I tried to explain my dilemma to my close friends and family members, they just didn't understand what I was talking about or they didn't feel it was important. The responses I got were "It's not that important," "You'll forget about it" etc. This happened when my boyfriend of one year broke up with me. I couldn't understand why and I had a terrible time accepting it. I tried to explain my feelings of anger, disgust, confusion, and hopelessness to my friends and family and I felt as though in the beginning they were sympathetic but were tired of hearing about it. I know I had to concentrate on other things, however, I felt as though I couldn't explain to anyone how much I loved him and why. Typical responses I received were that there are other fish in the sea and you are young. I didn't feel that my friends and family were intentionally belittling my problem. I feel they honestly felt that way about it. It's really easy to say something when you aren't the person experiencing it. It is always easier said than done as the saying goes.

#134 A's view: I am a very closed person to begin with, so there have been numerous times I could not express my feelings or things that are bothering me. If I feel sad around my friends or family, I put a mask on and act happy or like nothing is wrong. I feel why should they deal with my problems when they have their own worries of their own. Besides, I don't like people knowing my personal ideas. If my mate asks me what is wrong, I always reply 'nothing.' We had a major dilemma a few months ago, or at least I thought it was, and I just couldn't tell him what was bothering me. I avoided all eye contact with him and avoided the subject completely. I couldn't talk to him or anyone else. My best friend and I went to lunch during this dilemma and I just couldn't tell her what was happening or how I felt. I just sorted things around in my head. I try to be tough on the inside and the outside so no one would worry about me. I guess there are many situations where I just don't tell anyone anything for I fear they might tell someone else, betray me, or I just don't feel comfortable enough to tell them.

RELUCTANT TALK: LUST, SEX, AND LOVE

Some find talk about sex and love to be extremely difficult or virtually impossible. Respondents reflect back upon the personal influences associated with growing up without ever once hearing another human being say directly "I love you" or "You are precious." One respondent reasons that when small children are never told explicitly that they are loved by those who are closest to them, they may grow up to become young adults who never say "I love you" because they are so scared the others will not say it back. To be denied love after you have stated it so bluntly is to risk total rejection and be found unworthy. The three little words signify that a source of care giving is accessible and close at hand.

The first time someone says they are in love with you is a moment that can seem like the most joyous thing in all the world. Falling in love for the first time can be so confusing. When intense feelings are so new and real, it is often hard to stay in control. Everything one sees or does may remind him of the object of passion, lust, or desire. One may want to express such confusing forms of love but not know how to put it into words. Fear of rejection is a major theme. No one wants to be made a fool or to be teased. It may be better to keep these feelings to oneself and just fantasize over the object of one's desire. Words of love may become mental dress rehearsals that lead only to kisses and hugs, but without verbalized expression likely to be heard. Others claim rejection over lost love is no big deal. It's crazy to love one who doesn't love you back. Some people are simply too immature to know what genuine love really is. After losing one's first love, unable to explain the utter hopelessness, pain, and hurt, it somehow gets easier after a long period of time. Nothing seems worse than the loss of one's first true love. The possibility lingers with the longing to overcome all the fear now held for love.

Others find themselves being told over and over that someone else really does love them, but they themselves can only think "What is love?" The more others talk so casually of love, the less one may be able to respond. Individual A, for example, finds it very difficult to express to someone else how much they mean or how much influence they have had in A's life. It is hard to feel and think what you cannot bring yourself to say. It makes A angry to be constantly saying to himself, "Just say it" when the words just will not come out. It is as if the words are stuck on A's tongue with Krazy Glue and won't come off. The key question is whether A will always have so much trouble expressing such thoughts or whether each situation really differs all that much.

Individuals A and B date for a year and a half, and their relationship becomes extremely close. Inexplicably, both find it hard to say exactly how wonderful it is, and both assume the other has not experienced the situation in the same way and therefore cannot make the other fully understand the beauty of it all. The happiness is discovered in all the little things that one would normally overlook—a smile, the look in a starry gaze, a rose for no reason at all, a surprise outing, or an unexpected kiss on the cheek. Many times the obstacle seems to lie with the one who is unfamiliar with a care-giving relationship. This can be the underlying reason for a lack of any visible sign of appreciation for such little mindless things. One may be afraid to say how well things are going out of fear of hurting the other person's feelings. One would not want to make it seem as if the other person is missing out on something so wonderful. Maybe it is the fact that all of these little things just don't have the same significance to another person and does not hold the same meaning in their eyes.

It is important for talk of sex and love to transcend a common level of thought. The risk here is that the person who is listening does not feel as deeply moved as the person who is speaking when the interaction is complete. The depth of feeling is what gets lost when only one source says it or when another person hears it. The embedded moods and textures play a key role. One respondent suggests that perhaps what the world needs most now is a love-amplifying machine, a neurological feeling/thought/talk communicator—something that we could just plug into our minds and then plug into another's mind and thereby effectively convey the full magnitude of what we feel, think, and say.

Individuals A and B date for two years without saying they love one another. They talk about it many times, and each time A says he doesn't really know what love is. Individual B in turn thinks that this means A wants there to be flashing lights and bells ringing. It is very difficult for B not to tell A she is in love with him, so A does not feel she was saying it in order for him to tell her the same thing back. For several months B has to constantly bite her tongue until A finally says he loves her, but it is a phrase that is seldom used in their relationship even though B knows that A and

B really do love one another. The situation is one that friends do not understand, and it is even confusing and extremely frustrating for B, who now finds it a big challenge to say those three little words even today. Unresolved hurts from previous relationships prompt both to come into the relationship with their guards up.

Not being able to express true love can produce a terrible feeling. Individual A and B date for three years and never once express how they feel about one another. She never tells him she loves him, and he never tells her he loves her. Moreover, neither one expresses anger or love except during sex, which is the only sign that they like one another. Individual A is not a person who has ever had trouble expressing her affections until meeting B. The reason is that B has such a difficult time expressing himself in any way. He has a lot of problems and keeps his personal feelings and emotions to himself. She thinks he is afraid of getting hurt, so he never does let go and express the affection he does feel. Individual A views B's actions as an indication of an inability to express his true feelings, and this makes A become very afraid to express herself as well. Both are now locked into a position where each is afraid to say how they really feel about the other because they intuit the other is too afraid to say "I love you" back so it never gets said at all.

Consider a situation in which person A is trying to explain something he feels (at least at the time) is truly meaningful (deep). Simple clichés such as "I love you" (to opposite sex) may fall pathetically short of the magnitude of one's longing and desire. Outside social pressures enter in as well. Why risk saying how much another person means in a way that will make you end up feeling like an idiot? Such differences are what make for an interesting world, even if it can get so confusing and mixed up, with so many mixed messages widespread throughout the social fabric.

So we may need someone else to perform our private love songs for us. One of the hardest things for individual A to express is her love for her husband. When it comes to birthdays, anniversaries, and special times in their lives, A tries to find cards that express her true feelings, only to discover each time that there is no card that could ever say it all. When she sits down to write one herself, she is at a total loss for words. She starts one and tears it up because it sounds too mushy. Then she starts another one and tears it up because it sounds fake. Then A gets mad at herself and ends up not giving a card. She only hopes that when she tells him she loves him, he only knows how much.

There is also an oft-repeated theme of loving someone dearly but knowing that to speak of certain matters would only hurt one or the other's feelings. One may find it difficult to tell about one's own goals out of a deep love for the other person. A's feelings of love for another person are overwhelming, and this dictates why the hurt and frustration must be kept within. Such intense and salient urges may intensify over wedding proposals, where no outside advice will help. There is so much joy in finding someone to share the rest of one's life. A sense of joy and hope the other will say "Yes" mix with the possibility the other will say "No—you are not the one." One may not even know when is just the right moment to ask. When the other does say yes, the strongest urge is to want to rush right out and tell everyone else the good news, but at such times no words do the emotions justice—to feel as though you are the luckiest man or woman alive. No words can describe the full measure of the love, happiness, and joy.

Wedding days qualify as well. The bride and groom are so beautiful and accepting of the outpouring of love shown by all the family and friends assembled during one very traditional ceremony and reception. The mother of the bride wants to add to the remarks of welcome offered by her husband (the host), but no words could possibly capture the joy, so she decides not to express herself at the time. The dream she would not allow herself to dream for so long finally comes true, but only she can know the depth and pride and joy of the moment, and she could never say it so others could understand something so incredible.

ARTIFICIALLY INDUCED DISTORTIONS

#135 A's view: Last summer A had the opportunity to trip out at a Grateful Dead show at Alpine Valley (an experience in itself even without the help of hallucinogens). One hour after dropping the drugs A experienced severe paranoia and complete insanity for three hours. The trip was so intense A could not explain even to A's own self let alone others. Fantastic imagery blazing with colors intoxicated each thought. To this day A is still unaware of what went on during this experience.

#136 A's view: I remember being with some friends that I hadn't seen for a long time and we had been drinking all day. By say 8:30 that night I was pretty well intoxicated and up for just about any new and exciting challenge. One of my friends had just gotten a big bag of mushrooms and we decided to eat some. Because I had never done any before, I didn't know how bad the side effects would be. Friends say I ate probably three grams which I guess is a lot. Because I was so drunk, the mushrooms had an incredible effect on me. I remember going to a graduation party and everyone I talked to seemed blurry. I was very nervous and kept running around frantically, not realizing what I was doing. I would look at people and the bottoms on their shirts were like neon lights. I kept hearing weird noises in my head. It seemed like I was in the middle of a screen of a Pac Man game. Then when I finally got home that evening and went to bed, really weird shit started happening. It felt like I was dead, and I could hardly move my body. It seemed as though I would fall into these trances and would have to physically bring myself out of it. This was quite an experience for me and I have never done it again since that time. In a way it was sort of neat, but in other ways it was really scary.

#137 A's view: During high school A starts to experiment with drugs. For a year he uses marijuana and hashish and finds it stimulating and enjoyable. One night someone sells A some acid. A has heard of acid, of course, and has been with friends while they were tripping out but has not tried it out. But this particular time A is feeling adventuresome, so A buys a hit and swallows it. At first it isn't unlike being very high on good hash. Later, however, strange things start to happen. Geometric patterns appear on the floor, and A can't believe how neat it is. A is at a bar, and nobody knows A is tripping, but A would see these things and break out laughing. Then someone would say something really innocent like "How are you?" or something, and A would say "Like right now, as a primal animal, or superior being?!" Others laugh hysterically. Well, of course, eventually A realizes A is getting out of control and that people are noticing A is not exactly himself. So A excuses himself to go to the bathroom and slides out the door. Fortunately A lives close by, so he just walks home. To this day it's hard to describe how beautiful it is walking home on a cold winter night and feeling so outside of A's "normal" state-of-mind, walking through a park on the way, the moon shining through the trees onto the snow and hallucinating even more stunning colors, patterns, and so on. After he makes it home and marvels at the things appearing on the walls, A eventually falls asleep. Upon awakening the next afternoon, he feels a deep disappointment in the mundanity around him. The things he had experienced the night before he knew were drug induced, but he missed them. Looking back, A feels he has gained some real insights into the world we don't normally see. The end result is that A quit doing pot and hash, telling others he couldn't afford it or whatever. But the reason is that A knows he had experienced a special time, gaining important insights into life and his social circle, so he doesn't feel the need to experiment with drugs anymore.

#138 A's view: The only time I could not express what I was feeling was during an LSD trip. Even today it is difficult to describe. At first I enjoyed it, but after perhaps an hour, strange things began happening. The only way I've been able to describe it is that it felt like my brain was exploding. I was in the back seat of a car at night and the oncoming headlights scared me really bad. I felt as if they were penetrating me. We then became stuck in a traffic jam and I felt very claustrophobic. My mind was going so fast I didn't even know what I was feeling. Even today it is difficult to describe what a terrible feeling it was. Shadows were the worst as they seemed to be attacking me. Colors didn't bother me much though, although they seemed to blend into a large mass. Probably the weirdest thing, however, was the TV. A man was wearing a tweed jacket and the jacket seemed like the feeling you have when your foot falls asleep. It is one experience that I will never feel again.

#139 A's view: One year ago I had a terrible experience with drugs. I felt at the time that it was impossible to express to anybody and in a sense still do. I was unable to express what I was feeling at the time in part because I felt everyone was against me—feelings of extreme paranoia. I don't think I've ever encountered anything remotely like it. For a fact, I myself have trouble understanding exactly how I felt. Occasionally, though, I find myself reliving the feelings vividly and inadvertently. The memories come flooding back unintentionally. I am almost glad of it. Although I can never express the experience to anyone else, or ever impart what I have learned for someone else to use, I retain the experience as almost an integral part of myself.

#140 A's view: When I was in high school I was involved with a group of kids who were into a lot of drinking and drugs. In high school there was never a real problem, but once I started college, I knew that I needed help. My parents convinced me to join AA when I came home after my freshman year of college. Most of my friends and my family knew that I was joining and would ask me about it. I had a difficult time explaining what I was feeling and going through. I knew that a lot of my friends were worried about me, but that just made things more difficult. I didn't want them to pity me because I had a problem. At the meetings I was more comfortable with discussing it because I knew that none of the group had a right to criticize or judge me. But I still could not really talk to them about my life—only the problem. Usually I felt like I was being analyzed and didn't want to say anything that could be changed around. After a couple of months things got better. At the beginning though I felt totally alone because people tried to put me in this group like I belonged but I knew that no one was exactly like me, going through things exactly the same (as I) was.

#141 A's view: When I first started seeing my girlfriend, it was at a time when she was into drugs. I have never done any in my life and it was a rather uncomfortable situation at times. This doesn't sound all that strange but here is why it was. I met her at a summer camp and people usually refrain from anything (substance wise) while being a counselor. Anyway things were fine for the summer. It was when we got home that I had my problem. She got back into her drugs (nothing really bad) but it made me extremely upset and uncomfortable. I felt as though I really couldn't confront her with it and most of my friends really couldn't understand what I was going through. They all felt I was making too big of a deal about things. I tried explaining to my friends in more detail and really tried to show them how she was affecting me. People continued to tell me I was making too much of an issue and every time my girlfriend and I talked about the subject I would burn up inside. I was never more unhappy with a feeling than that one. I'm not sure why I had such a terrible feeling but I'm even more confused about the reactions I got from my friends. I guess the combination of the uncomfortable feeling I got from my girlfriend and the fact that I felt my friends really couldn't understand me makes me feel as though NO ONE really was there for me to express myself to. I'm usually the kind of person who needs to go to others for advice or at least just to talk. This was one of the worst experiences for me ever—to have to deal with this situation entirely on my own.

#142 A's view: When I was in elementary school my father had a very bad drinking problem. I would wait up every night for him to stumble through the door so I could put him to bed before mom and him got into a fight. I spent many days in school wondering what would happen when I got home and where I should hide the knives tonight. I felt I couldn't express my fear, anger, hate, and confusion to anyone. This was mainly because my sister and I were told we couldn't. My family of four became very good actors and should have won an Emmy. Instead we won ulcers and nightmares. In fourth grade I started attending Alateen, when I realized I wasn't alone. There were millions of people out there living with the same illness. I learned that I didn't cause it and I sure as hell couldn't cure it. Since then I have always had this support group and today Alanon has given me a place to express anything. And there I am completely free.

#143 A's view: Just last weekend I went home for a visit. On Friday night I made plans with my friends to go out to some of the more popular hangouts. I was excited to go out and see some of my old high school friends and have a few drinks. About 9:30 that night a couple of my girlfriends came and picked me up and we headed straight downtown for a night that I thought would be full of socializing and excessive drinking. However, when we walked into the first local bar I saw a familiar face—it was that of my dad. Seeing him in the bar wasn't what shocked me. My mom and dad got a divorce because of my dad's excessive drinking problem. What shocked me was the fact that my 47-year-old father was flirting incessantly with one of my friends from high school—and she didn't seem to be too bothered by it. The feeling I was experiencing at that particular moment was something that I can't really put into words. Not only was I shocked by what I was seeing. I was disgusted by it. In my state of confusion, I walked slowly toward my dad. When I finally approached him he reached out to give me a hug but I moved away from him. I didn't want him to touch me. Not when I was so disgusted by the way I had just seen him behaving. So he then proceeded to introduce me to his flirting partner but I quickly interrupted him saying that I already knew her. When she realized who this man was she looked down at the bar feeling a bit embarrassed. After a very brief conversation with my father I returned to my friends down at the other end of the bar feeling embarrassed and mad knowing that my friends had also seen the suggestive interaction that had been taking place upon our arrival at the bar. It would not have been so bad if I or my dad would have left the bar shortly after this little incident but unfortunately due to circumstances beyond my control I had to stay right where I was for the two hours that followed. My dad also remained at the bar for those two hours, wandering around in his drunken stupor, trying to talk to and 'hang-out' with people I had grown up with. I sat on my barstool watching my father try to fit in where he did not belong. He would occasionally buy a drink for someone hoping they would reciprocate but from what I observed, none did. People would say a few words to him if he hovered over them long enough but would then turn themselves away from dad hoping that he would take the hint and leave. I went home that night with many feelings I couldn't express to anyone. I felt like no one could understand what I was feeling when I saw this grown man, whom I loved despite his faults, wandering aimlessly around with such a pathetic look on his face, hoping someone would acknowledge him in a setting that was full of college students who wanted nothing to do with him. I had known for a long time that my father spent much of his time in bars but seeing him like that was a whole other type of realization I had to come to terms with by myself because none of the people I was with could identify with me or relate to how I was feeling at the time.

The subject of intoxication is incredibly complicated. Generalizations are hazardous because the center of the action is so context specific and situationally dependent. A broad spectrum of forces and factors separate the domain of use from those of misuse, or abuse. At issue are complex linkages between what one drinks, eats, inhales, or injects and subsequent alterations (or transformations) in the construal of interaction between oneself and others.

Artificially induced distortions alter the level of connection and synchrony between interactants. As the occasion for playful creativity, imagination, and innovation, states of intoxication produce temporary diversion from conventional sense-making practices while casting them into sharp relief. The recreational use of drugs and alcohol provides radically different ways of looking at the world and a measure of relief from the rigors of the day-to-day grind.

While under the influence of mind-altering substances, some respondents find some forms of communication to be easier than before. Retrograde bar talk, as a case in point, tends to revolve around either trivial matters that require minimal communicative skill or more important concerns expressed through slurred talk, blurred vision, impaired hearing, and babble without meaningful substance. However, the lowering of inhibitions is also equated with an inexplicable urge and willingness to discuss what matters most in one's own life. Increased comfort coincides with diminished concern over the consequences of what one might say or do. Temptations and libations help break superficial barriers that people put around themselves and their feelings.

Alcohol acts as a social lubricant. It is highly tolerant of loose talk and wagging tongues. In effect, the appearance of openness and candor can be chemically induced in a legally sanctioned manner. People who drink together may retreat into their own little worlds and not even think about their own communicative behavior at the time. Personal problems dissolve while fears and anxieties subside. It may take until the morning after to experience any negative reaction to how one behaved before others the night before.

Sometimes shared distortions work well for all concerned. People forget about their troubles and fill the air with the sounds of laughter and gaiety. Everyone has a good time, and no one is hurt. The world is magical, childlike, and alumnus. Fantastic images blaze with colors and richly textured thought. Music comes alive, stimulating, animated, and enjoyable. A cold winter night is transformed into a briefly inspiring cosmic journey. Induced distortions help one celebrate what remains mysterious, miraculous, and ultimately unknown. What unfolds from nine to five pales by comparison.

Nonetheless, no medication is risk free. The misuse and abuse of mind-altering substances has incredible, irreversible side effects. It takes a tremendous toll. Instead of opening up possibilities for communication, the process may close them down. Precious human resources go down the drain. What is so poignant and striking are the basic mechanisms designed to ensure that matters of chemical addiction are treated as an unspeakable subject.

The edges of abuse spill over from the participant to the observer. What follows is an understated reconstruction of the generalized sense of interactive abuse as framed from the position of second-hand parties. It is virtually impossible to stop some individuals from becoming totally intoxicated. To tell the truth would only bring out the threat of further reprisal. The operative rule is to stay away. There is to be no mention outside the immediate circle. No one else ever needs to know. The weight of the unspoken secret falls mainly on those who would intervene if only they could. Some addictions grow out of control. Mental dress rehearsal: don't talk; don't feel; seek refuge in silence, however weak a defense it turns out to be. Above all else, don't breathe a word. Talk of intervention is strictly out of the question.

NONSENSE: WHEN NOTHING MAKES SENSE

#144 A's view: When my friends and I start to argue, no one really says what they feel and most of it is just gibberish, total nonsense. While I listen to everyone bitch and carp back and forth, I just think to myself, "Why even say anything?" But the others get pissed off at me for not saying anything at a time when no one knows what they are talking about. You can't win. Well I finally say something but it is not what I really feel like saying. I want to say, "You guys are a bunch of assholes and I really don't give a shit one way or another." But of course I say, "Well, let's talk sense and compromise."

"Nonsense" is the name of a strategy under which are subsumed several communicative tactics. The overarching raison d'etre for this strategy is the internal demand that boundaries between self and other be erected and maintained or completely eradicated. It is, of course, possible that the language and metalanguage of the respective parties is so removed from the subject at hand and its contextual referents that meaning is either lost or rendered unobtainable. Some individuals who suffer from psychoses will often employ neologistic language and, in addition, may be disoriented from time and place. Consequently, neither the content of their language nor its context are able to give clues as to their intended meaning.

When the strategy is oriented to maintaining boundaries, a variety of pernicious tactics is possible. Is it possible for person A, for instance, to refuse to interpret the messages of person B? Since interpretations are essentially predictions of meaning based on necessarily incomplete data, A is put in the position of constantly needing to clarify and specify her/his meaning and intent. The more persistent A is in his/her refusal to interpret, the more distinct from meaning B becomes. Should B attempt intentional metacommunication, A will in all probability continue to refuse to interpret B's request. The form of refusal to interpret frames the discourse and places a stylistic demand on B. Consequently, if A says of B's statements, "That's nonsense," and offers no further explanation, if the subject and its context offers no hint of meaning, B will be adrift in what feels like a cosmos of nonmeaning, nonreference and nonstrategy for communication of intent.

It is also possible to create nonsense by opening the boundaries of meaning to a kind of surrealistic struggle to admit every possible mean-ing—hence no meaning at all. Each one of us has experienced conversations with those who accept every meaning we offer without equivocation, evaluation, or judgment. Under these conditions, everything we say has the same meaning, salience, or valence. Consequently, we lost the intent of our messages and soon experience the strange sense of being lost through the looking glass of meaningless. With this tactic, the participants refuse to punctuate communicative sequences into components and hierarchies of meaning. Since it is impossible to both communicate and intentionally metacommunicate the respective weights of the meanings of the stream of messages, we have to depend on the other. When they refuse or are unable to punctuate, we are lost in mapless territory, our shared forms of expressed activity grow increasingly nonsensical.

In Albee's play, *Who's Afraid of Virginia Wolff?* George asks, "Truth and illusion, who knows the difference, eh, toots?" When people convince themselves of the truth of anything, they begin to move inexorably toward the need to define, describe, and defend their truths at all costs. Hence, they may soon reach a crossing point beyond which arguments regress into infinitely spiraling forms of nonsense. As the other communicants challenge the arguments and the tenaciously held truth, they find themselves in a web of nonsense and begin to say precisely what they do not mean. One may hear passionate liberals espouse the most reactionary political arguments in defense of a radical "truth," while the other party blathers liberal certitudes even though they are consummate conservatives, all in their nonsensical defense and attack on "the truth."

Nonsense may become the rule of the tithe of conversation, held purely and simply for the sake of initiation of a relationship. It is the sort of form of exchange in which the information is of little or no importance. What is central to the tithe of exchange is the willingness to make contact and connect. Meaning lies in a discursive and dialogical process and any specific bit of content may have little or no meaning. Compliments, nonsense syllables, clichés, and euphemisms often fall into this category and are merely conveyances for contact.

FATE

#145 A's view: I guess the simplest way to explain is by using the word "fate." Whenever I think of all the reasoning behind my existence on earth, I often become speechless—as if the way I grasp things is inexpressible to another. Here's an example. Sometimes I wonder if the world is just a figment of my imagination. I mean, maybe I'm the only person really living and everyone I come into contact with and everything that I see or think about is all really there because it's there to affect me. For example, this questionnaire is just being filled out because it's a part of the master plan in *my* life—but nobody really exists—they're just here to play a part in my life. And after they do, they don't have separate lives—they just don't exist except to affect my life.

Fatalism may perpetuate miscommunication as a way of life. Others are encountered from the stance of a pure spectator. Human dialogue unfolds on every side and all around, but none of it really matters. It is almost as if one is resigned to sit on the sidelines and passively watch the game in a manner of resigned acceptance. Fatalism over interaction rests on the presumption that nothing can be done. Through participation in the perpetuation of tradition, habit, custom, and routine, one may become encased in a protective cocoon that constrains or prevents movement toward new and more effective modes of human interchange (Giddens, 1991). Unless routinized but ineffectual modes of exchange can be called into question, participants are in danger of living a fatalistic life.

The refusal or inability to discuss friction, strife, and strain further legitimates the sense that none of it can be overcome. During hectic or pressurized activities, it is important to reassess the driving fatalistic forces that dictate the course of life and adapt personal needs and desires according to personal priorities rather than allow frenzied circumstance to control the definition and direction of one's life. For interactants to overcome the self-imposed invisible walls involves great risk because one's sense of security can be easily threatened. Individuals who do not tolerate feelings of vulnerability may take refuge in acts of minimum disclosure during interaction.

Matters of security and risk enter into the calculus of fatalism in those situations where expressive acts have little or no power to alter the outcome of events. Heavily filtered messages complicate and encumber the process of interpretation. Respondents are prone to utilize a fatalistic outlook when dealing with others over great distances or time frames, when struggling over crisis, or when failing to know how to react to unanticipated or unwelcome complications in conversation. Missing is the recognition that those who blame their own involvements with problematic communication could be relying on those very same forces as a solution. According to Giddens (1991), fate has a unique relationship with risk because "fateful decisions are usually almost by definition difficult to take because of the mixture of the problematic and consequential that characterize them" (p. 114).

Fatalism undermines efforts to play a more active role in shaping events in one's life. What is required is the resolve to reevaluate any ineffective or burdensome mode of human interchange or whatever has been taken for granted or merely accepted as an expression of the way it is. At issue is the opportunity for renewed search for alternative frames of reference and trajectories of action that facilitate better adjustment to the realities of everyday life and promote unconditional regard for the expressive freedom to live by one's own standards. Finally, matters of security and risk need to be acknowledged for one to decipher what aspects of problematic interchange need to be addressed. The immediate objective of the shared movement is toward a communicative environment in which each participant can feel safe and secure. The urge to overcome risk enables one to come to terms with fear and acquire a more sustaining level of security and well being. The pursuit of optimum conditions is what enables the respective parties to remain open to the possibilities of discourse and dialogue, despite the countervailing force of whatever would hold anyone back.

REFERENCES

Atkinson, J. M. & Heritage, J. (Eds.). (1984). *Structures of social action*. Cambridge, MA: Cambridge University Press.

Becker, E. (1973). *The denial of death*. New York: Free Press.

Giddens, A. (1991). *Modernity and self-identity*. Stanford, CA: Stanford University Press.

Sperber, D. & Wilson, D. (1986). *Relevance: Communication and cognition*. Cambridge, MA: Harvard University Press.

7

Symbolic Violence

C. David Mortensen with Carter Morgan Ayres

REAL VIOLENCE

If we want to make the world a better place, we must be prepared to construct less violent means of cohabitation and communication. At issue is the universal struggle to understand, access, and mobilize affordable personal resources into communicative activities that contribute to the urge to make love, not war. After all, personal expressions of love and war are extraordinary sense-making achievements. Each operates at opposite ends of the spectrum of affection and disaffection. The main difference is that love preserves strong ties between individuals while war annihilates those same possibilities. The focus of this chapter is the movement away from the radical disaffection implicit in acts of physical violence and toward their plausible symbolic counterparts.

In the study of human problematics, every member participates in the collective definition of violence. We will examine violence as a meaningful construct within the context of human relationships; within this framework, acts of violence consist of whatever is life-threatening in human interaction. In its truest sense, the term "real violence" implies a *dynamic interaction* between destructive thoughts and abusive acts, and between confused thought and emotional pain.

Real violence acquires definition through the impact of feeling and thought on speech and action in human relationships; likewise, the process is shaped by how what is said and done affects what is thought and felt. Such an integrated notion provides a dynamic way of conceptualizing the sources of pain and injury in human relationships; it recognizes that complex urges, sensations, feelings, thoughts, and goal-directed actions determine whether our relationships prevent or encourage interpersonal understanding and support in everyday life.

Generically speaking, the term "real violence" refers to all outcomes of our interactions and relationships that have the power to hurt us. Because people experience real violence in a totalistic and synthetic manner, we will focus upon linguistic and psychological hurt and injury—we call it "symbolic violence"—and describe its dynamic connection with physical violence. The term is an acknowledgment that words and gestures are weapons (and a defense) that have the power to inflict serious injury and intensify the immediate effects of physical force.

Acts of symbolic violence may be expressed in a litany of verbal and nonverbal forms; they also involve the meanings we crystallize directly from personal experience. When we experience violence in its symbolic (transliteral) sense through our interactions with others, we visualize, think about, feel, and internalize or project hurtful meanings; when we initiate acts of symbolic violence, we produce words or make gestures that convey hurtful feelings to others, who then visualize, think about, feel, and internalize our hurtful intentions toward them. Regardless of the initial source of reference, collections of individuals are involved. Symbolic violence creates resentment, contempt, disgust, loathing, and hatred that permeates our manifest relations with one another, and our implicit feelings for ourselves.

Unlike the observable outcomes of physical violence, however, the hurtful and injurious effects of symbolic violence are almost always hidden from sight. In this chapter, then, our goal is to discuss the central dynamic of symbolic violence, and how violent images and meanings hurt and injure all of us. In this way, our study of symbolic violence will illuminate the militancy of the expressive environment, and its damaging effects in the lives of people from every walk of life. Only when individuals understand the basic mechanisms of symbolic violence are they in a position to create a life-world within themselves that, when shared with family, friends, and the community at large, encourages mutual understanding and compassion in interpersonal relationships.

Warfare takes place in a massively destructive environment where symbolic violence takes the form of deeply troubling images that will not go away. Consider the following experience related by a participant of an aerial assault in Vietnam. A twenty-year survivor of the war, he was sitting on a park bench when approached to make the statement presented below. For him, the war has continued to impact directly in the form of violent images recalled from inescapable thoughts and feelings that have lingered for more than two decades.

#146 A's view: There have been many instances in my life but one that stands out above all the rest happened in 1970 while serving in Vietnam with the Marine Corps as a door gunner aboard a Ch-46 helicopter. Six helicopters from our squadron were assigned to extract a company of Marines surrounded and under heavy fire in the

Que Son mountains west of Da Nang. As the first helicopter approached the landing zone, it was shot down. The second helicopter was also shot down as it approached the zone near the first helicopter. A third helicopter was making an attempt to get in but came under such heavy fire that it was forced to abort and return to Da Nang. Now it was our turn to start in the zone but we were instead asked to fly low-level through the zone to draw fire so helicopter gun ships could locate the heaviest concentrations of firepower. As we started through the zone (fifty feet off the ground at one hundred and eighty mph) we came under intense fire. At this point all ground fire was directed at our helicopter and machine gun fire and tracer rounds exploded everywhere. So many rounds were hitting our helicopter that it sounded like a hundred men beating on the helicopter with hammers. As we started to lift out of the zone into a max climb, the crew chief, Scott Wheeler, turned around to say something to me and at that point was shot in the back of the head. I started to tell the pilots Wheeler was dead but they already knew because there were pieces of flesh and blood everywhere, even in the cockpit. We immediately headed back to Da Nang. After we landed, we put Scott's body in a body bag, patched the bullet holes, and hosed down the inside of the helicopter. With a new crew chief, we were back at the landing zone in less than an hour. Before this mission started, Scott and I had been on standby at a small fire base near the Laotian border. We were drinking a can of Coke and talking about our plans after we had returned to the U.S. As I helped load Scott's body into a body bag, conversations among the crew kept going back to the way it had been only fifteen minutes before. How do you express what you feel through all the numbness, anger, and outrage? What or who do you tell? How do you explain to those who could not possibly understand how it feels to put your best friend in a body bag? It took fifteen years for me to even tell my wife these things without going to pieces, much less relate the experience to someone at the time.

In this Southeast Asian jungle setting, real violence unfolds in the form of a rescue operation deep in a firing zone. The drama takes place within a much larger killing field which eventually produced fifty-eight thousand American casualties and the mass destruction of several hundred thousand local inhabitants. Machine guns on all sides fire at point-blank range and helicopters fall from the sky. The terrible images of a friend instantaneously becoming splattered blood and ragged chunks of flesh are still indelibly imprinted on his consciousness.

While the Marine's written response is full of images, their meaning becomes partially obscured as his writing style impresses the reader with its mechanically specific, almost dry, recollection of the facts surrounding the hideous battle. He conveys very little personal feeling until the end of his response. One central reason for such numbed description is that violent dangers were everywhere, and they have shocked the writer's mind into a state of contrived calm. For him, "heavy fire" is a safe technical term to convey his experience of hundreds of machine gun shells smashing and slashing their way through American helicopters and the men inside them while still preserving his publicly expected persona of personal sanity.

The images storming through the mind of the respondent, however, are neither technical nor socially acceptable; they are overwhelming. Guiding them toward personal meaning and emotional agony are powerful beliefs in the inexpressibility of their visualized violence and emotional impact. These conceptualized images of a close friend's violent death are unspeakable in their horror, and the pain they create in the center of this man's being remain his alone; they smash through his emotional defenses and leave him staring numbly at a body bag that, just fifteen minutes before, was the furthest thing from his mind. As he struggles to reconcile his thoughts of what transpired fifteen minutes ago with Scott's sudden and total absence, grief and outrage permeate his body, mind, and spirit. Even revenge does not take away the pain.

For this marine, all that is left are more years of unresolved grieving over indelible images that painfully play over and over again in what has become the battlefield of his mind and memory. To this day, no one, it seems, has been able to recognize the agony in his eyes; he, in turn, presumes that no one else is caring or capable enough to appreciate how this physical and emotional horror penetrated a relationship of infinite importance and transformed it into unending emotional suffering. Under such conditions, it is little wonder that he finds it impossible to say anything meaningful about his traumatic experience to anyone else.

All of us have difficulty when we try to translate the eloquence of the images we perceive and feel so that others around us may hear and understand. Mental images often speak the truth of personal experience far more easily and eloquently than do words and sentences; indeed, they have the power to create a nonverbal reality that can upstage anything words can express. Images are eloquent and codify meanings far more clearly, quickly, and completely than verbal abstraction. To attempt to translate images into words and sentences seems to add confusion and inaccuracy to the understanding of others, and added frustration for oneself. Better perhaps, and more accurate, to allow our screaming and crying to identify the existence of such eloquent images as framed from within, even if these sounds do not tell others much about the emergent framework of our own personal reality.

As a result, most of us perceive words as a limited means for translating our inner sense of poignancy, harrow, and loss to others; the fact remains that it is difficult to explain the meaning of the images to ourselves, let alone to someone else. Besides, grieving encourages a person to withdraw toward internal images and meanings, there to lovingly languish over them; because the images and meanings are built into so many intimate reflections, it is hard to believe that someone else could conceive of them, much less care about them. In the interactive emptiness, all that is conveyed comes from mass media coverage that, at least for a time, broadcasts images and words that portray the illusion of the necessity and importance of war.

The aftermath of war's violence gives rise to fatalism and resignation, which in turn solidify the decision to remain silent. War's violence kills quickly, completely, and with utter finality; violence is impatient, but once it is over, it is over. At war's end, the casualties list at the war memorial reads like a final statement of the war's meaning. "These men were brave, and served their country well." Of course, those who were killed can no longer present their own thoughts and feelings; nor can they see, hear, feel, move, or touch in relation to the activities of any other person or source. The images and meanings they once struggled to convey are now and forever beyond reach because each man is now a symbol of a condition of eternal nothingless and loss. There will be no more arguments, conflicts, disputes, or intractable problematic issues. Death has overturned the purpose and possibility of communication. There is no more possibility of interplay between discourse and dialogue. The circle is broken.

Real violence, of course, is not limited to wars overseas; it is indigenous to day-to-day experience and our interactions with others. After three decades to remember and forget, the linguistic war at home continues, unabated. It is a far more subtle kind of war that is desensitizing and numbing in frequency, duration, and intensity of occurrence; moreover, its methods often revolve around the use of physical force. Here is where conspicuous modes of miscommunication gradually increase over extended time frames without much public fanfare, depending upon one's position in the increasingly stratified social hierarchy. Those citizens most likely to experience interpersonal violence are usually those who are least able to cope with it.

Violence follows impatience associated with deprivation, neglect, inequity in social status, and glaring disparities in the distribution of financial resources and employment opportunities. Thoughts of violence proceed from the fact that linguistic, economic, and material resources are unevenly distributed throughout the social fabric. Because of these disparities, poorer and less powerful citizens make better victims than others. Indeed, it is those who are most lacking in linguistic resources such as problem-solving strategies that are the most seriously disadvantaged when it comes to matters of barter and negotiation over vital economic and material interests.

For this reason, a physical crime against the state (for example, stealing) turns inward and finds some of its antecedents in a form of symbolic violence against single individuals (for example, being told one is "not what we want" when applying for a job for which one is well qualified). As a result, the type of language that cannot be used to work through problematic concerns is what becomes apparent in the behavior of the interactants. Discourse and dialogue are totally constrained within narrow expressive and interpretive roles—holdup man/thief and police officers/protectors. Verbalizations are not geared to the state of a troubled and frustrated individual, but rather to a man, already judged to be a criminal, who has two choices—to calm down and surrender or to die.

#147 A's view: At age thirteen A witnessed an event that left him speechless. The event occurred at a Poppy's restaurant. It was a hot sunny day with no wind. A black man was holding up the place at lunch time. A lot of people were running around screaming. The police were just arriving on the scene. Soon it was swarming with police cars. A huge black truck appeared on a side street. Out of this black truck came a lot of men with rifles. They dispersed all around Poppy's. People with megaphones talked to the holdup man and tried to calm him down and reason with him. Then the holdup man began to shoot. This was followed by a resounding series of bangs. The man fell dead. Individual A felt numb for several days afterward. Important things became less important. Individual A hasn't told anyone about the shooting until now, and just thinking about it makes A wonder.

The language employed is what defines the level of violence that took place. In fact, there was only one goal of this conversation—to stop him one way or another. In this case, language sets the scene for the police to win. All there was to be determined was the degree of violence required to get the job done—symbolic threats or ritualized threat and physical violence combined.

In contrast, there are times in which acts of violence in society result not only from social inequities and the resulting frustration but from the very absence of human contact itself. Independent decisions made on an individual or group level can have negative outcomes that accumulate over time and predispose individuals to engage in acts of symbolic and physical violence. This results from the fact that segments within the society at large are predisposed to solve communal problems violently rather than through the consistent use of individual inquiry and open discussion. In the following response, a calculated risk involving the withholding of new information sets the stage for a violent encounter. Here, the fear of openness preceded the encounter, providing a clear indication of why lines of open communication need to remain both openly available and actively reassuring to members of the wider community at large.

#148 A's view: This has something to do with interactions with some of my blood relatives. The family has a son. The son and I were getting along pretty well but soon my father and I discovered that the son was involved in drug trafficking. The first thought was to expose the whole issue to the entire family but after careful consideration we decided not to bring it up. The family in question had a very good reputation and great status in our community. By exposing the issue we were afraid we might ruin their reputation and respect in the eyes of others. We thought that we were making the right decision. But after a few months, we learned the son was killed in cross-fire with police. Suddenly we wished we could run the clock backward and have talked directly to the family. We felt quite guilty over this incident as if we participated indirectly in the killing of the son by not reporting the incident to the family. Our family still carries the guilt to this day through much of our daily lives. It is not pleasant to know we lost the opportunity of a lifetime by not expressing something that should have been discussed in spite of uncertain cost.

At risk here are ways in which what we say or don't say can affect personal and social realities in quite fundamental and profoundly important ways. What we think and say or do as a result has the power to create violent (even death-dealing) interactions between individuals and groups. It is this type of personal violence that has its roots in the experience of persons who replay over and over violent thoughts and picture violent images of human destruction. Nowhere is this more evident than in the following description of how a life-threatening fight erupted from the negative and predetermined conceptions of the interactants. Once again, the process is that of ignoring—or being totally unaware of—the possibility of mutually supportive interaction in favor of an ultimatum. Following this, a fight erupts, filling the minds of those present with images of unspeakable violence. These images in turn escalate the level of actual physical violence until it is almost lethal. The participants approach the outer limits of what is possible.

#149 A's view: We were drinking at a party in a bar and everyone was pretty drunk. Well, four bikers—dirtballs—Mexicans, or whatever else they were, walked into the place and refused to pay. They pushed their way to the bar and started to grab some of the girls. Three other men and I went over and asked them (peacefully) to leave. They refused and one threw a punch. The house was completely packed. Eight guys started to fight all at once. We pushed the fight outside and one girl started to scream. The guy I had been fighting left and I ran over to see my friend. He was laying on the ground bleeding to death. Three of the motherfuckers had pulled knives and stabbed him in the shoulders and the arms. Once we saw what those bastards had done, we went after them. Three got away but were later caught by the police. The fourth we caught and almost beat to death. He was hit with a tire iron and other things. I hope the vengeance and hate that was generated never comes back to me or my friends because the next time the man will not be alive. I have not talked about this matter except to the police. My friends know well enough to leave it be. In no way am I a weak-minded person but the complex feelings surrounding the experience are something to be forgotten.

The last three entries underscore important themes. Notions of 'sheer physical violence' are a misnomer here. Deep personal injuries acquired during interaction are never merely physical. Even acts of physical brutality reveal a deeper, hidden truth—that acts of physical violence emerge from acts of symbolic violence and vice versa. In this way, acts of murder and suicide draw tacit inspiration from the surrounding communicative milieu, while painful and injurious attitudes result from the emotional impact of physical violence.

These dynamic interactions between physical and symbolic violence have very negative outcomes. As we have seen, a respondent who served in Vietnam agonizes for decades over the death of his friend. Another respondent watches a man who needed money risk and subsequently lose his life. Even people who avoid risking life or limb can become hurt and injured because there were very few communicative options from which to choose. For all of these people what has happened cannot be erased. Neither privilege nor power can rebuild the shattered dreams, retrieve the precious resources, or actualize the unique potentialities of those who have been injured or killed.

It is very common in our society for symbolic and physical violence to be encouraged by the frequent use of alcohol and other drugs. With a sufficient supply of just the right mix of lubricants, your anger and rage can easily predispose you to picturing images of yourself killing whatever moves, whatever gets in your way, literally anything in sight. Underneath overt acts of hitting, kicking, stabbing, wounding, suffocating, shooting, and killing may be located a substrata of nameless, tacit acts of unresolved symbolic injury accumulated from the past. It is ironic that the same acts of physical and symbolic violence encouraged within society are precisely those one must also suffer, and perhaps die for in the end.

The whole issue of hurt and injury may be construed in terms of victims. They are the underdogs, the persons to whom our hearts go out. When we hear about suicides through the media, we often think of those who kill themselves as victims of intolerable conditions. They are not understood, we may think, and so they had no confidence with which to weather the difficult periods in their lives.

While this point of view has merit, we will focus on the survivors of suicide as victims, and on the hurt and injury that they endure. Individuals who are personally related to one who has suicided suffer through endless year of pain, guilt, grieving, and a profound sense of loss. For this reason, we suspect the self-inflicted deaths of relatives and friends of our respondents are correctly interpreted as acts of personal expedience as well as of personal desperation. In this sense, acts of suicide become acts of symbolic violence against family and friends, as well as acts of physical violence against the self. Consider, for example, the following response which provides evidence of selfish violence on the part of a brother who totally ignored the impact of his behavior of every other member of his family.

#150 A's view: There have been times in life when I couldn't even explain what transpired to *myself* let alone express such vital matters to anyone else. From about age four to age seven, I was sexually abused and raped by my brother who was five years older than me. I wanted to tell someone but he either would threaten me or say that if I told anyone something bad would happen to him. I *did love* my brother. I only hated what he had done. So I remained silent. Once, I threatened I would finally tell. I think I was about seven-years-old at the time. Anyway, he got very upset and ran off. I found him later in his room with a belt around his neck and fastened to the door knob. He was laying on the ground just appearing to be dead.

I started to cry and yell his name. He opened his eyes and started to laugh at me. I just cried and went into my room. Two years later, moments after my parents had returned from shopping, I opened the door to my house and there he was, with a rope around his neck, tied to a chinning bar that had been a Christmas present a few days before. He didn't open his eyes. I knew this was for real. Being the only one inside at the time, I ran to the door to keep anyone else from entering. Needless to say, it didn't work. The tragedy goes on but that is the brunt of it. I didn't express anything really, except gut feelings left over from what had transpired. My feelings weren't expressed until six months later when I began to cry for no reason. Hell, I didn't even go to the funeral because I wanted everyone else to be able to express their feelings without worrying about me. I am still sorry for that. Right now I can't *express* any more of it or it may become a vocal rather than a written expression. I will tell you though that I am angry, I am hurt—it will *never* be alright. I will, however, survive.

In this situation, it is evident that the respondent's love for her brother remained true despite his constant manipulation and self-serving cruelty. Indeed, a love that survives even repeated rape is real—and, under the circumstances, all the more vulnerable. Even a masquerade of death brings out feelings of desperation and dread, followed by feelings of relief mixed with an ominously strengthened sense of helplessness.

The subsequent symbolic damage to this respondent and her family is horrorifying in its suddenness and completeness. His parents saw their gift—an expression of their own love and encouragement—turned into a gallows. His sister saw her love for him turned into indecision and guilt as to what she should do to protect herself as well as to help her brother. After his suicide, this shattered seven-year-old would try to help others with their grief and pain—again, at the personal cost of being absent from the funeral and the chance to close this very painful chapter of her life. The respondent still cannot express her pain and sense of hurt even from a distance without fearing she will totally break down with the relentless grief and pain.

For the brother, there is nothing more to be said or done. He has created the irrevocable conditions of his sister's emotional burden. He has abused her body. Now he has made it impossible for her even to resolve her relationship with him through some form of open reconciliation in which forgiveness is penitently sought and freely given. He now remains the abuser, not only of his sister's body, but her mind and spirit. That abuse continues to return again and again in the form of painful thoughts and guilt-producing images that intrude into consciousness when she is alone and further distort her relationships when she is with others. For this respondent, only the most sincere caring and competent understanding will bring her to the point from which she can begin to heal and to move ahead once again with her life.

The emotions of an individual who survives the suicide of a loved one contain the most complex feelings and experiences imaginable. They swirl around in the mind in all-consuming guilt and withered hope and often lead to frustration that is very difficult to resolve. The following respondent describes his experience with this kind of hurt and emotional injury. While able to get some relief from deep personal loss by expressing anger to a friend, he is unable underneath to determine how to understand and resolve the violent changes that have transpired in his life.

#151 A's view: At the funeral of a good friend I was speechless. She had killed herself and I was very upset. I had dated her many years before when she first had problems with depression. We broke up a few months after she left the hospital. However, we stayed very close. I really loved her very much as she had gained considerable control over a very difficult life. In my eyes she had conquered all the problems that drove her to contemplate suicide. So when she died I was angry with her. She had accomplished all I feel you need to be a success. She was in many ways an idol. I wanted to be like her. When she killed herself I didn't cry or anything. I was hurt but also mad and stunned. I thought she had it all and threw it all away just because she had a bad couple of days. I know it can't be that easy but I still am mad today. She took a lot from me when she died. It's the wrong opinion but when I visit her grave I still get angry sometimes. If she came back from the dead, I'd chew her out and hug her and we would start all over again. I still can't explain how I feel. It's a combination of shock, sadness, anger, and guilt. It feels dull.

The final response in this section graphically describes the profound degree of hurt that survivors of suicide experience. The apparent message is that there are few communicative alternatives for complex personal problems other than suicide. Alienated persons may perceive suicide as an acceptable alternative to the process of having to invent a way to deal effectively with others. After all, why bother with something as undervalued as the transparent expression of one's own lived circumstances? Why not simply punish everyone around for the unfairness of one's troubles? Why not just get the point across in a painful and injurious way others will never forget?

#152 A's view: I was in the state of New York visiting relatives. One day I went to Niagara Falls, both the United States and Canadian sides. When I got there and saw all that water, all that force and the large number of people looking at the waterfall, I couldn't speak—it was the greatest experience of my life. I couldn't express how I felt at that moment. I just stared at the falls. I was speechless. I couldn't even say "Wow!" to my parents who were standing next to me. It was just the greatest sight and it made me feel really good inside. But then another incident left me even more speechless. Something tragic happened. A young boy about the same age as myself, twelve-years-old, started to climb the five-foot safety fence. This young boy who had been standing five feet from us suddenly climbed to the top and just jumped! I couldn't believe my eyes. I couldn't believe someone would jump and end his life like that. Neither my parents nor myself could say or do anything but leave. We didn't even know this person but we felt like we did. That ended our day at Niagara Falls and it was only 3:00 p.m. I couldn't look or talk about the Falls because it reminded me of this boy jumping. This is something I will always remember and at the age of twenty-two I still can't talk about it very easily.

Respondent accounts of the suicides of others provide an instructive case in point. Those who commit suicide do not just passively respond to their own inner pain; in addition, they may plan to die a death sure to make a lasting impression on those around them. Their desperate formulation: better get it over with than to take a chance on living one's life and confronting its inevitable problematic concerns. Hence, the meaning of the distorted message is framed within the profound ambivalence of the messenger toward the possibility of a stance of openness and receptivity toward others.

One thing seems certain—developmental damage accumulates. Unresolved conflicts coalesce into formidable burdens. Alternative feelings of love and hate, closeness and alienation, turn into a tumble and tangle of excessive, oppressive, or intolerably complicated sets of lived circumstances. Such conditions are prone to reintroduce definitional and directional confusions in otherwise life-giving interactions between needy and even desperate individuals and those who can help them. Extreme feelings of divergence, disagreement, misunderstanding, and failure are all too often the final realization between troubled and potentially supportive interactants.

So why not? Why not jump into a mighty river? Leap off the highest mountain? Hang yourself with a short rope? Shoot yourself in the mouth? You've read the papers; if you want to be sure to get people's attention, kill some cops on the way out. Small children make easy prey. Old people are especially vulnerable. After all, the potential payoff is the momentary experience of being in full control, even if it means nothing more than the presumption of the right to let one's pent-up frustrations fly for all to see before checking out early.

There are potential sources of the unspoken. Developmental damage in expressive and interpretive practices accumulate over time. Inarticulate feelings of powerlessness increase. And what lies beyond? If the essential presumption—the negative, sustained, self-critical message—does not change, then this hurt may result in one of two broad types of injury: (1) interpersonal and social violence, along with the possible death of others, or (2) withdrawal from others, with accompanying inner suffering, psychic damage, and possibly self-inflicted death. Both social violence and social withdrawal are radical and extreme attempts to align one's self-conception with one's place within the larger social hierarchy. For alienated individuals who insist on the constant reproduction of tacit pain and suffering, it is only a matter of time before their inner (private) reality is expressed in public terms.

At this point, let's turn from the problem of suicide and look at three different views of rape, and how each one evolved into an extended and alienating experience based on protracted episodes of symbolic violence. The first respondent is a child who witnesses a rape in a park. The second is a woman who is raped at gunpoint and who subsequently finds that no one can or will understand. Finally, a third rape victim not only finds herself unable to share her confusion with others; in addition, she starts to blame herself for her predicament and becomes suicidal. In each case, invasive violations of one's personhood begin a long period of searching for understanding and effective problem solving, only to find none. Indeed, it is the symbolic violence that precedes and follows each rape that has the most devastating effects on the women who suffered.

#153 A's view: At age seven I was a young, virtuous, and sheltered child who had not experienced much of life as yet. I took my daily skip to the park with my white kitty Tu Tu Belle. As I proceeded to slide down the slide with my kitty in my lap, I glimpsed over the swings and sandbox and saw a young man and young girl playing in the grass. All of a sudden a quarrel broke out between the two. The man raised his hand and struck the young lady. Then in a fit of anger he removed the lady's blouse. I became terribly frightened and crawled backwards down the slide. Slowly I crawled into a bush to hide. The lady was screaming for help and I couldn't help. I was frozen in my thoughts and actions. I watched a man rape a woman. I couldn't express the incident for months in my own head yet it was on my mind constantly. My thoughts were buried like I buried myself in the bush at the park that day. This brutal man displayed so much hate and anger while unveiling himself for his own pleasure. He did not stop to think about the pain and emotional heartbreak experienced by this lady. Another woman who viewed the incident called the authorities and upon their arrival I came out of my shelter, only to view a lady bleeding from all parts of her face—blood from her nose and a deep gouge of blood seeping out from her lower lip. She slowly gathered her rags which were once a blouse and skirt; ashamed and embarrassed, she was taken away by the ambulance. As she left, the look on her face was so striking it will remain with me forever, never to be revealed to anyone.

For this young girl, sheltered innocence is the broad causeway through which a profoundly disturbing sight rushes in and changes her world forever. Violence arrives in a scene that moments ago was playful and fresh. Anger creates fright in a child observer, let alone in the victim of the rape that ensued. The child cannot even admit to herself what has happened. The impact of the rape comes back to trouble her hour after hour, day after day, week after week. And it doesn't have to be clearly understood as sexual violence. The rapist's anger and hate have become an obsessive thought that will not leave this child alone. The young lady's emotional heartbreak, particularly as evidenced in her facial expression, becomes a young child's first glimpse of womanhood. A bloodied face replaces a pretty one. A fresh blouse and skirt become stained and sullied rags. Playing has become a blood sport, and the lady has become the victim. As the little girl sees it, trust in her partner led to her shame and embarrassment.

In the face of physical violence, a child observer becomes the victim of the significance of what she sees. No one has to say or do anything cruel to her. All that is required is for her consciousness to witness the unthinkable; that done, the unthinkable becomes violent meaning. In the moments that follow, violent meaning becomes all she thinks about. Her mind now knows violence, but the girl herself cannot fully explain it, not even to herself. Because she cannot explain the incident in clear terms to herself, she struggles to define what transpired. All she can come up with, however, are thoughts that remain buried, unexplainable, semiconscious. For this girl, the incident's violent meanings remain frozen in the unexplained images that play over and over again in her mind.

When violent meanings attack the thought processes over and over again, one can never be assured that things will get better simply because the act of physical violence is over. Violent thoughts and images can be just as powerful in their effects as the physical violence that surrounds them. For the young girl, the alien voice of her thoughts and feelings strongly promotes withdrawal from others; it especially encourages withdrawal from herself via the processes of emotional repression. Under these circumstances, there is no way she can ever reveal the ongoing anxiety, guilt, and confusion of her experience. Whenever violence and confusion replace innocence and happiness, we are likely to become closed off from others who can help us. We and they become mutually inaccessible and isolated. While our own personal search for understanding goes on daily, we remain vulnerable to being further shocked into a profound state of silence. For all of us, withdrawal from what others think, say, and do can easily become a very common refuge in which to survive.

The following response reveals the degree to which a woman can become hurt and injured by the vicious realities of rape. It is a statement which helps us realize why the young girl in the park is so profoundly affected by the rape she witnessed in a public setting and in subsequent reflections and mediations. But it is much more than that. It is a statement showing how the meanings we attribute to our experience—both from within ourselves and as the result of our interaction with others—can have just as lasting and pernicious an effect as the act of rape itself. Indeed, the careless comments of a few are enough to persuade this respondent that no one can understand or care about her deepest anguish.

#154 A's view: When I was twenty-one I was raped at gunpoint by two men. No other incident in life has made me feel as vulnerable, frightened, angry, and unable to convey as this one. It was late at night and I, with the sense of invulnerability found only in the very young, was walking to my car. San Francisco has hills so steep that some sidewalks are sheer flights of stairs. I was walking up one of those stairs that night. I heard footsteps behind me, so I glanced back and saw two nice looking black men. I continued climbing the stairs and noticed that the footsteps came closer, giving me the first indication I might be in trouble. I increased my pace, heading for the all-night attended parking lot where I'd left my car. I didn't make it. Suddenly, they were right behind me and there was something hard against the small of my back. I don't know why but I turned to face them. The man holding the gun raised it to my face. I held out my purse, convinced it was what they wanted but they didn't take it. I couldn't scream—I couldn't even speak. They ordered me to start walking again and told me they would shoot me if I didn't do as they told me. We passed a number of people and I was amazed that they couldn't, or wouldn't, see the terror in my face. We continued to walk until we reached a dark, deserted lot. It was there they took turns, one holding the gun while the other raped me. The second man kept insisting I tell him I loved it but I was still unable to speak. He kept hitting me and demanded that I say I loved it but I couldn't. When they finally finished with me, they ordered me to get dressed. They said they were going to take me to the "Tenderloin," one of the areas of the city known for its nude bars and prostitution. I was to make $150 for them or they'd kill me. At this point, anger began to replace fear and I began to think of ways to escape the entire situation. As we walked toward Polk Street, I saw a taxi parked across the street. By this time I was so angry that I didn't care if they shot me, so I ran, screaming, to the cab. The doors were locked and the driver wouldn't open up, so I continued to run back to the bar where I worked. I didn't know it at the time, but I was spotted by two cops in a squad car as I ran screaming to the taxi. As I reached the bar the squad car caught up with me—they'd followed me for five blocks. I slapped one of the cops because he touched me. Somehow, they talked me into getting into the squad car. The police report described me as "incoherent." They finally figured out what had happened and asked me to show them where the assault took place. I was too upset to find it, so they took me to San Francisco General Hospital. The doctor gave me an injection to calm me so I could be examined and talk to the police. There weren't any "Rape Crisis" people in those days, but the police were very gentle, guiding me through the process of giving my statement and looking at mug shots of hundreds of sex offenders. My friends, however, were not as gentle. I had only lived in the area for about six months, so my "friends" were fairly new to me. When I tried to talk to them about what happened, their reactions were similar—they didn't want to hear about it. My boyfriend, on the other hand, seemed to be getting some sick thrill out of it so I couldn't talk to him about it either. Six months after the assault, I flew home to my parents. I knew I couldn't tell them what had happened but I thought I might be able to discuss it with my best friend from high school. I was wrong—all I could do was cry. I knew that if I told her—or anyone else—what had happened, they would change the subject or reject me as my "friends" in San Francisco had done. She kept asking me what was wrong and I could only shake my head and cry. She became frightened and called her neighbor, a doctor, who took one look at me and gave me an injection. He also wrote a prescription for Valium. The next day I returned to California. For ten years I didn't discuss the rape with anyone. At first, I had nightmares every night and I was afraid to go to sleep. After a few months, the nightmares became less frequent, occurring only when something reminded me of what had happened. During those ten years I got married, divorced, and returned to school. I was unable to discuss the matter with anyone until my best friend and I shared our experiences with one another. She had been raped too so finally there was someone who *knew*. I listened to her and she called the Rape

Crisis Center and eventually we both joined a group to discuss the rage and fear that never completely goes away. I am still afraid to go out alone at night, which is a perfectly legitimate fear, but it makes me angry that I feel so unsafe. I did survive and I've learned to be able to talk about it but one who hasn't experienced it directly can't really understand the feeling of violation a survivor of rape is forced to live with.

This young woman is, for some ten years, totally unable to tell anyone about the violent rape she was forced to endure. She has tried, but friends regard her painful experience as either an uncomfortable imposition or a salacious anecdote. That is evidence enough—she now knows she will be humiliated if she talks about her pain and injury—even to friends and family. All she feels able to do is cry, and to keep her problems to herself. Following her return to California, this young woman survives rather than lives. Like the young girl who witnessed rape in the park, her own rape defines her outlook on life and keeps her a prisoner of her secret.

So far, we have seen how physical and symbolic aspects of rape interact dynamically to cause years of painful and injurious experience in the lives of two respondents. They have been wounded by repetitive cycles of anxiety, shame, embarrassment, confusion, and alienation. Even so, these individuals knew they were not responsible for what had happened; they only knew they needed to receive help from others and that, so far, they simply had not met the right people who could understand and help them.

A third respondent also tells how she was raped; this time, however, the victim is in even more danger as she feels herself close to suicide "so many times." While others have forced themselves to go on somehow with their lives, this young woman is still living on the brink of taking her own life because of continuing self-criticism and feelings of depression in the aftermath. Pain and injury take on new dimensions and new meanings as this young woman, who is now engaged to be married, struggles to keep her secret to herself even though this decision continues to endanger her life and her close ties with others.

#155 A's view: When I was sixteen, I was raped. Nails were driven through my hands and I was left for dead in a ravine behind my high school. I was attending Catholic high school. It was enough of a disgrace that the whole school, parents, and friends knew I had been raped. After I was discovered by a student in my school, I was rushed to the hospital. My blood pressure was so low that they couldn't do a D & C on me. Needless to say, I found out that I was pregnant a couple of months later. I felt that I had hurt my parents enough already so I didn't tell them. I was also sufficiently disgraced at high school. I couldn't tell my friends. I had been a virgin before this happened and my clean reputation was tarnished. Don't get me wrong—nobody treated me badly or said it was my fault. It was just that everyone knew I was no longer a virgin and I didn't know how the school or my parents would respond to my decision to have an abortion. I felt torn and I was depressed. I'm surprised I didn't finally commit suicide because I was close so many times.

One day I drove myself down to Chicago and went to a clinic on Peterson Ave. I remember screaming and crying. Everyone there was very nice to me. My blood pressure had fallen so low they wouldn't let me drive home. I laid in that room developing a story to tell my parents about where I had been for the day. To this day I am still scared. My fiance and I now live together. Sometimes when he touches me, I am just ice. I know he suspects something but how do you tell someone you love (and want to have his kids) that you are a rape victim who had an abortion. I can't.

For this respondent, the rape has become a source of shame and guilt that has left her emotionally paralyzed and in danger of dying from self-inflicted wounds. The violence of the rape has been magnified by her pregnancy, for now she must risk losing unqualified support from family and community. She was afraid of having an abortion that placed her in direct philosophical conflict with family, school, church, and community.

It is here that the role of personal meaning—the symbolic aspect of real violence—becomes very apparent. After the trip to Chicago, she struggles with reflective and anticipatory thoughts all alone. The framework of her thought and feeling is self-inflicted violence at its worst. She has come close to suicide many times because of her growing sense of anxiety, guilt, and confusion over the handling of her pregnancy. It is no longer the rape itself, or the nail marks in her hands, that endanger her now; rather, it is the self-critical meanings that her pregnancy and its ending have for her. Unless her interpretation of her experience and the present situation changes, she may live in crisis for a long time.

It is clear at this point how violent and intractable self-criticism and psychological injury can become. Over and over, the symbolic violence of nagging sentences grate against her consciousness: I have hurt my family— I am a disgrace at school—My reputation is tarnished—I have screwed up my life—I want to die. As we have seen, symbolic violence develops (1) from the hurt and injury that physical violence engenders in observers and victims alike, (2) from the attitudes and statements of significant others to whom we reveal the consequences of exposure to violent acts, and (3) from the severe, oppressive, and unrelenting forms of self-criticism and self-censorship injured and alienated victims may inflict upon themselves.

So far, we have seen how physical and symbolic aspects of rape interact dynamically to cause years of painful and injurious experience in the lives of two respondents. They have been wounded by repetitive cycles of anxiety, shame, embarrassment, confusion, and alienation. Even so, these individuals knew they were not responsible for what happened; they only knew that they needed to receive help from others and that, so far, they simply had not met the right people who could understand and help them.

It may well start out quite playfully—giving out even an aura of seduction. Then suddenly tensions break out. The male is more likely to strike first and talk later. He also may be tempted to rip her clothes off and make her scream for help. Masculine brutality is unveiled for its own purposes—the infliction of so much physical pain, emotional injury, and spilled blood on the female. Rape may be accurately seen as a clear example of how violent perpetrators strip personal power from their victims by overcoming them with coercive words and invasive acts. Either one will create great pain and suffering at the expense of the quality of life, and even the possibility of life itself. Indeed, it is the rapist's intent to cause his victims to lose control through the impact of his murderous attitudes.

It is instructive to look at aspects of symbolic violence in rape to see how central the quest for power is whenever violent perpetrators are involved in grabbing it for themselves. Of interest is the interplay between discourse and dialogue and critical differences in what perpetrator and victim express to one another. Cited entries provide a small glimpse. The perpetrator: threatens the victim to say nothing or bad things will happen; raises a gun to the victim's face; claims she will be shot on the spot for not doing what he demands; kidnaps her and moves into darkness; laughs and ridicules to humiliate her; relies on verbal abuse; hits, strikes, and rips off her clothes; makes the victim bleed; engages in death rituals; torments the victim by driving nails through her hands; impregnates the victim; insists that the victim say she "loves" it; takes turns with another rapist until finished; and leaves the victim for dead.

In sharp contrast is the expressive slant of the vocabulary of the victims, for they tell of how powerless they have become as a result of their ordeals. Of interest are the ways in which rape victims: remain silent at all costs or; threaten to tell; walk past bystanders who do not see any sign of terror in the victim's eyes and face; cry and yell out; are not able to say much of anything; feel anger at the full magnitude of one's wounds and injuries; scream for help to no avail; bleed profusely; surrender, become helpless; lose virginity; become impregnated; become incoherent; run away screaming or are left for dead; come close to dying; live with a tarnished reputation; go through a painful abortion alone; cry later for no apparent reason; and think of suicide.

What is striking is the degree to which the respondents lose their own sense of personal control over their intentions, thoughts, and actions. Clearly, symbolic violence is just as capable as physical violence of stripping strength and control away from those upon whom it suddenly descends. Indeed, symbolic violence is what perpetuates emotional hurt and injury long after the physical hurt and injury has ceased to exist. It can also determine whether our involvements with others will be helpful and supportive or alienating and damaging.

In this first section on real violence, we have identified complex ways in which acts of physical and symbolic violence combine to cause severe and often protracted periods of hurt and injury within an individual, between individuals, and between groups. We have termed this interaction between physical and symbolic violence *real violence* because, in real life, one usually combines with the other in complex outcomes that can be most difficult for an individual to understand, let alone to express to anyone else. For understanding to occur, individuals often need to interact with someone who has had a similar experience (for example, rape) if they are to understand the full magnitude of what had happened to themselves.

In the sections that follow, we look at different manifestations of symbolic violence that occur in individual experience. It is our hope that, by describing a spectrum of episodes, we may facilitate deeper insights into the ways in which symbolic violence can lead to interactive and relational madness, often with intensely harmful and injurious outcomes.

COOL VIOLENCE

In the last section, we saw that the concepts of physical and symbolic violence may be defined in relation to real violence. In this section, we elaborate on how violent personal experience has been further described in respondent accounts. Some involve passive forms of cool violence, while others involve incidents of direct physical aggression. Regardless of the degree to which physical violence is represented, symbolic violence exists in every case, with painful and injurious results.

Interestingly, the exchange of money can become a source of symbolic violence. Money is an international medium of exchange that affects the distribution of personal power and resources; thus, when people are deprived of money, its absence can introduce systematic distortion in every aspect of life. Unfairness and inequity in the distribution of the power and resources required for survival can lead to despair just as easily as can rape or warfare. This hurt and injury is then extended into the community, with further physical and symbolic violence as a result.

#156 A's view: My parents separated during my senior year in high school. It left my mother living all alone on a farm in the middle of nowhere (in Wisconsin) once I had moved back to school in Madison. My dad packed up and left us but didn't go too far away. Just far enough that the lawsuits for small business fraud were left with my mom. These lawsuits were criminal lawsuits filed by many people who had been swindled out of thousands of dollars by my dad. I have no idea what he did with the $$$ but he left my mom in the middle of a farm foreclosure and barely enough $$$ to buy heating fuel and other essentials for a bitter cold winter. My mom was devastated when he left and became somewhat anorectic. I went home every weekend to buy food and try to get her to eat but she wouldn't and kept getting sicker and sicker. My steady boyfriend from high school couldn't deal with my constant stress over my mom, etc., and broke up with me after a two year relationship. This devastated me even more because he was the one source of support I had counted on most. He broke up with me but dragged it out for months (while he went out with others and I kept hoping for another chance). Some of the people suing my father came to the farm one weekend and announced that they would be getting a court order to take my horses, car, and savings away from me b/c my father was on the verge of bankruptcy and they wanted some $$$ back from what they had lost to my father. They backed these threats with the fact that the operation my father had been running was registered in the family's name and I was responsible for the swindling too! In a panic I moved my three favorite horses to another farm where they ended up being stolen. I felt like I was going crazy—bad things kept on happening. My mom was threatening suicide. I felt like a complete failure b/c I couldn't help her. I didn't make any new friends at school b/c I was always going home to try to help my mom. My friends from high school had been alienated by my long and serious relationship with my ex-boyfriend, and I really didn't have a family left. I went to a university counselor in an effort to try to talk with someone but the counselor's answer was that I had so many problems that perhaps I should just drop out of college! That just scared me away from reaching out to anyone else. I didn't feel that anyone else would be able to understand the pain and confusion I felt nor the risks and changes I was facing. Not too many people are eager to get into a friendship or relationship when one individual feels so unstable. It's much easier for me to talk about it now b/c all of that happened two years ago and I've been able to work through it. It's an accomplishment now but at the time I felt it was too overwhelming.

#157 Once A's best friend is involved in an insurance rip-off. A becomes extremely angry, disappointed, alienated, and leaves feeling worthless, as if everything was worthless. It is as if the thoughtless, ignorant, stale bastard of a friend had permeated into A's own close, immediate world. A loses trust in everything. He can't even talk to his friend. A never once tries to tell his friend how he felt.

Cool violence is violence in disguise. Hot violence insists on instant gratification while cool violence thrives mostly on delayed gratification. Moreover, hot violence yearns to get it over with while cool violence is bent on prolonged suffering, slow-motion torture, and protracted agony. Cool implies the right to pack up but not go too far away. Cool implies the need to take advantage of others before they take advantage of you. Cool implies the intention, means, and determination to drag unresolved conflicts around for days, weeks, months, years, decades, generations, whatever it takes. The whole point of cool violence is to forget your loved ones while you live just long enough to outlive your rivals, foes, and assorted enemies.

Cool violence perpetrates psychopathically camouflaged forms of thievery and fraud that wreak symbolic havoc in the lives of its victims. Take the money and run. Be prepared to abuse and abandon the ones who depend on you to provide shelter from the storm. Avoid exposure to legal documents that might indict you somewhere down the road. Let others starve to death if necessary out in the middle of nowhere. Take your own kin to the verge of bankruptcy. Implicate family and neighbor in dismaying arguments over misplaced financial responsibility. Take everything in stride—even the threat of suicide, so long as it comes from someone else. Let offspring fill the void. Make it impossible for your children to reach out for a helping hand. And why not? No one is likely to understand the full magnitude of their silent suffering. Cool violence leaves those who are thrown along the wayside feeling worthless. They lose faith in everything and take a lifetime to recover.

AGONISTIC RITUALS

The term "agonistic rituals" refers to the ways in which conversations and interactions, discourse and dialogue, can become frustrated by the realization that, regardless of the verbal content of the message, very little of one's meaning is being conveyed to the other. No matter what one says, the meanings are not being evoked in verbal form. What often results is a situation in which people partially withdraw from one another, while still trying to maintain a weak level of interdependence and mutual influence. Inevitably, they may be frustrated with each new attempt, with the result that the degree of withdrawal increases. Even positive experiences can be difficult to convey, as the following response indicates.

#158 A's view: My number one pastime and major source of satisfaction comes from hunting, in particular, ducks, geese or deer. Every time I head out, it is a new experience, in many ways different than any previous trip, but all are related. So far I have never been able to explain to anyone else the pleasure I derive from each trip. Sure, it is easy to tell them what animals I saw, people I saw or didn't see, where I went, and what I shot. But none of this can come close to explaining the whole experience. There is so much more, in fact, the majority of each trip, that must be experienced directly to be fully appreciated. I can easily explain the sunrise and sunset, but I can't tell anyone what it was really like to see the whole scene. I can describe the smells, wind, bugs, and sounds but of course the listener finds all of this totally useless. The biggest myth held by most non-hunting individuals is that during each trip something must die for it to be successful. Nothing could be further from the truth. On some trips I will pass up a perfectly good shot and simply enjoy the opportunity to watch an animal without ever intending to shoot it. I cannot explain such matters to anyone else because I can't even explain them to myself.

A theme repeats itself here—the necessity of common ground. If person A wants to be understood, then person B must have had a similar experience to which s/he may refer. In this way, interactants may bridge the verbal gap between them by referring to a body of common knowledge and sense experience. Without some overlap in mechanisms for making sense, interactants are prone to perpetuate basic misunderstandings, such as the idea that animals must be killed if a hunting trip is to be successful. They also cannot increase their own self-awareness and self-understanding through the sharing of empathic dialogue. As the following account demonstrates, frustration associated with attempts at mutual understanding can lead to angry outbursts and sullen retreat from one another. All of this emotional give-and-take results in much pain and injury to the interactants, and strain in their relationship.

#159 A's view: A tends to be the sort of person who keeps everything inside, all bottled up. When there is far too much going on inside, A tends to explode. It's because A doesn't express A's lived circumstances well enough most of the time. A is easily intimidated by other people. A also likes to be looked at as easy to get along with. In a nutshell, the situation consists of a tug-of-war with A being the person tugged on. It has become progressively worse over the past three years, finally hitting rock bottom this past summer. Others have changed their view of A drastically, and that in turn has made it very difficult to interact with anyone else. A has tried many times, but when A is hurt, A keeps it all inside. A chokes and doesn't know why. Attempts at rational discussion end up with the participants able to communicate less and less.

Agonistic rituals are not solely defined in terms of agonizing attempts to communicate. As one member of the relationship withdraws further and further from the other, s/he can begin indulging in neurotic and ritualistic thought patterns that symbolically adjust and resolve perceived tensions, problems, and (especially) personal shortcomings over short periods of time. The payoff is a heightened sense of one's own importance, and the uniqueness of the experience one has given up any hope of explaining. The danger here, of course, is that such thought patterns encourage personal withdrawal, and a resigned belief in the pointlessness of new communicative efforts. Such extreme withdrawal can have neurotic and self-critical consequences for the individual.

#160 A's view: Now that I look back, it seems rather silly to take a curling iron to my back over such a little thing but I felt so low and unworthy and didn't want anybody to know what I was feeling, somehow punishing myself. Usually I purposely don't eat when I feel like this but I guess that particular day was worse than other days and I needed to know that I had suffered acutely for what I had done. I felt I needed to feel the pain. I happen to be a very dramatic person so a certain part of me is thrilled by the romance of having such a "deep dark secret" to hide. It's all too complicated to explain—which is why I've never told anyone except for my journal. So I deal with feelings of unworthiness when all alone when they are at their most destructive. I think back to what I have done during the day when I'm alone and the feelings swamp me in their murkiness. So much so that I need to hit or scratch or burn something immediately.

Agonistic rituals reproduce largely ambivalent forms of miscommunication. Those who participate are not sure where they stand with one another. The definition and direction of such relationships is often up for grabs. Conversations characterized by such pronounced levels of disagreement, misunderstanding, and failure of realization may be called into question because of a mutual and largely unstated sense of so much tacit confusion below the surface. Agonistic activity produces conversations with ill-defined and incommensurate focal points of interaction. Dialectical tensions abound. Participants take turns being construed as in or out of sync with the intentions, objectives, and goals of one another. Essential movements: up (superior) and down (inferior); close together (involved) or far away (detached); for (convergent) or against (divergent) matters to be affirmed (pro) or denied (con). Push and pull. Back and forth. Round and round. The respective parties are not able to come together nor to pull apart. The main participants may be pragmatically interdependent one moment but romantically dependent and needy the next. This in turn may lead to unexpected transitions into intractable narcissistic postures, such as detached indifference.

Agonistic relations help individuals avoid harm's way by serving as a medium for airing uncomfortable, unsettling, or disquieting issues such as explaining the joys of hunting to non-hunters. They are less successful as safety valve mechanisms when verbal conflicts escalate to the point where what is felt, thought, or said is no longer tolerable to the respective parties. The concept of "tough talk" refers to speech acts in which multiple references to threat and danger intensify to the point where what transpires no longer makes much sense to anyone. Here miscommunication is what stands out as the respective parties reach their limits of forbearance. As the heat is turned up, the coherence in conversation goes down. Fights qualify as terrible at the very point where (1) the participants cannot stand to be in the presence of one another or (2) one insists, demands, or forbids others from leaving the scene until certain demands or stipulations are satisfied.

TOUGH TALK THAT LEADS TO TERRIBLE FIGHTS

When agonistic relations stop working as partially effective buffers and coping mechanisms that lessen frustration in human relationships, one may assume that a transition from self-centered withdrawal to other-centered symbolic and physical violence is taking place. Such a transition toward alienation invokes a rite of passage into uncharted territory. The borderline is the periphery, the outer fringe of interpersonal tolerance where verbal resources are tested to the outer limits of human capacity. With time, however, signs of tolerance and compatibility diminish, while growing feelings of intolerance and incompatibility develop to a point at which acts of verbal force give way to multiple displays of physical force. Often the intensity of physical force is related to whatever magnitude of verbal force has preceded it. The moment when one can no longer talk back is precisely the point where one may be the most tempted to strike back.

The transition from verbal to physical modes of response to perceived threat and danger operate in the manner of a court of last resort. Here is a mythos where the potential for symbolic violence and physical violence are pitted against one another in a win/lose situation. At some point the statement "I am going to kill you" does or does not fulfill the verbal mandate. This suggests that one may think of symbolic violence as that which does not go all the way to the outer limit of what is still possible or imaginable. Symbolic violence here manages somehow to stop short of the mark. From this perspective, human beings may be viewed as civilized predators. We civilize one another with our collective legacy: clothes, body armaments, expressive styles, language, manners, deference, demeanor, customs, ritual, tradition, and ceremonies that quell the primitive urge toward all-or-nothing solutions to interactive complications that multiply along the way.

People surrender in strange and mysterious ways to the tug toward physicalistic solutions to verbal problematics. Commonly reported scenarios depict slow motion build up of implicit tension, strain, and discord into a moment of crisis. In the beginning is the semblance of normal appearances. Small mercies abound. Coordination prevails. Chaos is kept to a minimum. Minor disturbances are dismissed as trivial. What is wrong is not worth talking about. Violations are few and far between. Better to say nothing than risk a small fuss. Suppressed hostility is favored over overt acknowledgment of low-grade tension, strain, and stress.

Slowly the magnitude of what remains as the unacknowledged trouble spots begins to increase. Interaction now becomes an incremental burden. One may be tempted to start going through the motions and, in the process, water down the truth. Duplicity and self-exoneration follow. Get used to cover ups; at all costs, preserve the illusion that things are really getting better all the time . . . then, inexplicably, out of the blue, suddenly and unexpectedly, interaction reaches the breaking point.

One aspect of verbal conflict that hastens the development of physical violence often occurs when one person believes s/he is totally right and the other is totally wrong. Screaming and shouting center on what the one at fault has done incorrectly, imperfectly, improperly, inappropriately, and either too soon or too late. Words and gestures now become weapons—that is, both resources and liabilities at the same time. Any accusations from the one being blamed are drowned out by the barrage of blame from the other, who believes the illusion that his or her own reality is virtually faultless, and not at issue.

Regardless of these manipulations, each member of the relationship continues to believe it is the other who has undermined and subverted the relationship over long periods of time. "How could it not be so?" each one asks. "No matter what I think, feel, say, or do, it has always been impossible to talk to him (or her)." Each member of the relationship feels as if the other is preventing the expression of truth or reality; after all, each has a stake in blaming the other for the litany of problems present, rather than in accepting the probable truth that it takes two, not just one, to create an intractable communicative mess.

Deception and pretense thoroughly permeate the relationship as each interactant approaches the threshold of physical violence, causing one to back off at terrible emotional cost while the other thinks of him/herself in terms of clear superiority. Consider the following account, which gives expression to a pattern of verbal conflict that soon reaches a crisis when the possibility of physical violence becomes real, followed by the painful withdrawal of one interactant who struggles in a sea of self-blame and guilt:

#161 A's view: Heated verbal disputes turn into protracted power struggles as uneven layers of expressive and interpretive irregularities and discontinuities continue to multiply. One moment of subversive conversation leads to another and, before long, someone is out of control. Soon signs of threat and relational turmoil abound. Late into the night tempers flare and folks start to fuss, shout, hiss, whine, and blame in an unending stream of one-sided accusations and unremitting abuse. What registers as the most painful moment is when the participants shout, cry, curse, and scream so loud that one or the other must leave.

#162 A's view: The fine line between verbal fights and physical abuse is crossed far too many times. It may be the slightest of margins at first, followed by episodes of temporary relief. Then, before you know it, one starts to push and shove—to throw the other against the wall to emphasize a point and to reduce opposition. Soon the other is enveloped in a state of utter fear and silent terror at the thought of seeing the enraged face, hearing the sound of the menacing voice, and feeling the severe impact of hand and fist. Literal and metaphoric wounds and injuries multiply. The one who is the more abused remains silent out of sheer fear that others would overreact to the news. As days, weeks, and months go by, each one hopes the tough talk and terrible fights will finally stop so that things can get back to normal. The only trouble is that endless talk of trouble prevents 'normal' from ever coming back again. Now, alcohol and drugs mix with hate in fights that go on most of the night. Each one ends up the same way. In the early light of dawn the weaker, more vulnerable interactant breaks down, exhausted, and unable to ward off the terrible actions of the first. If one tries to break it off and escape, the other has a fit. Verbal harassment and mutual intimidation continue unabated amidst a concerted effort to change the other's mind once and for all. Slowly, the more abused one is run into the ground, cries a lot, and begins to think in confused ways. A neurologist says it's stress, but the real damage is spiritual—the sense that the subject of abuse is trapped and will not ever be allowed to be alone again.

#163 A's view: A terrible fight three days before Christmas between family members leaves the smallest children feeling guilty for getting the parents started into something that no one could stop. There is widespread fear that everyone would be hurt, the parent's divorced, and the entire family wrecked. All the fuss gets started just because some little kids fooled, fussed, and got into a shouting match. Afterward, no one can find the words to talk about either what was spoken or what was left unsaid. No one on the outside must ever know the perfect little family isn't quite so perfect any more. Now, each year, the children walk around the blazing lights of the tree and hear the inward echo of the very words that started a silly and foolish fight that did not stay silly and foolish for very long. No one can speak of what was spoken. It's a chilly feeling—Christmas has not been the same ever since.

#164 A's view: Individuals A and B were once very close but grew distant from one another over a long period of time. It reached a point where they practically became strangers all over again. The fighting would begin with simple disagreements. Gradually each one would begin to realize how different each one has become and how severely each disapproves of so much of what the other does. Verbal disputes undergo a gradual, almost imperceptible shift, a transformation in the interplay of personal conduct. Initial fights are mainly over specific, tangible things. Slowly a disturbing space separates each one from the other. The gap prevents the mutual expression of anything personal. Each one is too uncertain of the other. Neither one can clearly explain what is wrong amidst so much suppressed discontent located just beneath the surface and boundary lines of public appearance. Eventually neither can turn to the other one. Even a fifteen-minute conversation becomes virtually impossible to sustain. So A and B adapt expressive styles designed to perpetuate a mechanical, forced, happy acquaintanceship that leaves each one feeling increasingly isolated and massively guilty. Thereafter each one presumes a state of mutual love that simply cannot be revealed at any cost. There seems to be an invisible wall between them. What remains so inexplicable is the sheer magnitude of repressed guilt, anger, sadness, and madness built up within the lived circumstances of each one. Misinterpretation produces reams of heated arguments. Each one thinks that the other can't see what is really going on between them. Within the person who becomes withdrawn and silent, there is a sharp awareness of the negative outcomes associated with personal revelation. This person "knows" (in reality, *assumes*) that the other won't understand when told troubling matters. The following two accounts underscore some of the pitfalls.

#165 A's view: Something starts to bother one person who assumes others won't understand if they are told what is really bothersome. During fights, one person starts to think about many things from the distant past. It is stuff buried so deep that if anything were to be said, the other would just sit there and fail to grasp or comprehend the intended meaning. The fights are trivial in one sense; yet there are a lot of connections with deep meanings within. So there is a strong tendency to clam up in fights out of private concern over grave potential misunderstandings. Thereafter, each one thinks of the other in a certain way when, in reality (from their own vantage point), they are not that way at all. Such fights call into question who is in control of what and whom and at what price. It would cause a big disruption and uncontrollable conflict if either one knew what the other was really like.

Heavy fighting injures sensitive people. In close relationships, the most sensitive interactants rarely say what they really want to say—especially in conflict situations when it just seems to be too much of a risk. One respondent is most afraid of being left alone by a dominant individual who could take off in a fit of anger just because his or her true self is expressed exactly for what it is. In such intense fighting, nothing works out until or unless the most sensitive one is totally submissive and utterly silent. It makes the one who must surrender feel beaten; even so, it usually seems better to feel bad most of the time and say nothing so that the other won't get up and leave, walk out the door, and refuse to come back again. To the sensitive one, such intense fighting is so anxiety- and guilt-producing because neither one can agree or resolve anything unless the strong one always gets his or her own way. Honesty really hurts—yet so does dishonesty. Telling the truth can become so confusing. For those who most hate to fight, it continues to seem easier not to say anything at all.

#166 A's view: About a month ago A's boyfriend's sister announced that she was getting married. Her boyfriend has been invited to the groom-to-be's bachelor party. When he first mentions this to A, it takes her a minute to realize this has really upset her. A has never thought about bachelor parties much before, and she is surprised it bothers her so much. A couldn't really say anything to her boyfriend because he has to go to the party anyway. But still she feels shitty. A wants to tell him that the very idea of his being at that sort of party scares her, among other things. At the party (which excluded women) men would be celebrating male exclusiveness and female exploitation (in the form of blow-up dolls and a stripper). She takes for granted the degradation and objectification of women in this context. A feels that if he went to this affair, he would be buying into such an attitude; in fact, this possibility is the one that scares her most. The most important thing in a relationship to A is equality. Many men frighten her with their assumed dominance over the women they date. (Dominant thought: could her boyfriend possibly be like this deep down too?) A becomes self-censoring and decides that this topic is too trivial for her to make the effort to think about how to put it into words. She also thinks that maybe part of her concerns are based in jealousy on her part for not being invited to a party where a lot of her male friends will be in attendance. Finally A tells her boyfriend just to look at the party through women's eyes "now and then" when he is there. As it turns out, B attends the party alone and ends up getting into a fight with a guy who has been doing obscene things with a blow-up doll that was supposed to represent B's sister. At least A gets some satisfaction now. A hopes all of the thinking she did (instead of talking) about this issue will prepare her to talk about these pent-up feelings in the future.

This last response has something worthwhile to teach. The girlfriend avoids discussing her concerns beforehand and afterwards feels justified when her boyfriend sees her concerns acted out at the party itself. All too often, men and women alike refrain from discussing issues of real importance to them—all the while hoping solutions will somehow spontaneously appear. If individuals are to lessen their pain and injury in relationships of primary importance, it is essential for them to speak out about their anxieties and concerns. An assertive frame of reference may keep lines of communication open so that problematics inherent in all human relationships have a better chance of being resolved.

VERBAL OUTRAGE

It is instructive to examine venues in which symbolic violence makes its persistent advance from a state of verbal violence to a state of physical violence. Interactants are unwilling to take on a passive or reclusive stance in relation to the other. Each has issues, and each is prepared to express them symbolically so that there is no mistaking where a given participant stands.

A ream of resolution, however, stops just short of physical violence. This is not because the interactants don't want to fight; it is just that they extend the expression of symbolic violence to include the message "If I could fight you, I would; since I can't, I will show you just how powerful my anger has become. After that, I should be feeling somewhat better about life in general." Since each one is sending the same message, each reinforces the other until the ritualized give-and-take becomes a short-lived blizzard of violent messages that ends with each interactant assuming that he or she has won a symbolic victory over, if not an actual solution to, pent-up feelings of anger and frustration.

This kind of symbolic aggression is plainly visible in the following account of conflict acted out by two men driving in separate cars. Neither one can physically injure the other without injury to himself as well; for this reason, the tacit agreement to stop just short of physical violence is balanced by symbolic acts of aggression with no holds barred. Instinct replaces thought as each man's frustrating issues are translated into universally recognized signs of anger, hate, and violent aggression. The sights and sounds are so violent in and of themselves that they bring each man within a hair's breadth of actual physical combat.

#168 A's view: Once upon a time, I went out to dinner with my wife and another couple. During the course of the evening I drank wine to the point of moderate intoxication. It was certainly not to my capacity but it was too much as far as my wife was concerned. Nonetheless, I had the car keys and I wanted to drive home, so I did. While we were on the highway some "anus" in a Trans Am and his Heavy Metal passenger barreled up on my tail and wouldn't back off. So, I flipped him off out the back window and hit the brakes. Hard. Well, that successfully pissed him off and my wife too. After we had chased each other all over the highway for a mile, my ugly friend threw a beer can at me and they took off. My wife was hysterical, screaming at me about drinking and driving, and teasing the two assholes. She reminded me that she was pregnant and that we already had one baby and on and on and on. There was no way I could express my logic and instinct not to be fucked around by two goons on a Saturday night after partying. She wouldn't listen. I couldn't explain, nothing worked until the next day when I said, "You would've done the same things" and from her look I think she probably would have.

Verbal outrage is a point at which one passes over the line. It denotes the unspoken agreement of two individuals to act out their frustration over personal, family, and work-oriented issues which they believe cannot be discussed or resolved with any success. Usually, interactants feel, on an individual level, that each has tried hard to reach some kind of resolution. Such personal impressions encourage a warfare mentality in which each one fights the enemy of personal powerlessness just as a knight would defend his king to the death. Specific issues are not shared; the focal point of paramount importance is the unremitting frustration of life's problems and concerns.

For these reasons, two men engage in ritual combat as if they were top gun fighters engaged in an aerial dogfight. The size of their car engines, the speeds they are able to reach, and their wild dodging and maneuvering attest to their prowess as combatants. Unfortunately, the fact that they solve nothing substantive attests to the futility of their efforts—a reality our respondent continues to deny as late as the following day. Even so, externalized anger and frustration through the rituals of vicarious warfare with a counterfeit "enemy" is better than sitting at home and suffering inwardly; after all, feeling more powerful is a heady (if brief) fix for savage inequalities in the apparent distribution of personal power.

There is something else of interest as well. Beyond the threshold of immediate awareness, each man needs the other to play the part of the linguistic enemy within himself that he seems unable to defeat. While their problems may be quite different, the fact remains that each man has been suffering a similar degree of emotional pain and injury. It therefore becomes possible for each to find common ground with one another in the arena of symbolic warfare. As a result, each one becomes an "ugly friend" for the other, and provides the opportunity to show that he is capable of challenging and defeating the dragons that would rob him of a solidly masculine sense of personal power and social control. Having an agreeable scapegoat with reciprocal needs works out well enough—at least for the moment—as both claim victory and speed off into the night.

In this way, verbal outrage becomes the average man's victory over a life in which civilized words and gestures do not convey the full spectrum of personal experience (especially those aspects deemed socially inappropriate) with any success. Achieving a symbolic victory over a vicarious enemy is a rough and ready way to feel better fast; as in real warfare, however, symbolic warfare endangers civilians caught in the cross fire. The respondent's wife pays a high price when she understandably becomes quite frightened because her own safety, and that of the family as a whole, is being put at risk.

The most that can be said for verbal outrage is that it remains a simple safety valve for those who need to keep the ever-increasing pressure of personal issues at a more or less manageable level; the bad part is that verbal outrage is habit-forming at the expense of more productive approaches to personal problem solving. It also puts interactants and observers alike at risk. In the absence of any obvious means of engaging in successful dialogue, verbal outrage serves as a simple and easily understood means of venting ongoing frustration. All that is required is a release of inhibitions and a flash of anger, and the stage of engaging in symbolic warfare is set. In our society, such a release can be triggered by buying and consuming several bottles of one's favorite intoxicant.

THE FINE LINE BETWEEN VERBAL AND PHYSICAL ABUSE

At issue is the transition from symbolic to physical forms of violence. The base points in such a transition are instructive. Somehow the force of words and gestures congeal and pile up in partially suppressed, unarticulated, or unresolved forms. Salient motives involve protracted states of impatience over expressive and interpretive relations between the respective parties. It is striking that human beings have acquired the capacity and willingness to talk themselves to death. In the land of opportunity you can get shot in the twinkling of an eye over what you say or how you look when you say it.

Accounts of murder and suicide center around discursive practices that leave the participants without sufficient personal resources to contend with the full magnitude of symbolized discontent that arises between them. Ordinarily, the intensity and pace of discourse and dialogue begin to speed up. Thematically, there is an emerging sense of risk and urgency over the impending consequences of such a sustained breach of trust and care.

Of course, considerable physical force registers in the escalation of verbal force. It takes a great deal of physical energy to scream and shout. Sometimes people wear themselves out from fighting during the night. The confrontational potential of words and gestures reaches a point of yielding to a more severe and less open-ended solution or search for resolution whenever the possibility of sustained talk is overturned. The line is crossed when displays of verbal use slip into forms of neglect and abuse that, in turn, provide much of the pretext for outbreaks of physical abuse.

At such times a war of words may culminate in acts of physical assault. Here the volatility of the encompassing symbolic environment serves both as cause and justification for multiple lines of physical coercion. Constructive human activity may produce a rough mix of constructive and destructive consequences, both intended and unforeseen. The point of departure is the moment when the framework of multiple sense modalities shift focus from acts of talking and listening to those of hitting, kicking, stabbing, or shooting. To understand how and why such extreme acts of physical violence occur, it is necessary to search for clues within the surrounding communicative milieu.

#169 A's view: Consider a situation where four individuals live together. Two members fail to hit it off from day one. The respective parties are quite different with opposing likes, dislikes—you name it. Whatever the case, A and B always seem to disagree. Now the strange thing about this is that A and B knew early on but continuously covered it up in discreet ways. They didn't want the other roommates to know the way they felt about one another and so no one ever knew until A and B finally had it out! Everyday A would wake up and pray that B would be gone before A came out of the bedroom, or was at least on B's way out. When A would get home from school or work, A would be hoping B was going out with some friends after work, which B usually did anyway. Have you ever known someone who just did things that ate away at you bit by bit until it pissed you off so much that it got your heart beating faster and faster and you knew if you didn't avoid the situation that you'd both be at each other's necks? Right now, when A thinks back over those times, it still makes A mad. A feels B tried to take something from A but

A was damned if A was going to let B have B's way. B's sister and A were very close until B came into town and temporarily ruined A's friendship with her sister (C). Maybe A was just a bit jealous of how close B and C were. A felt like B was rubbing it in A's face too. So A grabbed B and pushed B up against the wall and scared the hell out of B who was in shock. B was so upset that B started to cry. A was crying too. It was so crazy because both of them were screaming their lungs out. A couldn't believe that A could act like a crazy psycho, totally out of control, shaking terribly.

In fact, the violence comes from feelings of powerlessness that have increased over time. It is as if the violent response just "comes out of nowhere." Suppressing worked for a while but did not resolve the problem. One thing is for sure, however: A responded violently to a trigger mechanism that B tripped. Pushing B up against the wall was a highly symbolic act, the result of a sudden, spur-of-the-moment decision. It was as if A had pictured this act in her mind, in the manner of a mental dress rehearsal centering on the notion of being in total control. Now the right moment for such a preconceived strategy had come to the surface. The fury pounded forth as A lunged to take back the control she felt was rightfully hers.

Something similar occurs in the next respondent's account. In this case, the trigger mechanism is a punch in the mouth that stops one interactant in his tracks. Then, suddenly, the respondent expresses physical and symbolic violence in return; his "friend" has become the enemy. Spontaneous outbursts of physical assault, once begun, are difficult to turn off. Complex thoughts confuse and disorient, and the respondent now becomes angry with himself as well as with the one who hit him. Suicidal thoughts critical of the self mingle with angry thoughts that are critical of others. Personal control is lost once again, leaving the respondent to scream and cry.

#170 A's view: I was at a party one weekend. The pressure had been intense for weeks so we were having a get together at this girl's condo. I had a few beers, two or three. There was a guy who was a friend/enemy—it depended on our moods. I made a series of remarks which set him off. He came over and gave me a shot in the mouth. I just stood there, dumbfounded. I could not move for five minutes. Then I slammed my bottle into the sink and pounced on him. We were split up and I stormed outside. In the ensuing twenty to thirty minutes I just stormed around outside, ranting and raving like a madman. I was so angry and outraged, I couldn't express it. I felt like exploding, like killing everybody, like killing myself. I'm not a violent person and all this fury couldn't come out fast enough. Then I just started sobbing and couldn't stop. I was disappointed in myself for losing my temper but at the same time angry because I hadn't done more. The only way to describe it is to say I didn't know what to do or how to feel. It was beyond utter despair. I felt like nothing I did had any meaning. Nothing meant anything anymore.

There is a striking similarity between the first and second responses in this section. (1) Pressure builds up as the respondent suppresses feelings of discomfort and annoyance. (2) The sudden pressure from the other's expression triggers a cognitive/emotional switching mechanism. (3) The switching mechanism releases the respondents suppressed fury. (4) Both attacker and victim are hurt and injured. In the second instance, the attacker turns his aggression inward as well as outward and becomes self-critical and suicidal as well as extremely sad, angry, and frustrated. As this happens, feelings of powerlessness and despair become dominant. A similar experience unfolds with the following respondent, who decided to use suicide as a way of punishing a boyfriend; for her, however, suicide was also a mechanism to convey the pain she was experiencing but felt unable to communicate with him.

#171 A's view: The time I am recalling is when my boyfriend and I were breaking up. It was a difficult time letting go. We had gone out for five years. For the first year it was great and then it went downhill. Change is inevitable and that is what happened. He began to drink and hang out with his friends more. It got to the point where he never really seemed to want to do anything with me anymore. Sometimes he would date other girls but would try to hide it from me. He didn't want me to date others even though he never seemed interested in being with me. He was the first person I had sex with which made the process of breaking up even more difficult. It seemed like I took what we did as being more serious than he did. We still slept together but we never really did go out. It was hard because he said he still loved me but that he needed to be free. I had difficulty understanding this. I thought he would want to be with me if he loved me and I thought he might change. In many ways he gave me mixed messages about what would happen to us in the future. It was his way of holding on to me psychologically, I now realize. Anyway, there was a time (I am ashamed of this now) when I attempted suicide. I couldn't handle the "games" anymore. He would let me get close one day and then push me away the next day. It was Halloween. He had been drinking. Earlier in the night one of my friends saw him with a girl sitting on his lap. Later I saw him at a frat party. He totally ignored me when I went up to say "Hi." He told me to go away. He went off to party with some buddies in another room. I ran back to my dorm room at Lake Shore. Nobody was home yet in the dorm so there was no one to talk to. Every time I thought of him I would get so angry. I hated him for hurting me all of the time. I wanted to hurt him like he had hurt me. I took a lot of aspirin that night. I started to get scared so I called a friend who came right over. I went to the hospital and they took care of me. Looking back now it was a very stupid thing to do. I thought I had run out of options. My friends were getting sick of hearing my stories and my family didn't like him. It hurt me that I was hurting myself. I couldn't understand myself. I was in a relationship that was psychologically damaging. Now I know that I would never allow anyone to do that to me. I am more important.

It is clear how sudden changes in one's environment can become triggering mechanisms that subsequently alter short-term interactions and long-term relationships toward the perpetuation of physical violence. Fortunately, the third respondent gained insight into herself and discovered that she was good, important, and worth protecting. Many others, however, are not so fortunate. Their injuries are not resolved following fights of massive proportions. Instead, their wounds and injuries fester with time, resulting in disaffection of mind and spirit. Periods of protracted agony, rather than periods of acute frustration, become the end result when resolution is apparently nowhere to be found.

WOUNDS AND INJURIES

There is something unusually poignant and particularly painful about the kinds of emotional wounds and injuries that are unexpected, ongoing, and unresolved. Interactive tensions become chronically painful as interactants feel more isolated and alone. Interactants may feel criticized for being themselves or being unvalued or unlovable in the eyes of others.

Wounds and injuries of this kind often trigger outbursts of righteous indignation; the criticized person feels personally violated, untrusted, misunderstood, and even manipulated. "How could this happen?" is the dismayed voice of pain and incredulity; "What have I done to deserve *this*?" Feelings of being so undeserving of pain and injury are rife within the minds of the interactants. Painful states of anxiety and guilt may quickly develop. What is most frustrating is that there seems to be literally no way of successfully resolving the problems that exist. Because of this, anxiety and guilt may lead to a chronic state of deep sadness, confusion, and alienation that is particularly painful and undeniably injurious. Witness just such a process and outcome in the following account:

#172 A's view: My parents have been happily married for the last twenty-six years. I've always felt proud of them because of this (in a world of divorce) and their respective accomplishments in life—my mother is a well-known nurse and program coordinator for a cancer study and my father is an assistant professor in a world-class university. I am also in a unique position in that I work for my father. I see him every day—sometimes not ever talking to him and sometimes talking a lot. We, my father and I, also work with a beautiful woman. This woman is so caring and accepting that both my father and I let our individual friendships with her grow. Thus, the conflict began between my mother and father. On my father's side—strictly friendship—a running partner and a person to share confidences with, a person who filled some supportive needs that my mother hadn't been meeting. On my mother's side—jealousy, anger, and hurt that my father could be sharing any confidences or part of his life with anyone else. Then there is me—knowing that she was deeply religious, deeply caring and supportive—knowing that my father and her were just friends—I saw my mother force the friendship to an end by telling my father it was either the end of the friendship or of their own relationship. And I saw my father honoring my mother and ending the friendship. I saw my dad lose one of his best friends, see my mother still very hurt and angry, my father hurt and angry, and both very alone, but together. Ultimately, though, I know my mother is hurting. I saw her push to get her own way. The hurt and helplessness I feel for my father is indescribable.

Symbolic violence invades, penetrates, neutralizes, damages, and destroys. It also leaves people unable to identify or resolve largely invisible wounds and injuries. It voices the threat of separation and divorce, abandonment and betrayal. Love feels lost or misplaced. Doubts and uncertainties multiply. Bitterness and mean-spiritedness abound. No mercy or forgiveness is found. The world falls apart when so much confusion and misunderstanding are in store. Losses multiply. Caring becomes an obligation that cannot be sustained deep down. Personal turmoil becomes very frightening as everything near and dear is either threatened or blown away.

The possibility of mutual understanding vanishes as each party sits alone and in silence and reflects on what went wrong. Each person struggles to comprehend without being in a position to talk about it. Separation from the other produces terrible strain once everything is over. Lament registers in the full magnitude of what can no longer be reclaimed. There are cries and whispers in the darkness and inner anguish in the light. It is almost as if nothing that actually happened really happened at all. One just keeps asking the same questions and coming up with very few answers. A sense of meaningless may prevail with resentment filling in love's vacuum as an answer to inexplicable loss and pain.

Because a pervasive sense of personal hurt and emotional injury are such persistent outcomes in hurtful family relationships, it might seem particularly difficult to understand how family members stay silent about what has happened, about what continues to unfold. Yet silence can easily become the very essence of strained family relationships when symbolic violence intrudes into the mix of discourse and dialogue. This was particularly true when alcoholism and drug abuse entered a family and began to destroy a young adult's highly valued parental relations. Inevitably, things became worse rather than better when silence, at least for one protracted period of time, frustrated proactive problem-solving efforts and overrode the desire to vent pain and frustration to sympathetic others.

#173 A's view: A grows up in a home in which both parents are chemically dependent. A is aware of the mother's alcoholism at around age twelve, and it is certainly five years before A can tell any friends or their families. The awkwardness of not having friends over or missing out on events because of A's mother seemed insignificant and painless compared to the pressure of feeling that family secrets had to be kept. As the mother denies her problem, so does the rest of the family. A can say happily that A was lucky or clever enough to recognize the unhealthiness of A's own home and to start spending a great deal of time with a friend and her family. It was with them that A began to tell the secret and then was reassured that it wasn't A's fault and was beyond A's control. To complicate matters, A's father also suffered from drug dependency and, being a doctor himself (and prone to depression and abuse), produced an issue that could be covered up or at least overlooked. For A and A's brother and sister, it was quite enough to have a drunk for a mother. If dad were a junkie as well, each one would surely be doomed. In addition to this child's perspective, there was the very real fear that if anyone knew about A's father, he could be in hot water with the medical association (lightly put). And then who would support the family? The father's practice (a psychiatrist, of course) seemed to be the only thing that A felt proud of and which seemed to give the whole "family" some sort of status and respect. Many years later the father's problem has come to a head. His license has been taken away—thank God—the fear of malpractice was another fear too great for A to bear while feeling at the same time not allowed to do anything. It is still hard for A to discuss and admit to the father's illness because as a child, in comparison to the mother, A had to believe that *he* was okay. A is learning, slowly, the empowering feeling of being able to discuss these things as it is only then that A can understand and reconcile the past and the effects it has had on A's life.

This account of effort to deal with parental alcoholism and drug abuse is an eloquent testament to the sense of powerlessness these practices inflict within the personal experience of adolescents. Through the most formative years of life, it is the child who has to cope with the uncaring and unpredictable behavior of the parents. Problem-solving efforts are undermined by the stress of keeping parental behavior secret from peers, the constant fear of embarrassment, and the anxiety surrounding the possibility of sudden unemployment and the state of vulnerability in which it would place the family as a whole.

It is such powerlessness that is at the core of all emotional wounds and injuries. The greater the sense of powerlessness, the greater the risk of long-term injurious impact. Words such as "chronic" describe this ongoing torment, with the wounded and injured child struggling to make sense of a world that is upside down. Sense-making and problem-solving efforts eventually result in fatigue and maladaptive coping strategies such as withdrawal from others. With time, coping strategies become hastily arranged survival strategies that become less and less effective; fortunately for the respondent, someone elses parents were nearby to encourage her to talk about her anxieties and concerns. Now an adult, she is still learning how to reconcile her childhood pain and injury with her life at present. Her account describes a similar type of anxious uncertainty and confusion. There are many parallels between entries #173 and #174. In the first case, a child lives from moment to moment in a world of uncertainty; in the second case, a husband struggles to accept a sense of uncertainty his wife's affair presents to him. In the first case, parents rationalize their use of drugs in efforts to justify it to themselves; in the second case, the wife rationalizes her extramarital affair to her husband. In both instances, acts of symbolic violence between family members stress those left behind to the point of agony.

#174 A's view: The thing I find most difficult to talk about to anybody else is my wife leaving me and her affair with another man. I even find it difficult to write about it here. I really don't know where to start. My wife and I were very close, probably too close to each other for a healthy marriage, if that is possible. We relied on each other for practically everything. We had so little confidence in ourselves as individuals that we relied totally on one another for moral support. Anyway, the point is—we were extremely tied to one another. For whatever reason, my wife left me. She has never given me a good reason for this. She says she saw us continually growing apart. Anyway, she had an affair and left me. The affair is still going on. She says she does not love me as a wife should love a husband. As far as I can tell, this seems to be one of the major reasons she hasn't come back to me. Well, I know that she does love me. I can tell when she's with me. I can tell by the way she tells me about things she does without me now. I don't believe I'm deluding myself but I could be wrong. She cheated on me. She left me. She has treated me and my emotions like so much dirt. In spite of all of this, I still love her and want her back. I feel very uneasy talking about this topic. It hurts very much. I have sought out one or two people whose shoulders I can cry on. As a rule, I feel very uncomfortable talking about it. I can't even discuss it with most of my relatives. It hurts too much to talk about it. Talking about it forces me to think about it. All the wonderful memories come flooding back. Talking and thinking about it just causes too much pain.

Our ability to think and feel emphatically makes a powerful case for finding ways to intervene on behalf of those who are suffering protracted emotional pain. For this respondent, talk is like a stab in the side; to cope, he must hang onto his memories, and his belief in his wife's continuing love despite her behavior. The tone of his response is dull and depressed. He feels confused about what to say or where to begin and questions the way in which he and his wife relied on each other for moral support. He wants to accept that she may not love him, but the very thought causes him to force the idea from his mind. His wife's uncertainty about herself, and her husband's uncertainty about why she left, leave him agonizing at his desk as he writes. To make matters worse, he has no idea what to do except to find some shoulder to cry on, and to cope somehow from day to day.

From this account of emotional hurt and injury, one can see just how agonizingly painful and emotionally destructive faulty interaction can be. Emotional injury lasts and lasts as if it were self-sustaining; not only that, but it can quickly influence the moods of others. The following response from a young woman describes how her parents' marital dissatisfaction and subsequent divorce caught her unaware and shook her sense of who she was to its very foundation.

#175 A's view: One thing I have not been able to express to anyone is the circumstance of my parent's divorce. Although it was eight years ago, it still affects me a great deal. I had never really imagined that my parents would divorce and when I questioned it my dad replied with, "I'll always love you." To me that was a "No, never." So I put it completely out of my mind. In fact, when I noticed my mom crying several times one weekend, a pregnancy was the only thing I could think of. My parents adored children, but I guess I figured they must have thought that it was not an opportune time for one resulting in my mom's tears. They left us in suspense for a couple of days before an appropriate time came to explain to us the situation. My dad began by saying that he didn't know if we had noticed but for the past five years he had not been comfortable in our house. I had felt that we were an upstanding, conservative, middle-class, very happy family. I was surprised and hurt to hear what he said. At that point I ran out of the room. When I returned, I was caught off guard by the words, "I have met another woman whom I love very much and plan to marry." At that point I ran hysterically to my room. I could not believe that this was my father—a wonderful man and a very successful corneal surgeon. How could someone so respected do this? I didn't have any close friends whose parents had divorced but certainly knew and respected families who were destroyed through involvement in an affair. I was so hurt and embarrassed because I couldn't understand why he, at least, hadn't waited until they were divorced. I was too embarrassed to tell any of my friends and even told my mom to tell her friends not to tell anyone. The affair was certainly something that would not be spoken of, and to this day, I have told no one. I know now that many people have assumed that it occurred but I have not discussed it with any of them.

Stress and strain in situations such as those listed so far in this section have the ability to hurt and injure individuals and relationships to the point where they break down. Nothing seems to help. Conscientious effort goes unrewarded, and the person may feel more and more powerless when nothing changes for the better. Reconciliation seems impossible as a growing sense of despair begins to evolve. As efforts to take the situation in hand result in considerable frustration, faith in oneself dwindles to almost nothing as self-criticism becomes more harsh and severe. This in turn escalates one's sense of personal failure, and makes future success seem very uncertain.

#176 A's view: In the first years after graduation from college I felt extremely frustrated with my life. I couldn't find a good job, I was living with my parents, and my boyfriend and I were not getting along. I felt that my life lacked direction and I was just biding my time waiting for something to change. I wanted to do something to change my life but I didn't know what. I tried to find a better job and I didn't have much luck. I felt like a child living with my parents and my relationship with my boyfriend was becoming nightmarish. When I tried to explain my frustration to others, I felt that I just sounded whiny and that I didn't really have anything to complain about. I figured if I said anything people would just think "Well, take control of your life and change it by yourself." That is what I wanted to do but I didn't know how to go about it. I was unable to find a job in my field, and the only jobs I could get were secretarial, which didn't pay enough to move out of my parent's house. I tried breaking up with my boyfriend, but he kept pursuing me and I always ended up going back to him. The frustration was so great I felt like I was going to explode. I thought about just leaving town, but I was too afraid to leave the security I had in Madison with family and friends all around. I remember trying to explain how I felt to my brother but I just couldn't put it into words. All I could say was "something's got to change."

This response shows how troubled relationships may predispose an otherwise intelligent and well-educated person to sit morosely at home waiting for things to change. As efforts to change her situation become more fleeting and less fruitful, this young woman sees herself as a victim of circumstance and unable to take control of her life. As her emotions vacillate between remaining inert or exploding in frustration, she may begin to feel depressed. The state of depression may be best understood not only in terms of severe emotional pain (anxiety, shame, guilt, and confusion) but also in terms of increasing alienation from others. In this way, depression and lack of interaction reinforce each other and result in a state of personal confusion and social estrangement from others, as the following account illustrates.

#177 A's view: During a conflict, I became extremely frustrated and felt like not even talking, especially when my views were not understood by the other person. It is not worth wasting my breath when what I'm saying isn't heard or is misinterpreted. My tendency is to simply stop talking so I don't perpetuate the supposed conversation. Sometimes I also need to stop talking in order to rethink what has been said so far. I may come to the conclusion that I will be more clear if I don't talk. Also, sometimes I may not talk so I don't have to listen to what the other person is saying when I "clam-up." Then the other person usually stops talking. If I become *so* frustrated by the other person's inability to listen and understand, I may sit back and stop talking so I don't get hurt anymore.

Once the person's sense of perspective with respect to personal and social realities dwindles to almost nothing, depression becomes alienation's crowning achievement. Psychological pain is of a kind rarely encountered before. Hearts break, spirits shatter, and faith in self and others no longer exists.

SYMBOLIC KILLING

#178 A's view: I was raised by my mother, who is 100% Native American. My parents were separated early in my childhood. My mother was raised on the reservation by her grandparents. She picked up their values as a child. She was raised in an extremely racist manner, hating white people for the atrocities committed against her people and the continuing abuses of the government. She did not have running water, electricity, heat. She was very poor and angry, growing up on a dead end street. Having been brought up by her, I shared some of her angers and desperation—the feeling of being treated as garbage, the disrespect and frustration of being hated. Needless to say, I grew up racist, not intentionally, but I could feel her hate and sorrow so vividly that it cut very deeply into my heart. It was so deep that it structured my feelings and views of a society that doesn't care. Being an insignificant statistic, my hatred toward white people grew. One day I looked into the mirror and realized that I am of the very race I despised with all my heart. My anger turned inward. I hated myself to the core. This was the feeling I cannot describe. I had an inner conflict of the greatest magnitude I have ever experienced. Frustration and my own ignorance still prevent me from resolving this conflict fully. My brother fought the law and the law won. I don't want my entire family to be destroyed by the hatred in their own hearts. I am taking a different approach by not allowing myself to defeat myself—half of the battle is already fought and won. Yet I get severe waves of depression at times because I know this issue has not been laid to rest in my heart. I not only experience racism one way, it is two ways. White people reject my ideology, my own tribe rejects my color. I am in the middle and quite alone. It is a very lonely experience that has drastically affected my life and the way I think. I am too proud to be beaten on a psychological level. I almost felt like crying thinking about this but I won't now. I will never stop fighting, whether gaining a firm grip on ideas, or using them to do something constructively. I am still in the process of finding my priorities, the values most important to me, and the incorporation of them into my ideology and lifestyle. It is very difficult to understand the magnitude of racism and to what extent it affects everyone, especially if you have not experienced it directly yourself. I was raised an Indian and many strong feelings are present. These feelings include resentment and anger toward the ignorance of other people. For example, people have made some very upsetting remarks to me about Indians, or even other minorities, not knowing of my background. Many are afraid of people of color because they are different. They look, smell, and act differently but should not be treated differently for they are all human beings. I ask people if they respect other cultures. I find that respect in this country is just a synonym for fear, i.e., people respect the law and powerful people. People don't want to know about anything that is different. Most people are even afraid to give their opinions about racism because, in a lot of ways, they don't have one. They remain completely ignorant of what is going on around them. It is time that people make an effort. Just open your eyes and look around. These feelings are not complete. I have not scratched the surface.

#179 A's view: A, B, and C are brothers. Over the summer A is to get married, and a conflict arises between B and C. It isn't the first conflict between the two brothers but it is one that B couldn't express because of extreme circumstances. Family and relatives are present throughout the weekend of the scheduled wedding, so B does not have an opportunity to discuss the conflict openly with C. The conflict involves differences in viewpoints and minorities. B is aware of what C is doing, but C has no clue about B's feelings. B sees C as very prejudiced, expresses it freely, and B can't stand it. Throughout the weekend, C bosses his wife, B, mother, and sister around as if they are animals. C expects this and forgets that he has two feet of his own to do anything he demands of others. All comply with C's demands, but B tries not to by ignoring him, but it is very difficult with all the company around, and C does not want to make a scene. C treats his wife the worst, and B feels the worst about it. It gets to the point where B would ask C's wife not to do things for C. Yet B wonders why he cares that she apparently likes it this way. The answer is that C is B's brother, and B can't accept C like that. At other moments B hears C cut down minorities in front of others, not even considering their views on the subject. C hardly knows anyone who isn't white, so how would he have any basis for saying some of the things he does? His range of thinking is so narrow. By the end of the weekend, B isn't even talking to C. At one time when B gets a minute alone with C, B tries to express what he is feeling, but all that comes out are frustrating tears, so he walks away. The ways his brother feels about issues like these and many others that deal directly with B's own convictions make B sad to this day. B does not feel the same toward C and is not sure he ever will unless he has a chance to express his feelings with his brother. At present B plays a fake role with him just to get by. Still the image of the wedding plays heavily on his mind.

#180 A's view: There I was, another evening supping at the table of my girlfriend's parents. All seemed to be moving normally, calmly—conversation was lighthearted and relatively low key. Unfortunately, the mood turned decidedly ugly when the subject became racially oriented. Starting with a seemingly innocent comment about the percentage of blacks and whites in the NBA (the only point in the conversation at which I intervened), the conversation deteriorated quickly into a debate between my girlfriend and her parents. I sat there frozen (verbally) as I listened to numerous racist statements and assumptions spew forth from the elders as never before, debated only weakly by the daughter. I felt acutely uncomfortable, especially since I'd never felt accepted either for my personal status nor for my opinions, I chose not to interject. My girlfriend was far less schooled in the subject than I was so I could only think of my responses to her mother's shrill demeanor. While I heard ineptness prevail, I felt like a traitor not only to all I've been taught and believe but to my friends who are black.

#181 A's view: There was an especially hard time in my life when I was attending junior high school. Even now it is sometimes painful to remember those days. I was a loner with hardly any friends. The school was located in a WASPish neighborhood. There were no visible minorities to discriminate against. Anyone who was even slightly different was the subject of daily public humiliation. Most people might say I'm being melodramatic—I'm not. One time a swastika was put on my locker door. The kids harassed me so bad on the bus that I fled to the seat behind the bus driver for several weeks. All my clothes were bought on sale and the kids at school made sure I knew that. Probably the worst thing was feeling sexual harassment for the first time. I was told over and over by boys just how ugly I was in rather obscene terms. It wasn't until I left high school that I began to feel attractive. During this entire time, my parents refused to believe what was going on. Over the years I have learned how to stand up for myself. To fight back then might have helped me—but I don't think so because it was always a group against me. Looking back, I've learned to accept what happened. As a result of my experiences I am acutely sensitive to the problems of minorities. I'm also a strong believer in people having a right to their own opinions. When people pick on others either physically or verbally, I always try to help out the underdog. Sometimes when someone is challenging me, they say I overreact but that's because of this past experience. When I left high school, I resolved never to be beaten down like that again. When forced with a conflict, I try to be as diplomatic as possible while letting the other person know I have limits.

#183 A's view: A is a white woman who has been involved in a relationship with a black man for four years. A comes from a very prejudiced family, and her parents are the most prejudiced people she's known. At one point her mother forbids her ever to speak to him again and never to see him or any other black person. Her father happens to be even more prejudiced than her mother and so the mother promises that they would put this entire experience behind them and never tell the father about it. If she refused such a deal, the mother said she would never allow her daughter in the house again. The daughter told her boyfriend what happened and that she could not see him anymore. However, she was miserable for the next month and had all this guilt inside as if she was doing something wrong. The relationship began to get more serious, and she realized that she truly loved him and didn't ever want to be without him. Last semester her boyfriend got drafted into the NFL. She moved back to Virginia, and he is still playing for Buffalo. She has experienced four years of guilt, shame, sadness, and unhappiness; the list goes on and yet she cannot share one moment of that with her parents or brothers and sisters. This hurts a lot, to know that the highest and lowest emotional points in life can not be shared with the people one loves and who mean so much. It is a heavy burden A will never be able to explain because her parents come from an entirely different generation and would never understand.

Language use opens up the possibility of misuse and abuse. The transition from constructive to destructive technique magnifies the risk and severity of impact. Words and gestures, after all, have definitional and directional force, and their aversive effects may be absorbed in a most forceful and injurious way. Instances of reported abuse frequently unfold in a militant, volatile, or even murderous symbolic milieu. Verbal aggression can become life threatening when encountered at its extreme. Communicative resources that could be used in life-affirming ways must be diverted to ward off danger and threat. The notion of symbolic killing calls attention to the place of deconstructive and disintegrative aspects of constructive and integrative projects and routines (Mortensen, 1987).

Old-fashioned midwestern racism is a case in point. At issue is symbolic killing with unbridled vengeance. The very possibility of construing certain persons as particular and specific individuals is destroyed through disintegrative and exclusionary logic. So, instead of being fully present for another equally distinct individual, the other is perceived as mere object—a nonentity unworthy of consideration as an alternative human source. At work is a symbolic personification and embodiment of all that is considered loathsome in the diverse modes of conduct of an entire class of individuals. In effect, one member of our collective humanity is transformed, in the manner of a grandiose illusion, into a spurious pariah deserving only of crucifixion for the secular sins of all members of that class.

An operational definition of symbolic killing: disproportionate exposure to developmental damage and early separation from love objects and care-takers; intergenerational poverty and collective devaluation; unresolved hatred over massive atrocities against one's own kin, flesh and blood, skin and bones; subject to perpetual abuse with no end in sight; inheritance and legacy of deprivation, scarce resources, and unfulfilled possibilities; a sense of personal worthlessness and insignificance, with outsiders remaining indifferent to the magnitude of imposed loss; dialectical tensions between private turmoil and public ignorance and ineptitude; self-destructive hatred and loathing for treatment as mere statistics, garbage, trash; rejection for one reason or another; fighting that doesn't stop, unspeakable burdens, and a torrent of words in protest coupled with feelings of powerlessness at being unable to scratch the surface; intolerable intolerance—rigid, inflexible, and narrow range of thinking; the imposition of fake roles just to get by; lost innocence followed by acute discomfort and public humiliation and the urge to escape and run away from all the profanity and obscenity; resolution never to be beaten again; ultimatums—forbidden to say a word and threatened with abandonment and banishment to wander in a foreign land.

It is important to look at peace and pain in human experience to try to discover the lessons the respondents want us to hear and to take heart from. It is from their comments that we may learn how symbolic as well as physical violence gives rise to protracted conflict, struggle, and strain. Respondents have told us a lot about *what it felt like* to be either the attacker or the abused, the critic or the misunderstood, and why they have reached a state where ineffective sense-making activities render them powerless. They also hint at why this perceived sense of powerlessness leads to our common inability to convey our personal experiences meaningfully to others.

Respondents tell about hurts that leave them unprepared to interact in meaningful and constructive ways with others. Each one was coping with his or her life more or less well (depending on individual circumstances) when violent things began to occur with such speed and intensity that it became virtually impossible to talk about such vital matters with others. These incidents were also very upending; men, women, and children alike reported confusion and disorientation that continued for months and years afterward. Each of them experienced violence as unexpected and incongruent with his or her surrounding circumstances. Each person's inability to talk to anyone about personal pain resulted in large part from the shattering and unexpected change in the world around each one of them.

Rage led some inward, some outward. Some respondents told about the ways in which their feelings of anger and outrage led them to retreat into themselves and think. Others told about actions taken when faced with protracted pain or frustration in relations with others. Guilt led some to suffer, not talk. These respondents told about ways in which a growing sense of guilt became disabling both in an individual and an interactive sense. These respondents felt an obligation to take responsibility for the well-being of others, even people who had been directly responsible for perpetrating the violence. It is possible to identify so strongly with a love object's need for help that one feels compelled to bear the entire burden of destructiveness by keeping a hurtful secret private. Such unresolved guilt makes it impossible to explain the nature and extent of one's problems even to oneself. Such a high degree of guilt seems to be indelibly written across the victim's increasingly shattered sense of self. Guilt accompanies entrapment in the form of obligations to others on one side, and by anxiety, guilt, confusion, and self-imposed silence on the other. Anxiety and guilt may intensify over time and become almost too much to bear. The decision to say nothing has the effect of focusing conscious and unconscious thoughts on a person's private sense of guilt, thereby amplifying it once again.

Some violent acts make no sense to the observer. Some respondents told about the ways in which they found themselves unable to explain the events they witnessed firsthand. Some felt totally at a loss, and very anxious, that circumstances at the moment of their encounter with violence did not make sense to them. This interpretive frame tended to confirm and extend a sense of disconnection, as well as to create it. How can it be that two polar opposites in human experience—a sense of wonder, and a conviction of total failure—exist side by side in the same social context? Here an encompassing sense of meaninglessness floods the field.

Certain emotional injuries result from personal beliefs. Some cling to assumptions, beliefs, and attitudes that brought on, or enhanced, their own deep sense of inexplicable personal injury. These beliefs are either governed by the specific situation or notions that people held in general. First is the masculine notion that men should be able to deal with intense feelings of hurt, anger, and frustration, rather than needing to spew them forth to someone else. Second is the tendency to generalize from unwelcome behavior of one source to every other member of a class, for example, Mexicans are "dirtballs," whites are racist, or black people are unworthy of friendship. The most frightening consequence is when such personal myths provide the incentive and justification for violent retaliation. In such cases it usually comes down to a matter of what they are doing to us rather than what we are allowing them to do to us or what we are doing to them in relation to what they do to us. Somehow the attributions of responsibility for violent conduct are directed outside the personal conduct of the observer and projected or transferred exclusively onto someone else.

Lack of communication correlates with the degree of difficulty in talking. When discourse and dialogue are problematic, respondents *presume* that they are unable to say what they think or feel because it is simply easier not to try. The required effort to talk through difficult or troublesome issues is measured and found wanting. It is important to notice how much exaggeration and fabrication occurs here. The talk does not seem to fit the circumstances or does not seem useful in any way. It is curious that individuals with 10,000-word vocabularies can be reduced to a point of being virtually mute. Notice how often respondents do not want to explain to anyone the nature of the very words and images that so poignantly describe their problematic relations with others. Some protestations are stated in very eloquent terms. Images may speak a truth for only one person to see. They may also speak the truth most easily, because they very efficiently present the whole picture at once, rather than the tedium of using one word at a time. If it is imperative that *some* form of interaction take place; one can still scream or cry. There is nothing tedious about a scream or a cry, but it too presents only a very general picture that has none of the detail of one's own visual images. Comments about imagery are quite telling. Images are so much more efficient and eloquent than words in some contexts. Pictures of experience present personal reality with ultimate clarity; they stand alone, without any need of interpretation, provided that one can gain access to them. Vengeance, in and of itself, has the capacity to limit though to a few basic images, and shut down effort to transform sensory activity into verbal forms. In this state of mind, the respondent shows, rather than describes, the intensity of what is felt at the time.

One's thoughts can become buried under unspeakable images in the mind's eye. It is these images that play and replay constantly in one's mind. Usually, we find that as we review them time and time again, we are unable to translate their eloquence for others to hear and understand. The fact that words can be so laborious to use (in comparison to the holistic images in our minds) that it is just not worth the trouble to relieve our suffering over an extended period to translate something that may register quite differently in the minds of others. Hence, real violence that arises in a given situation can reduce verbalization to a scream and to physical (evasive) action that is highly risky. Visual or spatial reasoning and memory may be adversely affected by exposure to acts of physical violence, such that one cannot remember where one was, how to get back there, or how to guide others to the spot.

One way to minimize gaps between interactants is to find someone who has had a violent encounter similar to one's own. This is because people who have had similar experiences do not need nearly so much explanation; they can *see* what the other person is experiencing because they already have a voluminous library of images that can be instantly recalled at will. Groups for victims of physical violence help them to talk again about their terrifying experiences with others who will know from experience what the traumatized person is saying. In these settings, words create images that are likely to be meaningful to those who are present. The power of visual imagery creates a nonverbal reality that can upstage what words are meant to do. These observations may help explain why we stick to images, rather than risk communication with something as awkward, and as prone to misinterpretation, as basic forms of shared deliberation.

Finally, notice how simple acts of miscommunication can be made all the more crippling than ever by the development of second-order complications such as anxiety, guilt, and confusion. In our view, they produce an inarticulate stance that transcends the inability to speak because of violent activity alone. Here we are referring to inexplicable frames of reference that linger over long periods of time. It is the sort of undefined state that keeps a victim of sexual abuse silent for weeks, months, and years after the rapist has left her for dead.

It is this second type of social inarticulation that is truly dangerous. To any victim of a violent act, it makes sense that the physical force itself does not make sense. What does not make sense is when such an inexplicable framework continues to weigh heavily upon individuals well after the immediate danger has long passed. It is then that people get frustrated with themselves, rather than with a temporary episode of dangerous circumstances. It is then when they question their own ability to solve problems, their personal worth, their intrinsic goodness as people, and their right to forgive themselves for what they perceive as damage they do to others.

It is this second order level of human problematic that leads to a linguistic game without end. The point is to know when and how to let whatever seems pointless fall by the wayside. What is needed is opportunity to return to the pursuit of optimum conditions, despite all that would hold one back. The cure is what facilitates restoration of faith in one's own expressive and interpretive capacities in relation to the surrounding community.

8

The Pursuit of Optimum Conditions

In human interchange there is only so much room to move in and out of problematic circumstance. Respondent accounts document an array of activities located toward or within, but also out or beyond the influence of unwelcome complication and encumbrance. The main point is to see how the mechanisms and devices used by individuals to get themselves into communicative difficulty hold the key to get them out.

The efficacious use of personal resources tends to promote favorable conditions for significance-making practice—where there is a tacit sense of common ground, reasonable clarity in matters of relational definition, and a sustaining climate of agreement and understanding. Under favorable conditions, a certain degree of disruption, confusion, and ambiguity is to be expected and tolerated. In contrast, the misuse or abuse of those same capacities may produce disruptive acts or episodes that register as neither inevitable nor necessary.

Human interactions are constructed out of the real-world conditions that give rise to them. First comes the opportunity to make sense together, then the actual course of direct or mediated contact, and finally the effects of living through the unintended and unforeseen consequences of one's own actions. In the center of a dynamic and evolving sphere of shared action—where there is no final authority nor supreme source of arbitration—the very definition of who conveys what with whom is open to renewed question, scrutiny, and review.

In complex encounters alternative versions of what takes place emerge in direct proportion to the total number of participants/observers who define the situation. Contested matters in this study clustered mainly around basic issues of incompatibility, miscommunication, verbal conflict, relational confusion, and unspoken apprehension over unfulfilled expectancies, strategies, or goals. Within such a complex and elaborated field of shifting reference points, the pursuit of favorable or optimum conditions is played out.

Respondent accounts document the protracted effort required to work through unresolved problems to the point where various members can live in reasonable harmony with one another. In the sharing of problematic concerns there is considerable negotiation over the severity of the demand characteristics to be imposed, by way of environmental and behavioral constraints, on the yearnings, strivings, and aspirations of the respective parties. On one side of the ledger are the communicative resources—accessible affordance, means of appropriation, and enabling modes of expression conveyed from one to another. On the other are the communicative liabilities—inaccessible skills or immobilized resources, means of misappropriation, and constrained or inarticulate modes of expression at work within the wider parameters of the system. From such a perspective, optimum conditions represent shared linguistic achievements of the highest order. They involve at minimum (1) considerable individual courage to resist whatever would hold one back from collective participation in (2) the wider communal effort to fulfill the potentiality of shared moments rather than let them be misused, abused, or merely wasted. Successful communication is shown to be an achievement, accomplished through hard work and mutual accommodation rather than merely taken for granted as an entitlement.

The major point of this project is to show how and why the appropriation of material, economic, and symbolic resources gets so entangled, interdependent, and intertwined in the execution of problematic concerns. Perhaps the way human beings treat one another, the use of words and gestures in public settings, establishes the primordial conditions and contingencies of the shape of things to come. In such a domain, favorable conditions revolve around the degree of compatibility of expressed interests with vested interests in sustained sequences of interaction in which the effective use of personal resources leads to the maximum fulfillment of mutual possibilities. In effect, the power of talk may be expected to sustain faith in the possibility of finding a way to work through unsettling problems or unresolved issues while there is still time/space to do so.

Some problematics are more amenable to resolution than others. So it is important to discover the magnitude of difference between the two. What appears as an obstacle may be envisioned later as a means of enablement. Hence, the acquisition of optimum levels of communicative competence involves the capacity and willingness to speak to, for, with, or against the vital interests of self and other(s). The center of the action is where the personal conduct of each one is supported and nourished for the welfare of every other one. In effect, individuals strive to adapt whatever communicative styles facilitate a sense of feeling safe and secure with one another.

In a world of uncertainty and unknown risk, there must be at least a thin veneer of shared presumptive ground for genuine human contact to occur. Such an affirmation provides the tacit basis from which to address the central question of what is to be said and done and with what implication and cost. The use of personal discourse for the purpose of sustaining a condition of mutual dialogue means little apart from the wider search for articulate, explicit, and fully manifest truth. Hence, a minimum degree of faith (or trust) in the tentative and provisional aspects of shared activity would seem to be a prerequisite for unconditional participation in the process. The ultimate litmus test is whether the words and gestures facilitate or undermine the reproduction of life-affirming signs. In effect, the ethical and ecological come together at the very point where sense-making practice supports or subverts faith in the efficacy of sense-making practice. At issue is the magnitude of resourcefulness in the interplay of source and subject matter.

What enables humans to endure does not ensure that they will flourish. Favorable relations between individuals within society require relatively free access to a diverse range of alternative sources and resources embedded within a wider set of multiple and shifting reference points. In such a domain there are three communicative luxuries: having access to an expansive community of individuals to turn to, interact with, and confide in. From such a perspective, optimum conditions evolve from having a wide latitude of access to shared activities in open systems of communication where respective parties help one another find the courage to say and do what must be said and done while the margin of opportunity still remains. This is what promotes a spirit of world openness at any level of communal affiliation.

HUMAN SURVIVAL SPELLED OUT IN LINGUISTIC TERMS

One's definition of personal reality is subject to considerable interpersonal negotiation along the way. What counts as real depends on what qualifies as a given for a particular subject. Presumably the development of living subjects cannot be readily disentangled from their respective involvements with pressing subject matter. The key presumption is that individuals move in relation to the distribution of collective resources and all manner of stylized contrivance and fabrication. We talk and gesture our way into an incomplete, uncertain, and unfinished future. The spinning globe changes under our feet. In the vortex of each one's own lived circumstance—the sheer constancy of what transpires in the absolute present tense—there are deep, implicit urges to be explicit, articulate, and make manifest. Thus, in the actualization of expressive and interpretive urges, the stage is set for the pursuit of optimum conditions.

Respondent accounts reference basic conditions to be satisfied for the members of a given speech community to be in a position to fulfill their promise to one another. Of interest is the center of the action where the 'real' and 'ideal' coincide. This presupposes the urge to fulfill the potentialities of the present moment is present at least as a plausible possibility. It also invokes the creative urge for human beings to wish for things to be what they are—opportunity for mutual fulfillment of sense-making practices conducted in a clear and transparent manner.

After all, it is relatively easy to build idealized and rarefied models of sense-making practice by taking refuge in highly abstracted notions of what it means to be a human being for other human beings. It may be tempting, for example, to appeal to the triumph of will or intellect, rationality or reason, or consensual visions of the good. It is much tougher, of course, to envision optimum conditions where the obtainable 'ideal' is grounded in the actual 'real' life situations of the particular subjects in question. So the point is to show why the possibilities for growth, emancipation, and liberation are strictly bound by time, place, and circumstance not entirely of any individual's own making.

At issue are the stockpile of complications, the magnitude of contingencies to be worked through for problematic interchange to achieve a reasonable degree of communicative success. Here favored conditions are earned, deserved, warranted, not merely assumed or taken for granted. Specifically, the pursuit of optimum conditions in this project center around four basic clusters of individual concern. Each one may be represented in terms of an expressive or communicative ability that is sufficiently life-affirming to alter the mix of discourse and dialogue. Such obtainable ideals are reached each time the respective parties are shown to be capable and willing to deal with problematic concerns in a manner that takes into account (1) the safety and security of each member; (2) the intrinsic worth of mutual exploration; (3) a stance of receptivity toward future interaction; (4) the courage to say and do whatever is required while there is still a margin of opportunity; and (5) a willingness to promote a spirit of world openness.

FEELING SAFE AND SECURE WITH ONE ANOTHER

If language is a resource as vital as currency and manna, then surely the linguistic parameters of human affairs make a difference not only in the reproduction of those conditions but rather in all levels of resource allocation and use—symbolic, economic, and material. Most decisive is whether the activity in question is sufficiently open to inspection to enable each source to call into question the physical and material well-being of one another. At issue are sources of deprivation that leave interactants feeling unsafe and insecure in their respective dealings with one another.

It is important to consider the long-term consequences of both favorable and unfavorable efforts at sense-making practice. In effect, danger and threat to the material and physical well-being of an individual serves to undermine (1) the amount of room to move and (2) the total latitude of expressive and interpretive freedom. The basic risk is that one gradually loses the capacity or willingness to speak up for one's own vital interests. Highly subordinated or marginalized individuals, for example, may be tempted to settle for fatalistic measures, short-term coping mechanisms, subsistence conditions, and meager gestures of compensation. In a fast-paced, high-tech society it can become more and more difficult to stand one's ground. An additional risk is that vital matters are covered up or buried over in acts of protracted silence, hinting, or implicative gestures—as in the manner of a symbolic cover. As a consequence, the one who would function as source and object becomes over time more object than source.

Perhaps there should be greater provision in the communal landscape for message makers who act on behalf of those who cannot or will not design such vital messages for themselves. Here heroic communication is cast into a universal idiom in which everyone is presumed to be worthy of inclusion. Favorable conditions: one gives explicit expression to the implicit, unspoken urges of self and others in a salient contemporary idiom. In other words, those who are most fluent and articulate give expression to the issues and concerns of those who lack the resources and skills to represent their own vital interests in any public setting.

This is linguistic achievement in which no one member is solely at the mercy of his or her own linguistic devices. Individual members speak to, with, against, and through unfinished, urgent, or compelling business. Such individuals engage in styles of self-presentation that seek to find a way to work through whatever would hold one back or stand in one's way. After all, there is only so much room for mortal beings to move about and only a limited range of opportunity to express, articulate, and make manifest. In effect, direct human contact is mainly what makes individual concerns better or worse. So the whole point is to be in a favorable position to make matters better rather than worse for all who are concerned.

Approximately one in seven respondents answer NO to the central question. None can recall any time/circumstance in which they were presumed to be incapable of expressing what was taking place at the time. This type of response is subject to alternative modes of interpretation. Most striking is widespread appeal to a long succession of direct contacts with other individuals framed in largely unproblematic terms. Descriptions bear witness to the possibility of overcoming periods of individual unsettledness and disconnection at strategic stops along the way. Considerations of lack of safety and security are presumed to be a direct function of the total magnitude of deprivation in one's own physical and material well-being. Therefore, it is important to find strength and determination to engage in the most resourceful and efficacious use of personal resources. Safety and security presuppose that the respective participants stand on solid ground while the opposite conditions signal a shift or transition to uncommon ground.

The absence of material and economic deprivation is what respondents who function well have most in common. Central icon: strong and solid families among whom the appropriation of collective resources enables each sibling to work, play, and rest in the relative absence of deprivation. Here idealized activities, routines, and projects are defined in terms of hard work and sustained effort that pays off with a trip to explore the Virgin Islands.

#184 A's view: Money is no problem. Lie on the white beach. Sip the best Piña Colada's made and swim around in crystal blue water. Roll a joint and run to the beach at the peak of sunset, smoke a dobe, and quietly listen to Moody Blues tapes until well into the night. Elation. Sheer joy. To this day the single measure of extraordinary activity in the life of one young adult is the vivid memory of one bright, shining evening on a beach in a tropical paradise. It is the type of place everyone should explore at least once in a lifetime.

Communicative competence is clearly manifest in families whose off-spring develop a strong sense of ontological security early on. It is this profound sense of personal security that allows each one to speak freely and not hold back in a self-disclosive sense. Favorable conditions are fostered in networks of communication with sufficiently high levels of care and support to fulfill the aspirations of the various members. The act of withdrawal or withholding of such vital human resources constitutes a severe liability for those who are dependent on others as heroic (emancipating) models of care, nurturance, and support. The following three entries are cases in point.

#185 A's view: If people rarely express what matters most, how can others get to know them for what they are? Anyone may be awestruck by a startling new experience but it is important to remember that every human being goes through similar things at one time or another. It matters to be able to say, "I am important but so is everyone else." The failure or refusal to express oneself in a clear and articulate manner only makes matters worse if vital personal interests are held inside too long.

#186 A's view: I must express myself and let people know who I am and what I want. Only then can they can know how to respond and what to do. I like to talk with others and see how they respond to various expressions of my own circumstances, activities, projects, and problems. It doesn't matter what the issue happens to be. I am the sort of person who has to get it off his chest. No matter what the magnitude of the puzzle or problem, I am going to tell others because I feel so comfortable with who and what I am.

#187 A's view: No matter what transpires, I've always had the feeling that I could talk to anyone else about virtually anything. I am truly blessed with the most understanding, loyal, and compassionate set of friends. Also, I have three beautiful sisters who differ in their perspectives on life, love, and everything else, but the one thing we have in common is unqualified support for each other no matter what. Finally, I am confident in God's ability to be omnipotent, so if I ever were to do something that couldn't be expressed to someone else, such a feeling would be in vain because my God knows all and sees all. Of course the people you interact with have a lot to do with what you may feel to be expressible or not. It's not even the people, it's your consciousness of how other people are conscious of you. So basically I see the issue as a matter of how you choose to express what you feel is most acceptable to others.

In effect, the optimum movement toward mutual exploration is enacted around the following themes: (1) the expression of what matters most; (2) the opportunity to get to know others for what they are; (3) the risk of interaction is viewed as less than those associated with the refusal or failure to engage in clear and articulate modes of self-presentation; (4) the state of being at ease facilitates the knowledge of how to act and react; (5) the faith that virtually anything can be conveyed one way or another within an inclusive atmosphere of care and concern.

THE LUXURY OF HAVING OTHERS TO TURN TO

The movement toward safety and security is fulfilled in the possibility of being able to turn to other persons for guidance and direction. The search for safety and security translates into flexible and open-ended opportunities for risk taking over matters of trust and reciprocity—where one can take the personal conduct of someone else at face value and thereby acquire an added source of consideration and council. This minimizes some of the deprivation and loss associated with the consequence of being left out. It also provides a measure of existential relief from the tension, strain, friction, and strife associated with isolation and disconnection with other living beings. During transitional periods, there is comfort knowing this too shall pass, however unfavorable the immediate interactive conditions happen to be. Even if there is no one to turn to right now, one can still envision future alternatives.

Prolonged exposure to unfavorable conditions is particularly risky when accompanied by an acute sense of fatalism—nothing can be said or done because it has always been this way between source A↔B. It is striking just how much of a person's own sense of security and protection is wrapped up not just in the *belief* but the *faith* that things eventually will get better and everything will turn out all right for everyone in the end. Unspoken faith in the possibilities for personal renewal serve as an antidote to fatalism at one extreme or the illusion of permanent connections at the other.

Prevailing images consist mostly of personal engagements in communicative systems that foster healthy, functional, and open climates in which each member feels free to express any salient feeling and thereby share deep personal concerns with others. Presumably the stakes are not reducible to a hidden agenda or big dark secret. Favorable conditions foster priorities, decisions, and choices firmly grounded in each member's life history. In such privileged domain there is no reason for shame and no cause to hide or escape.

There is comfort in knowing there are others you can turn to when in need of special care or concern. Granted there are times when you won't talk to a particular person about a specific subject. What cannot be expressed to one member may be discussed at length with someone else. After all, different people bring out diverse sides of one another. One can be serious with some friends and goofy with others. It is important to have faith that there will always be someone there for you. It is necessary to have access to those who never judge or complain so that one can go to them with anything at virtually any time. Occasionally, of course, one may try to figure things out all alone. At other times there is the need to keep personal events private and special. It all comes down to a matter of the way one lives through the unforeseen consequences of effort expended to sustain communal ties with others.

THE LUXURY OF HAVING OTHERS TO TALK TO

#188 A's view: A has never had a problem conveying personal feelings to others. There have been times when he has chosen not to express his feelings to others. This has been because he usually sees no reason to burden them with his problems, or it well may be that others might be severely hurt by the display of intensely personal feelings. At times he keeps vital matters private until they have been sorted out. Usually, however, the act of expressing personal feelings to others helps one deal with unresolved matters and put difficult circumstances into proper perspective. Through the struggles and strains of interaction, one is able to understand intensely personal circumstances with greater transparency and clarity than ever before.

THE LUXURY OF HAVING OTHERS TO CONFIDE IN

#189 A's view: I've racked my brain for two days trying to decide if there has been a time when I could not express a feeling to anyone and there has not been such a time. I've been in my share of conflicts and even then I can always find someone who will be receptive. If it isn't a best friend or family member, it is a stranger. There have been times when I should have gone to my own family to express my feelings but for some reason I found someone else to talk to. When I was a junior in high school my brother was killed in a brutal accident. I felt as if I had to be strong for my family because everything else was crumbling down around us. I felt that if I expressed my pain to my parents, they would start worrying about me on top of other things. I was too caught up in being strong to realize my lack of expressivity was a source of unspoken concern and worry to my family. I began to express my pain directly months later to friends. It was easiest to talk with them after we had a few beers. They were as anxious to hear about my unspoken feelings as I was to let them out. There were so many strong feelings held inside that it was simply easier to share with those who do not know me well. There is always someone and some way to express any sort of feeling. Such acts may not be the healthiest but they do help relieve a bad experience.

Under favorable conditions, the opportunity to interact directly with others is taken as intrinsically valuable. The process may be approached strategically, as a means to an end, but also as an end in itself. Hence, the urge to grant or deny access to others takes on a new meaning. Individuals are construed as resources rather than as liabilities or obstacles. Each one qualifies as an added source of consideration. Interactants address and respond to one another through the very center of each one's life history. Such a presumption of receptivity helps cast immediate difficulties into sharp relief. It is liberating to be in a position of not having to depend on any one single source to fill one's own cup and to know that individual joys and sorrows are collectively distributed.

RECEPTIVITY TOWARD FUTURE INTERACTION

Those who so describe themselves as receptive interactants equate a spirit of openness with access to close friends, tolerance of diversity, mutual respect, and personal engagement in networks of human relations that work so well that not every little thing can, should, or need be shared. Still, there is confidence in knowing there will always be someone who can know and understand one's deepest feelings. It is not always the same person, but many different individuals who behave in much the same way. What cannot be easily conveyed to some can be readily conveyed to others. It all boils down to being able and willing to explore different things with different people. Some can grasp and understand certain types of human concerns better than others. What is most deeply troublesome may well require access to someone who can really empathize.

What one seeks is basic human understanding. Therefore, one may sustain the rare achievement of being able to count on many people who take the time and expend the effort to talk, phone, or write. It is not a problem to express honest feelings to the right type of people. One should never hold something deep inside for any length of time (that is, a few days) without signifying something (verbal or nonverbal) to someone else. It soon becomes intolerable to bear such intense or acute feelings of anxiety and uncertainty, but it is still important to be able to tell even one other person what has transpired. If one expresses vital matters to those who will merely judge, criticize, condemn, or just misconstrue, one may become more anxious than before. It is valuable, therefore, to be able to convey personal matters well enough to sustain necessary and sufficient thresholds of sympathy and forbearance about one's position and place within a larger community of individuals.

#190 A's view: I am a very open and honest person who has never had a problem sharing things with other people. At times, though, I consider this a weakness. Very few people are as open. I trust people too easily. This is often bad because people ruin trust by telling others very personal, private, and sensitive matters. This is discouraging. Over time I've learned to hesitate and evaluate another's friendship before I begin to trust. However, there is a positive way to look at my openness as well. For example, when I meet someone who appears trustworthy, etc., I share and feel comfortable with that person. Yet many times this particular person will hold back or be less comfortable than I am when sharing so freely. When I interact with someone who appreciates a spirit of openness and opens up as well, it is a wonderful feeling to know because you act one way another person reacted differently. Out of this ease of sensitivity and trust I've developed some of the deepest of friendships and interpersonal relationships.

#191 A's view: I believe I have always been able to express my feelings no matter what the circumstance. I am extremely open and can convey thoughts and feelings easily to others. Sometimes I only relate certain types of events to select types of people. On the whole I believe I have been able to be quite expressive, depending on the situation. Sometimes, however, I do not want to relate my experience to anyone. I do not have a particular example for this, but sometimes I just don't want to talk to anybody about certain subjects. For these instances I would rather make the decision myself and think things through on my own rather than having somebody else's opinion. I trust myself a lot and I believe that is why I sometimes do not want other people's opinion. I have gone through some very difficult periods in my life that I would not have been able to work through without talking with others for support. During a difficult period, interaction with a wide variety of people allowed me to recover from extreme circumstances. I would not have wanted to work things out on my own because, honestly, I do not think I could have made it through. I really like to interact with other people and have not found a situation in which I felt I could not convey my experience to another person. I believe this is a personal strength of mine and I'm glad to have the ability to do so.

#192 A's view: Parents, family, and friends have provided me with a very open environment to talk about whatever is on my mind or whatever may be bothering me. My parents really emphasized, while growing up and even still, they would always be there for me whenever I need anything or just to talk. I am the sort of person who needs to be surrounded by people. I enjoy being with people and interacting directly with them. My friends and family are life for me. They make me feel that if I have a problem or just want to talk, they will be there for me. I like this feeling. The exact circumstance has a lot to do with whom I feel comfortable talking about a particular subject. I tell (a) the people who I think will best understand what I am going through at the time and (b) those who are not personally involved in the particular situation in question. My friends and family may not always know the best way to handle a situation I may be going through, but their listening and support are always offered. Sometimes just this is enough.

#193 A's view: I am always able to express to my loved ones and acquaintances exactly the way I feel. I am able to verbalize my thoughts freely, both in words on paper and spoken language. If I am confused about something—I am able to convey to someone what is so confusing about at the moment. I come from a family where we have been taught to express virtually everything verbally. We were positively reinforced as we were growing up. We talked about sex, drugs, crime, etc., long before I had any strong concern for the issues. Nothing is "taboo" as far as my family is concerned.

ON THE COURAGE TO SAY AND DO WHAT MUST BE SAID AND DONE

#194 A's view: After thinking about this question for some time, I conclude that I have always used episodes of direct human contact to make myself feel better, whether I wanted to share a happy, joyous experience with others or most often the need to participate in mutual dialogue with others when in need of advice, consolation, or basic help in sorting out my thoughts. If the experience was wonderful and exciting, I would quickly share the news as a means of sort of 're-living' my experience and ignite a spark which sets off some great feelings. Keeping things inside isn't as much fun. When I have experienced times of great difficulty or uncertainty, I just have to discuss them with others. When interacting with others I was reassured I'm not a bad person or that what I was experiencing was something others had experienced as well. Direct human contact is a way to keep my 'psychological' slate clean, if you will. I have great faith in this. I give expression to everything that has significance in my life. Holding things inside is something that is not natural for me.

#195 A's view: I come from a large family of very open, outgoing people. My parents have taught us to be very "down-to-earth." In our family atmosphere, we all showed every emotion almost the instant we felt it. Little control or restraint was exercised. While this characteristic may not be ideal, we all loved each other enough that we could forgive our own individual outbursts. A lot of times anger and judgment was placed on other members for their emotional state but unconditional love was ever-present. Having been socialized in my family environment in such a way, I've never been able to hold anything inside. People usually know exactly how I feel. I have no secrets. If someone wants to know something about me, I answer honestly. I do, however, tend to avoid talking about some things to some people. I don't see a need for lies or secrets. People should make their decisions about me based on the truth. To be honest, though, I find myself constantly concerned with whether or not people like me despite my lack of secrets. I know that I am not like most people. It seems that everyone has something they are ashamed of or have held inside. If they don't have that sort of problem, it seems people try to hide how they really feel about most things. I've never been like that. To my advantage, my personality allows me to form some really special, close friendships that involve lots of sharing, nurturing, and caring. To my disadvantage, the people with whom I have only surface relationships sometimes become uncomfortable with my outward displays of emotion. I probably should learn more self-control so that I may better appropriate my behavior to the given situation. Sometimes I wish my family environment would have taught me to keep secrets and show a more emotional level of self-control but overall I'm happy with the person that I am. I'm honest and straightforward and sometimes wish other people would be more like that too.

#196 A's view: I have always been able to express my feelings, that is, at least as well as any person can. One human being cannot know exactly what another may be experiencing, no matter how open two people are with each other. That's the beauty of being an individual—the only person who truly knows is yourself. There are, of course, many occasions in life when our feelings concern someone else or are of some importance to others for whatever reason. Expressing such feelings has not presented any problems for me. I believe that if a person can try to express his or her true feelings, either directly or indirectly through some type of example, the listener's imagination *will* and *does* complete the picture, perhaps drawing on previous experiences to produce a satisfactory level of understanding to the listener. Satisfactory is an incredibly vague term in this usage and it must be. Who cares about the *deepest* feelings or reactions of another person? A stranger may not care at all about what another person is experiencing but a loved one who has a much more intimate relationship with an individual will try to ascertain his or her feelings to a much larger extent. The situation can be considered a stimulus-response system. I have always been able to respond, whether the stimulus (questioner) is strong or weak. I must admit there have been times when I judged it best *not* to express what I was experiencing at the time in order to protect myself or others. This does not represent the inability to express myself. I feel that I have always been able to express my feelings to a satisfactory extent to me and/or satisfactory to whomever wants to know them.

#197 A's view: Despite the full range of human differences, personal concerns can be associated in a way that draws together unlike circumstances with similar results. This is what makes mutual understanding possible.

#198 A's view: It may take a while to get my problems off my chest but eventually it all comes out and everyone is better off in the end.

Perhaps it is possible to relearn how to employ words and gestures in a radical way—as if our very lives depend on the efficacy of their use. The way we present our lived circumstances to one another can make all the difference in the world. This suggests, in turn, that the movement in and out of the sharing of problematic concerns can be subject to refocus and reframing of troublesome modes of personal conduct. The alternative is to repeat mistakes in a robotic manner. To confront the full magnitude of what stands before us, it is necessary to be models of expressive and interpretive freedom, spontaneity, and creativity in the search for an integration and synthesis of existing possibilities. It is crucial not to underestimate the magnitude of unfinished opportunity for further expansion and elaboration.

ON THE SPIRIT OF WORLD OPENNESS

The distinction between relatively open versus closed systems of communication is very broad. It is important to recognize the difference between the two and to be in a position to act accordingly. One model at work in this study is oriented around the principle of life-affirming signs. Here one gradually acquires the personal resources required to sustain a generalized expectation of a demonstrated stance of competence and compatibility with others. The ideal interactant is receptive to the potential for integration, interdependence, and relational sensitivity and differentiation. At the level of personal implicature, fluid and provisional modes of dual patterning guide the complex interplay of internal standards with external circumstances. In such a speech community each member demonstrates an expressive or communicative style that is taken (1) as efficacious, coherent, and articulate; (2) capable of sustaining a deep level of integration between individual aspirations and commitment to others; (3) intent on fulfilling the potential of the shared moment by being fully present, mindful, alert, attentive, and clearly focused; (4) spontaneous, creative, innovative, imaginative, and capable of feeling a sense of joy, wonder, and awe that things are what they are—a set of miraculous, mysterious, and inexhaustible possibilities set in shared motion.

#199 A's view: In order for others to get the true picture, I feel that they need to know everything, all the details. It is always an accumulation of events and not just one occurrence that is at stake. Therefore, all details are important and that is the reason I make short stories long. To a certain extent, no one can completely understand anything in someone else's life because each person has their own life experiences. I believe there is a reason for everything that happens, even if I don't understand what transpires at a certain time in my life. It may take hours, days, months, or years but eventually I will figure it out. And my initial understanding also changes over time with greater depth of experience. I think I know the answer but because I realize nothing is permanent, I'm never completely sure. Overall I have found that expressing what you are thinking is usually better in the long run. The responses of others are exceedingly helpful and save a lot of misery in the end. I consider myself very fortunate to have so many people who are there for me to talk to and confide in. Communication is so important when it comes to peace of mind.

Respondent accounts help recast the problem of what happens when one source among many confronts a disruptive litany of elaborated complications. Successful communication is rediscovered not as total, infallible, or flawless, but rather as a confluence of accessible possibilities set into uncertain motion. It is important for each participant to be sensitive and tolerant of slippage, lapses, and departures from a stance of alignment, reciprocity, and symmetry. Each one is in a position to deal with the full weight of unresolved involvements and concerns because no one operates under the illusion of the need to express oneself in a perfect or flawless manner. What matters most is fidelity to the unfolding expression of implicit possibilities. Hence, the respective definitions of what takes place remain uniquely situated, spontaneous, and autonomous. Such a climate fosters the urge to become more mindful of what others construe as having any distinctive communicative value.

Complex issues implicate matters of risk and change. What needs to be fully articulated is how much risk of communicative failure is considered tolerable in collective negotiations over the significance of the larger communicative equation. Moreover, the urge to make personal worlds more commensurate and directly proportionate is to be encouraged, fostered, and sustained. Thus, the capacity to affirm, nurture, spare, and preserve seeks fulfillment in mutually sustained modes of inquiry, elaboration, and inquiry. Conversely, the capacity to negate, neutralize, block, or refuse to sustain the act of spreading the word risks loss of contact with shared possibilities in the here and now.

The universal task of creating a spirit of mutuality is a collective burden. Individual resilience merges with collaborative vulnerability whenever there is sufficient room to move and a goodness of fit in the mix of personal logic in matters where one source takes the place of someone else or something else. Successions of speech acts are designed to facilitate the future incorporation of life-affirming rituals, ceremonies, activities, and routines. An affordable supply of liberating words and gestures works to restore a more integrated sense of community between given sets of language users and other living creatures.

As a consequence, the one-among-many problem is recast in the manner of an unfolding discovery and evolutionary quest. Slippage is taken in stride, and life-affirming modes of free expression and interpretive response abound. What is manifest is widespread tolerance for alternative, misaligned, or disruptive methods of personal account. Others are viewed as resources rather than liabilities or obstacles. Members are models of taking into account alternative pathways and methods of self-expression. Fatalism recedes, and so does miscommunication as a way of life. Hence, there is room for exploration beyond protective cocoons that constrain or prevent movement toward new and more effective modes of human interchange. Here as well is the prospect of overcoming self-imposed invisible walls through acts of risk in which one's sense of security can not be so easily threatened. Where there is sufficient tolerance of personal weakness and vulnerability, episodes of problematic communication may be recast not so much as the source of blame but as the very method of cure. Such conditions enable the respective parties to remain open to the possibilities of discourse and dialogue despite the countervailing force of whatever would hold one back.

The pursuit of optimum conditions culminates in the desire to fulfill the potentiality of the existing situation and not let shared opportunities go to waste. Conversely, by implication, such a movement is intolerant of the waste of precious human resources. Specifically, individuals give unique expression to lived circumstances, relational definitions, and common understandings as well as they are able. Members who live largely unproblematic lives comingle freely with those who define life mainly in problematic terms. In the mix, the personal conduct of each member bears witness to an alternative model for dealing with unresolved issues and encumbrances.

In such a communicative milieu it is possible to address personal concerns of each member in light of the collective resources available to every other member. Thereby individuals teach and learn how to bear one another's linguistic burdens. Here the individual search for collective truth facilitates renewed opportunity to explore the mix of discourse and dialogue from every conceivable angle. No one is left out. Everyone gets a chance to set the record straight and say the way they think things are and what, if anything, should be done about whatever is still outstanding.

In effect, each respondent provides an alternative model of what makes life problematic or what can be done to ease the strain along the way. So instead of ranting and raving about the fallibilities, foibles, and vulnerabilities of human beings, discourse, language, or institutions, there is rather an inclusive communal spirit that resonates and registers with such force and determination as to not permit the risk of falling short to hold one back or stand in the way. Conclusion: within the protective cover of the surrounding ecological landscape, there need be no invocation to a higher power than what succeeding generations of interacting beings make possible—a linguistic vision of secular salvation—the opportunity for personal engagement in the universal struggle toward fidelity in thought, word, and deed.

Selected Bibliography

Aldous, J. & Ganey, R. (1989). Families' definition behavior of problematic situations. *Social Forces, 67*, 870–896.

Arndt, H. & Janney, R. W. (1987). *InterGrammer: Towards an integrative model of verbal, prosodic, and kinesic choices in speech.* Berlin: Mouton de Gruyter.

Babrow, J. (1992). Communication and problematic integration: Understanding diverging probability and value, ambiguity, ambivalence, and impossibility. *Communication Theory, 2*, 95–130.

Bavelas, J. B., Black, A., Chovil, N. & Mullett, J. (1990). *Equivocal communication.* Newbury Park: Sage Publications.

Brown, H. L. (1984). Incommensurability. *Inquiry, 26*, 3–29.

Burling, R. (1986). The selective advantage of complex language. *Ethology and Sociobiology, 7*, 1–16.

Callon, M. (1980). Struggles and negotiations to define what is problematic and what is not. In Knorr, K. D., Knohn, R. & Whitley, R. (Eds.), *The social process of investigation. Sociology of the sciences.* Vol. 5 (pp. 197–219). Dordrecht, Holland: D. Reidel Publishing Co.

Coupland, N., Giles, H., & Wiemann, J. M. (1991). *"Miscommunication" and problematic talk.* Newbury Park: Sage Publications.

Ehman, R. (1969). Privacy. *Man and world, 2*, 269–284.

Fischer, K. (1988). The functional architecture of adaptive cognitive systems—with limited capacity. *Semiotics, 68–3/4*, 191–248.

Giddens, A. (1991). *Modernity and self-identity.* Stanford: Stanford University Press.

Grace, G. W. (1987). *The linguistic construction of reality.* London: Croom Helm.

Grice, H. P. (1989). *Studies in the way of words.* Cambridge: Harvard University Press.

Hewitt, J. P., & Hall, P. M. (1973). Social problems, problematic situations, and quasi-theories. *American Sociological Review, 38*, 367–374.

Kaplan, S. (1983). A model of person-environment compatibility. *Environment and Behavior, 15*, 311–332.

Moore, A. W. (1987). Points of view. *The Philosophical Quarterly, 37*, 1–20.

Mortensen, C. D. *Violence and Communication*. Landham, Md: The University Press of America.

Mortensen, C. D. (1991). Communication, conflict, and culture. *Communication Theory, 1*, 273–293.

Petrilli, S. (1986). On the materiality of signs. *Semiotica, 62 3/4*, 223–245.

Platt, R. (1989). Reflexivity, recursion, and social life. Elements for a postmodern sociology. *The Sociological Review, 37*, 636–667.

Polanyi, M. (1962). *Personal knowledge: Towards a post critical philosophy*. New York: Harper and Row.

Porpora, D. V. (1989). Four concepts of social structure. *Journal for the Theory of Social Behaviour, 19*, 195–210.

Prodi, G. (1988). Material bases of significantion. *Semiotica, 69–3/4*, 191–241.

Scheff, T. J. (1990). *Microsociology: Discourse, emotion, and social structure*. Chicago: University of Chicago Press.

Schrag, C. O. (1986). *Communicative praxis and the space of subjectivity*. Bloomington: Indiana University Press.

Sperber, D. & Wilson, D. (1986). *Relevance: Communication and cognition*. Cambridge, Mass: Harvard University Press.

Steiner, G. (1975). *After babel: Aspects of language and translation*. London: Oxford University Press.

Taylor, T. J. (1992). *Mutual misunderstanding*. Durham, N.C.: Duke University Press.

Index

About the Author

C. DAVID MORTENSEN is Professor of Communication Arts at the University of Wisconsin-Madison. He is the author of many books on communication and social conflict, including *Communication: The Study of Human Interaction* and *Violence and Communication: Public Reactions to an Attempted Presidential Assassination.*